ASSAULT ON OLYMPUS

W. H. LEWIS

ASSAULT ON OLYMPUS

The Rise of the House of Gramont between 1604 and 1678

HARCOURT, BRACE AND COMPANY
NEW YORK

FIRST AMERICAN EDITION

Library of Congress Catalog Card Number: 57-6212
Printed in Great Britain

To

KELSIE and GUNDRED

FOREWORD

★

IN MUCH which has been written on the social structure of monarchical France, it seems to me that undue, and indeed exaggerated emphasis has been laid on its rigidity; class barriers, we are told, were insurmountable, and the gulf between the Court noble and the country gentleman was unbridgeable.

The facts do not bear out either statement; with class barriers we are not here concerned, though in passing we may notice that in 1629 economists were viewing with uneasiness the number of artisans' and peasants' sons who were passing through the universities into the 'white collar' class. And when we turn to the *noblesse* we find that, so far from being static, the whole corps was patterned in ebb and flow; new houses rising from provincial or bourgeois stock, famous names rotting into obscurity or extinction.

With these facts in mind, it occurred to me that it might be interesting to examine in some detail the transformation of a typical provincial family into a great House; and the Gramonts were selected for two reasons. Firstly, the wealth of literary material they produced during the period I have selected; the family is unique in that the Marshal-Duke, his son the Comte de Guiche, and his brother the Chevalier de Gramont, all either wrote memoirs or else provided the facts and opinions which were subsequently worked up by those who had known them. Secondly, because the Gramonts, unlike the majority of French nobles, were a travelled family; and consequently, instead of spending all our time in France, we see through their eyes a good deal of their Europe – Germany, Spain, England, Holland, and the Netherlands. It is my hope that this book may induce some readers to look into the Gramont contributions to seventeenth-century literature; I shall be surprised if they do not enjoy them.

My thanks are due to my old friend Gervase Mathew, who was good enough to read my manuscript, and make some useful suggestions; and to Joy Davidman for her patient kindness in pruning the first draft and recommending certain excisions.

Oxford 1955–56 W. H. LEWIS

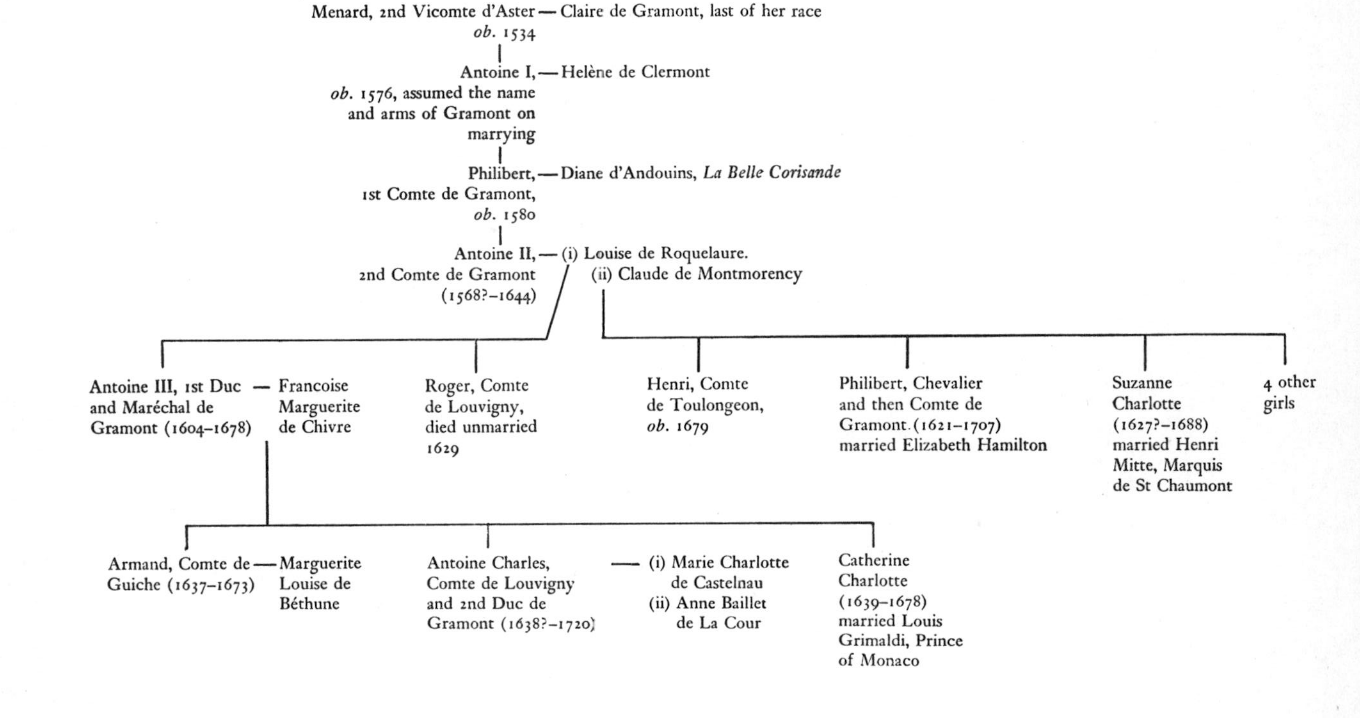

Menard, 2nd Vicomte d'Aster — Claire de Gramont, last of her race
ob. 1534
Antoine I, — Helène de Clermont
ob. 1576, assumed the name and arms of Gramont on marrying
Philibert, — Diane d'Andouins, *La Belle Corisande*
1st Comte de Gramont, *ob.* 1580
Antoine II, — (i) Louise de Roquelaure.
2nd Comte de Gramont (1568?–1644)
(ii) Claude de Montmorency
Antoine III, 1st Duc and Maréchal de Gramont (1604–1678) — Francoise Marguerite de Chivre
Roger, Comte de Louvigny, died unmarried 1629
Henri, Comte de Toulongeon, *ob.* 1679
Philibert, Chevalier and then Comte de Gramont. (1621–1707) married Elizabeth Hamilton
Suzanne Charlotte (1627?–1688) married Henri Mitte, Marquis de St Chaumont
4 other girls
Armand, Comte de Guiche (1637–1673) — Marguerite Louise de Béthune
Antoine Charles, Comte de Louvigny and 2nd Duc de Gramont (1638?–1720) — (i) Marie Charlotte de Castelnau (ii) Anne Baillet de La Cour
Catherine Charlotte (1639–1678) married Louis Grimaldi, Prince of Monaco

CHAPTER I

★

'It is my father's own fault that he was not the son of Henri IV.' Thus Philibert de Gramont, recalling that Henri had offered to recognize the second Comte de Gramont as his bastard, and had been met with an indignant refusal. His remark gives us the key to the character of his generation of Gramonts, unsentimental, acquisitive, unscrupulous, careerists to a man. In 1618 the second Comte de Gramont was a man in his late forties, head of the House since the death of his father in 1580. An unlikeable person, but the first Gramont to raise the family above the mere country nobility and give it an assured start on that long climb to Olympus which ended so brilliantly with Antoine III. It was in 1620 that the second Comte first came to the front by securing the government of Navarre; in 1636 he followed up this success by defeating the Spaniards at Roncevaux; in 1638 he became a Major-General; and he died a Brevet-Duc in 1644.

But the world of fashion looked rather askance at the second Comte, perhaps with good reason; for he was suspected of having murdered his first wife in 1610 by a trick worthy of an old-fashioned thriller. 'On some suspicion' he manipulated the floor of her bedroom so that when the unfortunate woman stepped on it she was dropped into the cellars; and Antoine II was free to make a more satisfactory marriage.[1]

Antoine III, Comte de Guiche, Gramont's eldest son, was in 1618 a lad of fourteen; a boy to our way of thinking, but to contemporaries a young man who should be equipping himself to take his part in advancing the family fortunes within a couple of years at the latest. The cult of the child had not yet been heard of; to hustle and flog a boy through childhood in the shortest possible time, to turn him into a family asset in his 'teens, was then the sole object of education. So Guiche was sent off to

[1] Tallemant des Réaux, *Historiettes*.

Paris in his fourteenth year; and the father equipped his son for the struggle with characteristic Gascon niggardliness. 'The fathers of those days', says Guiche in later years, 'did not willingly forego what was useful and agreeable for themselves in order to give it to their children.' With a change of linen, two indifferent horses, and a small sum of money entrusted to the old family retainer who was his guardian, tutor, and valet, Guiche left for Paris.

But if his equipment was scanty, he had at least the consolation of leaving home without regret; there would be no sorrowful looking back at the château of his fathers, for it is unlikely that he had ever experienced happiness at Bidache, except perhaps momentarily in the arms of a peasant girl. His mother had died when he was six, and his infrequent meetings with his father would no doubt have been conducted with that cold formality which was *de rigueur* among the aristocracy. For it is a curious fact that among the *noblesse* of the *ancien régime* we frequently find the father and son relationship obliterated in the common realization that both parent and child were first of all men of quality; even bad fathers recognized this, and whilst you might be tyrannical towards your son, it was a gross breach of good manners to treat him otherwise than with the utmost politeness. This was not a pattern of life calculated to engender much filial affection, and we are not surprised to find in Antoine III's memoirs no trace of it; when he set out for Paris he probably dismissed all thoughts of home from his mind before he was out of sight of Bidache. True, the world which he was about to enter expected that a Gascon, like a Scot, should be clamorously insistent on the delights of his province, and on its superiority to all others; but the time to shed tears over bonnie Gascony would come when he was firmly established at Court in a position which precluded any risk of his ever having to return to his native land.

1618 was a good year in which to turn one's back on the traditional life of the country gentleman and seek a fortune at Court. Richelieu was on the verge of power, the good old days were ending, feudalism was on its deathbed. There was to be no place in the new France for the provincial Governor who made war on the Crown 'for the redress of his just grievances', that is, blackmailed the King into paying him to disband his army of relations, connections, and peasants. Henri IV, in many ways the cleverest of the Bourbon kings, had done much to cut the claws of these satraps by transferring most of their powers to his own nominee in the province, the King's Lieutenant; though since his death in 1610 feudalism was enjoying an Indian summer under the feeble Regency of his stupid widow Marie de Medicis, 'the Florentine tradesman's daughter'. But it was the expiring flicker of the old order.

Still, if the life of feudalism was fast decaying, its outward trappings were yet to be seen on every side. The country through which Guiche travelled was the immemorial France; heavily wooded, sprinkled with privately owned and garrisoned castles; with unmetalled cart tracks, impassable in winter, offering a slow and costly means of communication; rivers carried the bulk of the heavy traffic; primitively cultivated, undrained, and with much heath and moorland; at intervals small fortified cities, held by a bourgeois militia, and with a civic pride as arrogant as that of the *noblesse* itself. Perigueux for instance, where it was an article of faith that the town had been founded by a great-nephew of Noah; and modest Lyons, which only claimed as its builder King Lugdanus, who died in 2335 B.C.

The nearer Guiche got to Paris the cleaner, or rather the less dirty he found the towns; for the cities of the south were notorious for their filthiness, even by the unexacting standards of the day. In most of them the houses, even those of the rich, had no sanitary arrangements whatsoever; family and servants relieved themselves on the flat roof, the cleansing of which was left to the rain. The unfortunate traveller, caught out of doors in a storm at Marseilles, may well have asked himself what the Egyptians had to grumble about when their skies rained blood.

Paris would not however have struck us as any startling improvement on the towns of the south; most of the houses had sanitary arrangements of a sort, this was the only difference. It was a city of stinking, narrow alleys, made narrower by the stalls of tradespeople lining either side; deafening the stranger with its innumerable bells; so terrorized by gangs of assassins that after dark respectable citizens dared not venture out of doors; and, even by day, victimized by bands of mendicants whose begging was in fact the extortion of money by threats. Until well into the reign of Louis XIV, not only was no effort made to deal with these pests, but their position was officially recognized; when Louis entered Paris with his bride in 1660 the Beggars' Guild was amongst the deputations which presented congratulatory addresses, 'all clothed in their richest costumes'.

The sights to be 'done' by the newly arrived provincial were the Pont Neuf, the heart of Paris; the Island, the original city, where were situated Nôtre Dame and the Archbishopric; the Châtelet, police headquarters, with its descending series of dungeons, including the terrible *End of Ease* which had never held a prisoner who had not either died or gone mad within a fortnight; the still unfinished Louvre; the Faubourgs, mainly occupied by religious houses, where the silence and the endless blank walls offered an eerie contrast to the comfortable uproar of the city proper; lastly the university, consisting of between thirty and forty Colleges, a place of little work and much privilege, where even the College servants got their wine tax-free and made a good thing out of selling liquor to undergraduates at a trifle below tavern prices. Every College had a horde of Fellows, a few scholars living on the Foundation, and a number of non-resident undergraduates drawn from all ranks of society. Many of the latter were the sons of small tradesmen, even of artisans, who were now going up to the University in increasing numbers. There would also be a sprinkling of young nobles, reluctantly preparing themselves to occupy the family bishopric in due course, and entertaining meanwhile surprising views on the type of experience which would best equip them for the pastoral office. Finally, and perhaps the majority, were the rake-helly sons of rich bourgeois, who cut purses, snatched cloaks, fought the watch, and to the best of their ability aped the dress and vices of the young courtiers.

If Gramont's idea in keeping Guiche short of money was to impress upon him the desirability of finding his feet with the least delay, he could hardly have chosen more wisely, and Antoine's thoughts from the outset must have turned to the problem of filling his empty pockets. And indeed his empty belly, for after tramping the city all day he would often come home to a supper of dry bread 'by the light of a stinking lantern, for he could not afford candles'.

Perhaps the boy had already received some formal education at home, for his father told him that he was being sent to Paris 'to learn equitation and other needful exercises'. By sixteen a gentleman was expected to have completed his studies in philosophy, history, and politics, and to be ready to take up the more serious matters of riding, the use of arms, and dancing. Faret, in his *L'Honnête homme ou l'art de plaire à la Cour*, describes the well-educated noble as 'dexterous in Dancing, at the Tennis Court, at Wrestling, Leaping, Swimming, Shooting, and all other Diversions . . . and not ignorant of the Plays of Hazard'. Here we notice a hint of a vanishing France in which the gentleman lived close to the soil and did not disdain to compete in village sports with his plebeian neighbours. Faret writes in 1632, and in less than thirty years a Versailles noble would have been both shocked and ashamed to learn that his grandfather had indulged in such clownish diversions as leaping and wrestling. As to learning, Faret says, 'It is sufficient that we have a tolerable knowledge of the most agreeable Questions which are sometimes debated in good company'. And there is no harm in being 'learned in the Spheres' or having 'an ear capable of judging nicely of the tones of Music'. Of two subjects however a gentleman must have complete mastery; he must know 'Addition, Subtraction, Multiplication, and Division', for without these he will be unable to understand the complex army drill of the period; and he must also acquire the art of letter-writing. No matter if your spelling be phonetic and your grammar non-existent, providing that you know the exact turn of phrase for a letter 'serious, complimental, or amorous'.

Thus equipped, Antoine may have crowned his education by a study of Refuge's *Traicté de la Cour ou instructions des Courtisans*; for the work appeared in 1622 when he was emerging from his apprenticeship. At first glance we think that the *Traicté* is a satire; and it is not until we have read it carefully that we realize that it is a serious work of instruction.

Here are some of the author's precepts for the budding courtier:

> Never express any opinion contrary to that of your Prince, and never give him a definite answer when he asks for your advice.
>
> Be all things to all men, never disagree with the Great, never argue with a woman, and never join in the secret pleasures of your Prince.
>
> Always speak well of everyone, whether the facts bear you out or not; and despise those of low extraction, whilst being free with your servants.
>
> Never contradict the opinions of a superior or of an inferior, for in the first case you give offence, and in the second you give the man an opportunity of appearing to be on the same level as yourself.
>
> Become adept at dissimulation; and never leave the presence of the Prince if you can avoid it, for if you do, the other courtiers will speak ill of you.
>
> The most telling flattery is that which cloaks itself as a bluff, soldierly independence of mind.
>
> When the Prince asks for your advice, remember that what he wants is an enthusiastic endorsement of the line of action which he has decided to follow.
>
> The quickest way to fall out of favour with your Prince is to let him see that he is under an obligation to you . . . above all, never let him suspect that you are cleverer than he is.
>
> Never ask a favour for a friend; keep your credit for your own advancement.

In 1621 Guiche was seventeen, handsome, witty, insinuating, and penniless; still apparently living on the same allowance which had been paid him as a boy, and constantly meditating in his unheated room on the problem of how to raise the wind. Not for him the solution so popular with the bourgeois undergraduate, which was to get a rich tradesman's daughter with child, denounce himself to the Church, be ordered to marry her, and then settle down to live on his father-in-law. For Antoine was a noble who would eventually become head of his House, and he intended to do better for himself than that in the marriage market. But what for the moment were his assets? None, so far as he could see, except that he was a Gascon.

But to be a Gascon was by no means a negligible advantage in this world which he had to conquer by his wits. Ever since Gascon Henri IV had unbolted the gates of Paris to his compatriots, an increasing stream of them had flocked to the capital and there made good, just as the accession of James I opened London to the Scots. And the Gascon, like the Scot and the Irishman in England, had been quick to realize that in Paris the way to turn toleration into affection was to create a comic Gascon, a light-hearted, reckless fellow as unlike the keen-witted *arriviste* behind the mask as an Irishman playing the buffoon for a roomful of English is unlike the same Irishman off the stage. A few pioneering years sufficed to build up the character to which every Gascon was thereafter to conform; he was naturally a man of the first importance in his province, where his home was one of the sights of the south; often his attic would be decorated with pictures of this purely imaginary building. He was also rich, though whenever you met him he seemed to be awaiting a remittance from that dilatory rogue, his Intendant. The length of his stay in Paris, he whispered to you, depended upon the secret business the Minister wished to discuss with him; and also on the caprice of a lady so exalted that he dare not even hint at her name. Finally, just as the comic stories about Scots are invented in Aberdeen by men who have remarkably little that is comic about them, so it was the Gascons themselves who invented the jokes which kept the stage Gascon before the public. One of them will serve as a specimen; a young Gascon in threadbare homespun is attitudinizing in front of the royal palace; halting a passer-by he says, 'Pardon, fellow, but I am looking for lodgings to accommodate my household this season; is this Hôtel to let?' All Paris laughed at the simplicity of the country cousin who proposed to rent the Louvre, and the inventor of the story laughed at the simplicity of all Paris. Professional Gascon, decided Antoine, was his rôle, and he was to play the part admirably for the rest of his life; though towards the end, unfriendly critics sneered at the circumstance that the longer he remained at Court, the stronger grew his Gascon accent.

But this was all in the future, and in 1621 the hungry Antoine, with the broken feather concealing the rent in his hat, was still one of the Gascon cadets of *Cyrano de Bergerac*, striving desperately for a foothold on the slippery ascent to Court favour.

He is discreetly obscure about his doings for the next few years; he was, he says, 'young and vigorous', and 'had learned to please some ladies of fashion'. Or in plain English, he was being kept by ageing beauties who in return for his services supplied him with clothes and cash. To us it seems more disgraceful than the marriage swindle of his humbler contemporaries, but no one in society would have seen anything blameworthy in his conduct; how else was such a man to live? Do we not all remember Porthos and his Duchess? As a profitable sideline he initiated young fools into the fashionable pastime of deep play, and with such success that before he was eighteen he was able to set up a household 'which began to have the air of that of a Seigneur'. He need hardly have troubled to tell us that 'some Béarnais, men of spirit, knowing that he had a little money, attached themselves to him'. For the clannishness of Gascony had its drawbacks; let the rumour spread amongst the host of poor relations that young Antoine was doing well in Paris, and distant cousins would descend upon him by every night coach. And Antoine was undoubtedly a man to whom it was prudent to attach oneself; the bed-sitting room had given place to a house in which every effort had been made to give at least the reception room a fashionable air; stands of arms on either side of the fireplace, birds in cages, cupboards containing curios, and perhaps a fake old master on the wall. His ideal being rooms which would seem to us 'fussy', but in which Queen Victoria would have felt comfortably at home; countless tables with mosaic-work tops, cabinets everywhere, gold and silver vases; ebony tables with silver legs carved into caryatids, loaded with bronze statuettes; yet more tables bearing rock crystal models of famous churches, little boxes of cornelian, agate, and amber; busts; mirror-panelled walls; and in every angle 'an admirable vase' standing on a gilt tripod and containing spare candles.

Gone too for Guiche was the nightmare of trying to dress himself becomingly, for his tailor's bills would now be the affair of his patronesses, and a very serious affair too. A complete outfit for a needy lover was a common gift from a rich mistress, and would cost at least £250 of our money; even so, one would cut a poor figure beside Bassompierre,[1] whose best outfit cost him about £14,000, or Cinq-Mars,[2] who died the owner of three hundred pairs of boots. But Antoine could be elegant, if not yet magnificent; no longer would he soil his stockings by tramping Paris, he would travel in his *vinaigrette*, a wheeled chair pulled by one man. As became a person of quality, he would dine between one and two and sup from eight to nine, on a scale of which we get a hint from the Edict of 1629, which limited the number of courses which could be served at either meal to eighteen. He would have a smart hack to ride in the Cours-la-Reine, and there would be able to offer his mistresses an *ambigu*,[3] a picnic meal of sweets, pastry, and fruit, with gifts of gloves, fans, and ribbons; and if he was in funds, enlivened by the music of the 'four and twenty violins', the only professional orchestra in Paris.

For the rest, the world in which Antoine found himself was a blackguardly, swaggering, noisy one in which a thin veneer of chivalry and gallantry barely hid a barbarity carried off with boastful ostentation. Society still took its colour from the vanished Court of Henri IV, which more resembled a barrack-room than a palace, a place where horseplay, practical jokes, and the grossest freedoms were permitted, and in which the King neither expected nor received more deference than was due to the oldest officer present; whilst his soldier courtiers 'would never stand but in the Posture of Bragadocio, their looks and gestures as fierce as if they came only to quarrel with their

[1] Bassompierre, François de Bestein, Maréchal de, 1579–1646, one of the most magnificent courtiers of the reign of Henri IV and Louis XIII.

[2] Cinq-Mars, Henri Coffier d'Effiat, Marquis de, 1620–1642, became the King's favourite, 1638; Grand Equerry, 1640; beheaded for treason, 1642.

[3] The *pique-nique*, at this time popular with the lower bourgeoisie, was not an outdoor meal, but a dinner to which each guest contributed his quota of food and wine.

master'. Amongst the nobility passions were uncontrolled; abduction, rape, murder and duelling were commonplaces, and every man daily carried his life in his hands. The duel was not a check on ungentlemanly conduct but an eagerly sought diversion, to be provoked on the flimsiest pretexts. Seconds fought as well as principals, and sometimes a duel would be a battle, with six or eight men a side; each of the assistants very likely fighting an opponent whom he did not know, in a quarrel which had been explained to neither. Worse still, the duel had as yet no code of rules, and was often little better than plain murder; if you were doing badly at swordplay, it was quite legitimate to throw away your weapon and try to strangle your adversary; one Le Sec ran his adversary through whilst he was trying to draw; another gentleman proposed to his opponent that they should take their spurs off before they fell to, and whilst the man was kneeling, ran him through the back. It is only fair to mention, however, that society murmured at his action, which was described as 'a little too princely'; which gives us a curious idea of the standard of conduct to be expected from a seventeenth-century prince.

In 1621 Guiche made his début as a soldier in the army with which Louis XIII in person reduced the Huguenot strongholds of St Antonin and Montpellier; and there he fought recklessly, for he was always ready to stake his life on a single throw, provided the stakes were worth playing for.

At Montpellier he had his reward, for the courage of the young Gascon caught the King's eye. But the Treaty of Montpellier in 1622 restored peace between the central government and the Huguenots, leaving Antoine at a loose end, and with some little reputation gained. 'He rightly thought that it did not become a man of his age to plunge into the delights of Court life when he might be learning his trade in order to qualify for the military rank to which one of his birth and courage might aspire.' So 'he took leave of the King, having asked his permission to hunt for some opportunity of distinguishing himself in Holland', where Spain was still engaged in its hopeless attempt to subdue the Dutch. There, 'in one of the most beautiful sieges ever made in the Low Countries . . . the Comte de

Guiche was everywhere at once, and the Dutch conceived a high esteem of him'.[1]

In the winter of 1625, after fighting under Créqui in Piedmont, Antoine made his début at the Hôtel de Rambouillet, an indispensable ceremony for those seeking to enter polite society, and one which, if the candidate met with a favourable reception, gave him the entrée of all the best houses. But unfortunately for Guiche, neither rank nor military prestige conferred upon a man the entrée to Mme de Rambouillet's salon;[2] charm, knowledge of literature, and the art of easy, graceful conversation were the qualities in demand, and in these, hampered by his provincial upbringing, Antoine was sadly deficient. Keenly alive to atmosphere though he already was, he had not yet sloughed off the teaching of an elder generation which had held that all a man had to do to impress women favourably was to extol his own power, magnificence, wealth, and bravery, spicing this with a few perfunctory and patronizing compliments. The Rambouillet verdict was that the young man smelt of the age of Henri IV; nor could the habituées detect in him any trace of that wit for which he already had the beginnings of a reputation. He was civilly ejected.

However, before the winter was out he had restored his self-esteem by the *éclat* of his first and well-publicised duel; after which he left the country hurriedly. For Richelieu was now in the saddle, and was making one of his periodical attempts to suppress duelling. The Bastille had no attractions for Antoine, and still less had the scaffold; so he fled. 'The role of a simple traveller did not consort with his character, so he decided to look for a battle in Germany under Count Tilly[3]... who received him with open arms and treated him like a son.'[4] It is a

[1] Gramont, *Mémoires.*

[2] Rambouillet, Cathérine de Vivonne, Marquise de, 1588–1665, queen of the Paris bluestockings from 1630 to 1645. 'Famous for her beauty, her virtue, and her exquisite taste'.

[3] Tilly, Johann Tserclaes, Count von, 1559–1632, a native of Brabant. Died 1632 of wounds received at Breitenfeld in 1631, where he had been defeated by King Gustavus Adolphus of Sweden.

[4] Gramont, *Mémoires.*

striking tribute to Antoine's heritage, the fascination of the Gramonts; for Tilly liked very few people, and Frenchmen not at all. A sinister figure, one of the most notorious generals of the Thirty Years War; a small, thin man, a pupil of the Jesuits, with a slit for a mouth; who lived in the field with the regularity of a monk in his cloister; practised mental and ejaculatory prayer on the line of march; was incorruptible; and perpetrated atrocities which made his name a terror fifty years after his death. The hideous cruelties of his sack of Magdeburg in 1631 were to shock even his fellow generals; but Tilly, when remonstrated with, merely replied coldly, 'My troops needed some recreation.'[1] Antoine, on first seeing him on his little Croat pony, dressed in a mixture of oriental costumes, thought that he had fallen into the hands of a lunatic; but he was speedily convinced of his error, and of the need for treating this terrifying little man with considerable respect. Later in the campaign Guiche was to serve under an even more famous general, Wallenstein, who 'recognizing... that here was a young man capable and worthy of employment... offered him an honourable post in the Imperial service'. But Antoine realized that if he took service with the enemies of France, he would sentence himself to a life of exile. He declined the offer, though until 1629 he continued to serve under Wallenstein, 'from whom there was much to be learnt'.

In 1626 Antoine's brother overwhelmed himself and his family with ignominy. Richelieu had by now become the best-hated man in the kingdom, and his conspiracy complex was fully developed. To win the King's friendship was to incur the Cardinal's suspicion; and to incur his suspicion was to invite your delation for treason by one of his spies. It is in the ignoble role of informer and perjured witness that we first meet Roger, Comte de Louvigny.

Henri de Talleyrand, Comte de Chalais, Grand Master of the Wardrobe, now in his twenty-seventh year, was an attractive, idle, intriguing sort of man, who had been the King's follower, then the Cardinal's, and had now secretly joined the 'malcontents', the party headed by Louis XIII's worthless brother,

[1] Villermont, *Tilly*.

'Monsieur'. Into this party Chalais had been seduced by his passion for the notorious Mme de Chevreuse,[1] the greatest intriguer in France; and he had committed the fatal error of making Louvigny his confidant. The plot, so far as it was a fact and not a figment of Richelieu's imagination, aimed at little more than procuring the dismissal of the Cardinal and his replacement by one of the conspirator's 'creatures'; probably it would have failed in any case, but what brought Chalais to the block was the fact that Louvigny, like himself, was madly in love with Mme de Chevreuse. Not only did Louvigny betray all his rival's confidence to Richelieu, but he invented and swore to the abominable lie that Chalais planned to murder the King with a poisoned pin whilst adjusting his ruff at the *lever*. And Chalais was beheaded on the 19 August 1626.

In 1629 the Gramonts had the good fortune to lose Roger, who was killed in a duel. He had been a heavy liability; that he was a scoundrel they might have lived down, but not the fact that he was a beggar, and looked like one. No one of his quality had ever before dressed in such rags, and he would have looked better barefoot than in the shoes which he habitually wore. He was the owner of one shirt and one ruff, which his valet washed for him by night, and once when he was sent for by 'Monsieur' he had to reply that he could not wait upon him until his shirt was dry. A friend, knowing the exiguous nature of his wardrobe, pointed out to him in the street one day that he was getting his stockings dirty; 'No matter,' said Louvigny, 'they don't belong to me'.[2]

Meanwhile Guiche, who was looking about for some fresh field in which to catch the public eye, had got a commission from the Duc de Nevers to go to Mantua and there 'annoy the Spaniard as much as lay in his power'. To the causes of the Mantuan dispute he was obviously heartily indifferent, and we

[1] CHEVREUSE, Marie Aimée de Rohan, Duchesse de, 1600–1679, married the Duc de Luynes, 1617; widowed 1621, and married her lover, the Duc de Chevreuse, 1622; alternately in favour and disgrace throughout her long life. 'There never was a woman who had a bigger contempt for duties and scruples.'

[2] Tallemant des Réaux, *Historiettes*.

can dismiss them very briefly. Charles de Gonzague, Duc de Nevers, a Frenchman by inclination and upbringing, became in 1627 heir to the sovereign Duchy of Mantua; but the Hapsburgs had no idea of allowing a Francophil Duke to make the Duchy a springboard for Richelieu's aggressive policy in Italy.[1] Richelieu had naturally supported Nevers' claim, and had succeeded in making him the new Duke; which was not only a diplomatic triumph, but a domestic satisfaction, for Nevers had been one of the most troublesome members of a very turbulent aristocracy. In 1614 he had shown his disapproval of the French government's action in sending a Treasury official to audit the accounts of his Government of Lorraine by arresting him, dressing the unfortunate man as a fool, and having him led through the province mounted head to tail on a donkey. Antoine rendered good service to his somewhat eccentric commander, holding Nice for him against greatly superior forces for three weeks before marching out with the Honours of War. But the situation worsened in 1630 when he found himself besieged in Mantua by the Austrians under Colalto,[2] and on Ascension Day 1631 in a skirmish outside the walls he was wounded and left for dead on the field. He was ultimately saved by the courtesy of Gallas,[3] the Imperial Commander-in-Chief, who had known him when he was serving as a volunteer under Tilly. Gallas had him carried in a cloak to headquarters, where the Prince de Bozolo treated him with a kindness and courtesy which Antoine remembered when he came to dictate his memoirs forty years later; kindness which probably saved his life, for, tough though he was, Guiche spent the next hundred and twenty-seven days in bed, 'without moving from that spot'. But when convalescence ended, the captive found himself transferred to very different hands. In accordance with the laws of war Bozolo was now

[1] Richelieu, *Mémoires*.

[2] COLALTO, Rainbold, Count, an Imperial General who made his name as one of Wallenstein's lieutenants.

[3] GALLAS, Wenzel, Count von, one of the most brutal German commanders of the day; he escaped liquidation after the murder of Wallenstein in 1634 because the Viennese Court thought him harmless, 'he being seldom sober, and with not enough imagination to be dangerous'.

forced to hand Guiche over to his actual captor, a Corsican named Ferrari, who imprisoned him in the fortress of which he was commandant; and there Guiche 'received the worst treatment that a prisoner of his quality ever endured . . . in order to extort from him a large and immediate ransom'. Here he remained for eighteen months, despite the expostulations of Ferrari's officers; in great discomfort, and with his pride bitterly mortified by the refusal of his father to render him any financial aid. He owed his release firstly to the sudden death of Ferrari, which put him once more into Bozolo's hands, and secondly to the exchange of all prisoners of war which followed on the Treaty of Cherasco in May 1631. Whereupon Antoine joyfully hastened back to Paris and 'was received by the King with all the marks of kindness and distinction which he could hope for, and in consequence, by all the distinguished Seigneurs of the Court'.[1]

[1] Gramont, *Mémoires*.

CHAPTER II

★

ANTOINE at twenty-seven was already a man of some importance, a rising soldier, known at least by sight to the King, the Cardinal, and the leading courtiers. He could no longer follow with profit the advice of Refuge, to be all things to all men; the time had come when he must enlist in one of the parties into which France was divided, for to endeavour to stand aloof would be to condemn himself to the obscurity which would result from his unimportance to all factions. He had to give serious thought to the decision forced upon him, for an initial mistake might well be irremediable.

He had three parties to select from. First the 'malcontents', those who rallied round 'Monsieur' and endeavoured to use him as a spearhead in a permanent opposition to Richelieu. A party to avoid, thought Antoine, for he was not important enough to conspire with a reasonable certainty that whatever the outcome of the plot, his head would remain on his shoulders. And could any conspiracy succeed which had 'Monsieur' for its chief? For in all France there was no more contemptible man.

In 1631 'Monsieur' was a flippant irreligious youth of twenty-three. Vain, touchy, and so restless that his valets had to learn to dress him whilst he flitted about his bedroom, he spent his days mooning about the Louvre with his hands in his pockets, hat on the side of his head, and whistling perpetually. By night he would wander alone round Paris, entering any house where there was noise and music, and there delighting to cause dissension in the family. Physically and morally he was a coward, and would have solved all his difficulties by the coward's weapon, assassination, had it not been for his terror of Richelieu. His life was one long series of conspiracies and rebellions against the Crown, and each of them ended in the same disgraceful way. No one more eager than 'Monsieur' to enter into a plot, no one made a braver speech to his associates, no one more skilful in planning an abduction or an assassination – until Richelieu, whose spy system was the best in France, decided that the nuisance of 'Monsieur's' latest treachery must cease. And he would send for him. Confronted with that pale, terrible, passionless man, armed with proofs of 'Monsieur's' guilt, Gaston would lose countenance, stammer, contradict himself, and then fall at Richelieu's feet in tears, pleading that he had been led astray by wicked men. And, once assured of his personal safety, the prince would joyfully turn King's evidence, pouring out what he knew would cost his adherents their lives. His confession once sealed and signed, Richelieu would contemptuously grant Gaston an increase in his allowance, and the wretched man would go home in the highest spirits. Rarely did he attempt to plead for those whom he had betrayed, and at the moment they mounted the scaffold 'Monsieur', without a care in the world, would be chasing flies in his apartments. But though the details of his despicable conduct always became public knowledge – Richelieu saw to that – Gaston was blessed with an irresistible charm of manner when he was determined to captivate; and he was one of the wittiest speakers in France. Consequently when he next turned to plotting he could always collect a formidable body of supporters, undeterred by the fate of Gaston's previous dupes, and convinced that this time 'Monsieur' meant business. It was a party which struck Guiche as offering a precarious opening to a man with his way to make in the world.

Then there was the party of the King, for as Richelieu was for all practical purposes King of France, the *de jure* King was forced into the position of leader of a faction.

Louis XIII, now twenty-nine, had been a childless husband for fifteen years, and was already a victim of the tuberculosis which was to kill him in 1643. His nominal reign had begun when he was nine years old, and his childhood had been spent in subjection to a bad-tempered fool of a mother and her low-born Italian favourite, Concini; the boy detested both of them, and it is hardly surprising that he grew into a cold, timid, peevish and suspicious man, cruel and undependable. Nearly as irresolute as his brother Gaston, he was predestined to be dominated by a stronger character, and he escaped from the rule of his mother only to fall under that of Richelieu, who governed him absolutely. Which was perhaps fortunate, for Louis' only piece of unassisted 'ruling' was in 1617, when he planned the murder of Concini and watched with delight whilst the victim was slaughtered in the courtyard of the royal palace.

In his cruelty and dissimulation Louis XIII was not a Frenchman but a Renaissance Italian, the true son of his Medici mother. Even in appearance he was a southerner, having black eyes, a haggard yellow face, Italian features, and an expression which was at once cruel and vacant. When we add to this that he was a stutterer, a bore, and a man whose timid flirtations were conducted with the clumsiness of a schoolboy, we can understand the contempt in which he was held by his Court, and why the nobility in 1642 'went to his funeral as to a wedding'. What was France to make of a son of Henri IV who opened a liaison with a willing lady by saying 'Now, no naughty thoughts!' Or who, when challenged to take a letter out of a pretty girl's bosom, did so – with the fire tongs? And to crown everything, he was one of the stingiest men in his kingdom.

Not unnaturally, he found it impossible to win friendship, and difficult to obtain companionship; for society he was reduced to the company of obscure young men like St Simon,[1] father of the memoirist, who would put up with his dullness and pretend to take an interest in his favourite pastime, hawking. Though this was by no means his only hobby, for he was a dilettante in many fields; he painted a little, composed, loved string music, was a good gardener particularly successful with early peas, a first-class chef, and a shoemaker. But none of these occupations enabled him to shake off the boredom which afflicted him all his life; '*ennuyons-nous*', let us bore ourselves, he would say, drawing some reluctant courtier into a window.

He is praised for retaining as his Prime Minister Richelieu, whom he hated; but Richelieu was saved, not by Louis' appreciation of his ability, but by the cowardice which kept the King

[1] ST SIMON, Claude de Rouvroy, 1st Duc de, 1606–1693, Page to Louis XIII, and his favourite, 1627–1636; created a Duke, 1635; retired from Court, 1643, and spent the next fifty years on his estates.

from murdering him. Like Gaston, Louis dreamed of a palace revolution which would rid him of the detested Cardinal, and he incited his courtiers to hint at Richelieu's assassination, enjoying the thought of the Cardinal dying as Concini had died; even going so far as to clap Tréville[1] on the back, saying, 'Here is the man who will rid me of the Cardinal when I give the word'. But in spite of such talk Louis generally found it expedient to betray his companions in discontent when Richelieu frowned; not only allowing him to behead Cinq-Mars, who passed for his closest friend, but in his last moments remarking with glee, 'M. de Cinq-Mars will be passing an uncomfortable quarter of an hour just now'. For Louis was as heartless as Gaston; as is evident from one of his favourite diversions, which was to stand by the bedside of a dying courtier and mimic his last agonies.

To Antoine, considering the matter, it must have seemed that there was little to choose between being a King's man and being a 'malcontent', and that he must perforce become a Cardinalist; he offered himself to Richelieu and was accepted.

Armand Jean du Plessis, Cardinal de Richelieu, now in his forty-sixth year, was the third son of a Poitevin squire who 'had not passed for a man of quality'. Originally intended for the army, he was in his last year at the Academy when a family disaster altered the whole course of his life. The eldest brother, a wastrel, had what family property there was, whilst the second, being feeble-minded, had been forced into the Church and given the Bishopric of Luçon; but in 1605 the Bishop vanished, and when next heard of had become a Carthusian monk. Whereupon the mother appealed to her youngest son to step into the breach and save the bishopric from being lost to the impoverished family. Armand readily made what he himself describes as 'the heroic sacrifice'. In 1605 he was nominated to the See of Luçon, and, his chosen career apparently ruined, found himself installed in 'the worst, dirtiest, and most disagreeable Bishopric in France'. There he vegetated until 1614, when he was taken up by the Queen-Mother, and thereafter his

[1] Treville, or Troisvilles, Henri Joseph de Peyre, 1st Comte de, a Basque who enlisted in the French Guards, 1617; Captain of the Musqueteers, 1634.

advancement, though chequered, was rapid. In 1624 he became Prime Minister. His old patroness, who was on the worst of terms with her son, had now become an embarrassment to him, and he set about ridding himself of her by systematically exacerbating relations between the mother and son; with such success that in this year, 1631, he had succeeded in driving her into banishment. And from now onwards he ruled France and the King absolutely until the day of his death.

Handicapped by chronic ill-health, Richelieu was a depressed, melancholy man, rough to those about him, and nearly always in a bad humour; indifferent to popularity, ruling by terror, and finding a grim satisfaction in the knowledge that 'all knees shook before him'; rewarding and ruining with an icy, still politeness more menacing than any anger. Almost the only relief he allowed himself was an occasional flash of frightening humour, as when he sent for Harcourt, who was under a cloud, and said in his coldest voice, 'Monsieur, the King orders you to quit Paris instantly' – adding as the terrified man left the room – 'to take command of the Mediterranean Fleet'. Life brought him fame, wealth, and a lasting place in history, but he was still tormented by an inferiority complex. His insignificant birth was misery to him, and his enemies were constantly rubbing salt into the wound; and his failure to make friends or win the love of women was a profound mortification; for he was childishly touchy about his own attractiveness. This man, whom one would imagine above foppery, was everlastingly changing his clothes; now the Prince of the Church in scarlet, an hour later the gallant in grey satin, and again the soldier in leather jerkin and buff gauntlets; and at Court he was even known to wear face patches.

That he had no friends is understandable, for he had no idea of the nature of friendship. Intimacy with him was as dangerous and exhausting as it was with Frederick the Great; the same tenseness, a veneer of good-fellowship, the same dilemma of how to treat the master apparently as an equal, whilst preserving that constant obsequiousness whose absence would have been so brutally resented; the same anxious watchfulness to keep in step with his changing moods; even the same need to produce at a moment's notice what looked like criticism but was in fact eulogy of the Cardinal's wretched plays and verses.

Why he was an unsuccessful lover is less easy to understand; for, in addition to his prestige, he was a handsome, virile man who had acquired the polish of the best society. Perhaps he was too abrupt and dictatorial, too much the sultan deigning to beckon an attractive slave; at any rate even courtesans like Marion de l'Orme jeered at his advances.

It is a commonplace to say that Richelieu laid the foundations of French greatness, but it may also be argued that by destroying the constitution and erecting a despotism on its ruins, he set the monarchy on the course that shipwrecked it in 1789. Could Richelieu come to life today, he would find himself in a congenial climate as the holder of an important post behind the Iron Curtain. One of his most revealing characteristics was his hatred of public opinion; any public opinion, for approval of his régime expressed by anyone who was not in his pay, annoyed him little less than disapprobation; 'respectful silence, as of a soldier in the ranks' was the only safe course if you wanted to keep out of prison. And as his grip tightened, it became a crime to publish anything which, in the opinion of the Cardinal – that of the Courts did not matter – was seditious.

One of Richelieu's first moves was to rid himself of the whole machinery of criminal justice by bringing his enemies to trial before Special Commissions, packed Courts of his own henchmen in which the Crown was both prosecutor and judge. In these new Courts there was generally an elaborate and widely publicised trial of the type with which we are only too familiar today, a trial in which verdict and sentence were arranged beforehand; as we may easily imagine when we come to Richelieu's own views on treason trials – 'in matters of State, conjecture takes the place of proof . . . any action is honourable and legitimate if it is of service to the Prince'. How many of the small fry were victims of Richelieu's special justice we do not know, but forty-seven great nobles were judicially murdered by this method.

Richelieu's greatness as a foreign minister must not blind us to the disastrousness of his domestic policy; if indeed we can dignify with the name of policy his empirical fumbling designed to raise the huge sums needed to make France the first power in Europe; a policy of opportunism, of illegal and tyrannical expedients. Perhaps the best criticism of his internal policy is that when he died, the State was borrowing – with difficulty – at twelve per cent.

But no consideration of Richelieu's merits or demerits would occur to Guiche in weighing the problem of how his own fortunes were to be advanced. He saw clearly the risks involved in becoming the Cardinal's 'creature'; but he also saw that the choice lay between submission to Richelieu and relegation to obscurity in the provinces. So he chose Richelieu:

> He made himself pleasant to the illustrious Cardinal, now at the height of his power, and who made much of those who had a name and some merit. The Comte de Guiche was assiduous in paying his court to him, and obtained his confidence; and the Cardinal, to give him a convincing proof of his esteem, decided to ally himself to him by marrying him to his niece.[1]

Thus Guiche himself, but the facts do not flatter him as much as we should gather from his own account; nor is he strictly accurate. What happened was that Richelieu sent for him in 1634 and said, 'I promised you Mlle de Pont-Château, but am sorry to say that I cannot let you have her'; (he wanted her for the purchase of a more prominent courtier, whose support was essential to his plans) 'I therefore wish you to take Mlle du Plessis-Chivré in her stead'. The substitute palmed off on Antoine was not in fact a niece of the Cardinal's at all, but the daughter of one of his cousins. However, it was all one to Antoine; he replied deferentially that 'he was marrying His Eminence and not his relations, and that he would take whichever lady it pleased His Eminence to bestow upon him'. And any chagrin which he may have felt at having to marry the less distinguished girl was dispelled by the marriage ceremonies, which were 'sumptuous, and in the highest degree magnificent'. And too by the fact that Richelieu, as a reward for his docility,

[1] Gramont, *Mémoires*.

gave the bride a 'dowry which would have reflected credit upon a Princess'.[1] As this is Guiche's first and last reference to his Countess, we may assume that she was of small importance in his life; but she was to bear him two sons and a daughter, all of whom later played prominent parts.

Antoine might now have felt that he was standing on firm ground, but he was too shrewd a man to presume on his position; he continued to treat the Cardinal with the greatest deference and adroitness. One day, entering Richelieu's room, Guiche found him in his shirt and breeches, engaged in the intellectual pastime of trying how high up the wall he could plant a kick. Now to surprise one of the Cardinal's morbid vanity in such an unseemly attitude was to incur a real danger; the slightest disclosure on Antoine's part that he saw anything ridiculous in Richelieu's amusement might well have been fatal. So without a moment's hesitation he threw off his cloak and said with his pleasant smile, 'I wager I can kick higher than Your Eminence' – and proceeded to lose his bet. About the same time one of his friends is shocked at his drunken rashness at a supper party where Guiche bursts out, 'Though I've refused to be his damned Gentleman of the Chamber, I'm for the Cardinal against any man, even against the King.' Drunken rashness? It would greatly surprise me if Antoine was drunk on this occasion; I rather see him practising the advice of Refuge, that a soldierly bluntness is the cleverest form of flattery. He knew that there was one of Richelieu's spies at this, as at every social gathering, and that his remark would be reported; as it was, and Richelieu took the bait, as he did on other occasions as well. Years later people would recall admiringly that 'Even with Richelieu, Guiche kept some shadow of liberty'. His dutiful marriage and his assiduous attentions to Richelieu were not to go unrewarded. Tension between France and Spain was steadily growing, and in 1634 news reached Paris that the Governor of the Spanish Netherlands was contemplating a surprise attack on Calais; Antoine, sent there in a hurry, took command. Though the threatened attack did not materialize, he was thanked by the King and given a handsome draft on the Treasury by Richelieu. 'Nothing,' he

[1] Gramont, *Mémoires.*

says complacently, 'sits so well upon a wide-awake courtier, or shows him off to better advantage, than to have as his protector a Minister of the first rank to whom the master has given absolute power'.

Throughout the next twelve months the Franco-Spanish situation continued to deteriorate, and on 19 May 1635 France declared war on Spain, thus making her formal entry into the Thirty Years War.

With the origins and progress of that immensely complicated struggle we need not concern ourselves any more than did Guiche, to whom it was merely a Heaven-sent opportunity to obtain those prizes which he so eagerly desired. And indeed even the well-informed of his contemporaries would have been hard put to it to explain a war which had already raged for seventeen years and was now continuing under its own momentum, as if war were in itself an objective; as indeed it was for the Generals of those hordes of unpaid bandit armies which were now ravaging central Europe. France, in alliance with Sweden, Holland, and Savoy, set out on her adventure with high hopes which were not to be immediately or completely realized. And the explanation is simple. With unimportant exceptions, she had not fought outside her own frontiers for seventy years, and she was now to pay for her lack of experience; as is always the case with a power, hitherto neutral, which intervenes in a long war in which her enemies have become seasoned.

The most serious French defect was the quality of the senior officers, who had nothing to recommend them but the reckless bravery of their caste; Major-Generals, says Richelieu, neglected their duties, could not pitch a camp, or even assure its safety when pitched. There was practically no discipline; in 1632 when 'Monsieur' was in command of an army, his baggage was looted by his own troops; and the officers' ideas of discipline were as curious as the men's; Arnauld, for instance, dislikes the habit of Court-Martialling a man for desertion, which he says, 'is, after all, only a trifle'.[1]

In 1635 Guiche got his first real chance when he was appointed

[1] Andilly, *Mémoires*.

Major-General under La Valette[1] on the Rhine front, Turenne[2] being the other Major-General. And it was lucky for La Valette that he had serving under him two officers who knew their business; for the initial French manœuvre, an advance on Mayence, at once revealed the weakness of La Valette's army. Guiche, commanding the advance-guard, says, 'it was the opening of the campaign, and everything appeared difficult to the troops, and even to the officers, who had lived softly for too long; the cavalry was not used to pitching camp, and did it clumsily . . . the army regarded it as a prodigy to have to pass four or five days without bread, and their attitude produced an almost general sedition . . . in which Guiche had to show much address in bringing the men back to their duty by his soft and persuasive eloquence'. 'Stronger persuasion' was needed to get them to cross the Rhine. And having crossed it, they showed such anxiety to put it once more between themselves and the enemy that La Valette decided to fall back on Metz – 'that memorable retreat . . . so well known to all the world, and which made so much noise'. As well it might, for it was the retreat from Moscow in miniature; roots and herbs were the French army's only food, the baggage was lost, the cannon buried, and men died like flies. It was a chastening experience for the raw French officers, who imagined that wars were fought like duels; 'they thought that as soon as they reached the front a challenge would be sent to Gallas; on the following day they would beat him; and on the next, they would set off for home'.[3] Only 5,000 out of La Valette's 12,000 men won through to safety, and even so Richelieu was thankful that things were no worse.

In 1636 Guiche was again posted to the German front; the Duke of Weimar having taken a liking to him, and having asked for his services.

[1] LA VALETTE, Louis de Nogaret, Cardinal de, 1593–1639, Archbishop of Toulouse; Cardinal, 1621; left the Church and married, 1622; a good second-rate General, commanded French armies, 1635–1639.

[2] TURENNE, Henri de La Tour d'Auvergne, Vicomte de, 1611–1675, son of the 1st Duc de Bouillon and the foremost soldier of his day, killed in action on the German front.

[3] Montglat, *Mémoires*.

It is characteristic of an unfeeling age that in reading Antoine's memoirs we get no hint of the nightmare that was Germany during the Thirty Years War; a country littered with corpses, 'their limbs and bowels torn and eaten by dogges and swine', where, as hope died, men were turning for help to the powers of darkness. As early as 1624 Sir John Hepburn, commanding the Scots Brigade, notes that throughout Germany enchanted bullet-proof armour was in keen demand, and two years later an astrologer recommends attacking without artillery cover because the enemy are wizards who can be killed only by being clubbed to death. As agriculture ceased to be practised and food stocks became exhausted, looting, murder, plague, and starvation became normal in any zone of military operations; and armies turned into mobs of ferocious bandits under a leader who, as he had no means of paying his men, had to let them live as they pleased. By the time Guiche joined the army of Germany, strategy had degenerated into an attempt to manœuvre the enemy into a district in which you could starve him without starving yourself, and tactics had become largely an affair of night raids to capture food. One recorded night attack had for its objective the seizure of a heap of decaying horses – 'We could smell our meat afarre off . . . yet we ate it savourly'. On several other occasions this particular force feasted on rats and mice, which our author calls 'unedible cattell'.[1] And this diet of the troops had much to do with spreading the plague throughout Germany; and what plague meant we learn from a grim contemporary description – torpor, sleep, burning heat, horrible pain, gangrene, death. Poisonous and insufficient food quickly reduced troops to a state in which 'if any Souldier were but slightly wounded, presently it became a maligne ulcer'. And even when food happened to be plentiful, every camp was a breeding ground for disease; for in unruined country the troops would slaughter cattle and sheep so recklessly that within a few days the camp would be surrounded by a wall of rotting carcasses.

What foraging meant to the civilian population we learn from

[1] Munro.

a vivid contemporary account[1]. The cavalry descend upon an isolated farm and begin by breaking all the windows and furniture; next, the copper utensils are beaten flat and loaded on the farm horses; all the livestock is then slaughtered or driven off, and a huge meal is cooked. After business comes pleasure; having raped the women, the troops proceed to torture the farmer and his sons to make them disclose the whereabouts of that 'hidden wealth' which the poor wretches almost certainly did not possess. Most of these tortures are too disgusting to describe, but a favourite one was to geld the farmer in the presence of his wife and daughters; another, to force victims dying under torture to pray to the Devil.[2] Those who would know what the eruption of troops into a hitherto comfortable district meant should look through the collection of engravings by Callot published at Paris in 1633 under the title of *Fructus Belli*; and particularly at the one called *Voyla les beaux exploits de ces coeurs inhumains*. Here we have the living room of a well-to-do farmer in the hands of the invaders; in the foreground some soldiers are busily engaged in making up the family property into bundles; to the right blazes a huge fire, over which hangs an elderly man head downwards, the head just clear of the flames; on the hearth is a younger peasant, held in the blaze up to his knees; and at the back of the room is the farmer's wife, held down on her bed, with a queue of soldiers waiting their turn to rape her.

In a captured town things would be little better than in the isolated homestead; once the preliminary ravishing and massacre were over, a deathly silence fell upon the empty streets, broken only by the uproar from some shuttered house from which proceeded drunken laughter and the screams of women and children. Only around military headquarters would there be some semblance of normal life, a coming and going of officers, wagons loaded with stolen wine and provender driving into the courtyard. For whoever else starved, it was not the garrison commander and his staff; one unforgettable picture has been preserved for us of a headquarters banquet in a starving town,

[1] Grimmelsheusen, *The Adventures of Simplicissimus*.

[2] Vincent, *The Lamentation of Germany*.

where host and guests vomit over the masses of untouched food which even German gluttony has been unable to consume.[1] Not always were the streets deserted; sometimes there wandered in them runaway children in terror of their parents – 'We doe heare daily of children crying about the streets and lamenting that they dare not goe home for feare of being eaten'. By 1636 cannibalism had become common in Germany; at Zweibrucken in that year a man was found eating his mother's corpse, and in the Lower Palatimate in 1637 women lured unwary travellers into their houses with a promise of food and there killed and ate them. At Worms in the same year there was a riot when the smell of cooking meat brought a mob of soldiers down on a house in which they found 'a human head that had been scalded in hot water, and so baked in an oven'. In some slightly less miserable localities where a brave effort was being made to preserve the rudiments of civilization, armed guards were posted on cemeteries with orders to shoot on sight those who came out after dark to dig up the dead.[2] When it comes to barbarity, there is little to choose between Protestants and Catholics; and the same is true not only of the German but of all other war theatres. Richelieu speaks with great indignation of the conduct of the English army at Rochelle in 1627, where, he says, it showed 'the cruelty and inhumanity customary amongst heretics'. No doubt Buckingham's rabble behaved ill; but here is the same Richelieu telling us what happened two years later when Catholic Austria invaded Catholic Mantua:

> Arson and murder were common . . . the soldiers . . . greased their boots with the sacred oils, broke images of the Virgin, fired volleys on the crucifix, polluted the Churches . . . and trampled the Holy Sacrament under their feet.[3]

Perhaps the balance is slightly in Catholic Tilly's favour, for in his army the sack of a nunnery with its inevitable sequel, the murder of the elder nuns and the transfer of the younger ones to the camp brothel, was often punished as a breach of discipline;

[1] *Simplicissimus.*

[2] *Lamentation of Germany.*

[3] Richelieu, *Mémoires.*

whereas the Protestant Mansfield kept squads trained in the outraging of nuns and children, and in the mutilation of priests. But the Protestant armies had no contingent so devilish as Tilly's Croat cavalry. Amongst the Croats a man did not rank as 'a jolly companion' until he could sport a hatband made of peasant's ears of his own collecting.[1]

With soldiers like these at work it is not surprising that in Bavaria in 1632 the Scots Brigade found the bodies of fifty of their comrades with the eyes gouged out and the noses cut off. The result was, as the Scots boasted, that they thereafter killed every Bavarian they could find. Nor was the miserable business of reprisal confined to the troops, for the hardiest of the maddened peasantry took to the woods, and the sick or lost soldier whom they captured died horribly. A cavalry foraging party once surprised some villagers burying a barrel; these fled at their approach and the patrol dug up and opened the barrel, only to find to their great disappointment that all it contained was one of their comrades, alive, with his nose and ears cut off. But in both armies the worst element was not the fighting troops but the horse-boys, valets, quack doctors, prostitutes, hucksters, and the 'death hunters', the terrible old women who murdered and stripped the wounded; amongst whom an officer called the Provost of the Harlots maintained some semblance of order by daily hangings without the formality of a trial. Only against Gustavus Adolphus' Swedes, who were well paid and well disciplined, are no breaches of the laws of war recorded.[2]

Guiche, like Gallio, cared for none of these things. To the insensibility of his century he added the arrogance of a French noble, and if he noticed what was going on around him at all, he no doubt shrugged his shoulders and reminded himself that these wretches were only Germans and Scotchmen.

Germany, though one would not guess it from Antoine's memoirs, was a theatre of minor importance in 1636, the disastrous 'Corbie year' when for a moment even the capture of Paris did not seem beyond the enemy's powers; and except for the capture of Saverne, where Guiche nearly got himself

[1] Noailles, *Episodes de la Guerre de Trente Ans.*

[2] Trench, *Gustavus Adolphus.*

drowned in the moat, little of interest happened in Germany. However, Guiche managed to extract a good deal of enjoyment out of cavalry skirmishes, in one of which the Duke of Weimar was so thoroughly beaten by a regiment of Croats that he called upon Antoine to devise some striking revenge. Fortune, as usual, played into Antoine's hands; a few days later he succeeded in beating the same Croat regiment and capturing all its baggage, including an ape as big as a man, dressed in hussar uniform, the property of the handsome young wife of the elderly Croat Colonel. Here was just the opportunity which Guiche had been looking for; he had the unfortunate animal castrated, and returned it by a flag of truce to the enemy Colonel with the Comte de Guiche's compliments.

In 1636 Richelieu found nothing on which to congratulate either himself or his Generals; he had barely held his own against the Spaniards, and elsewhere his plans had been frustrated by the glaring incompetence and lack of discipline which continued to be the radical troubles of the French army.

The annual retirement into winter quarters brought Guiche not a holiday but a change of work, which elated him as showing his increasing favour with Richelieu; he was ordered to try his hand in the diplomatic line by opening negotiations with 'Monsieur', to whose Court he repaired in December. 'Monsieur' had spent what was, even by his own standards, a discreditable year; he had done a little amateur soldiering on the Flanders front where, to say the least of it, he had not added to his reputation. And in October he had been the mainspring in a plot to murder Richelieu, which had failed only because 'Monsieur' himself lost his nerve at the critical moment.[1] He had then left Paris in a hurry, and was now skulking at Blois in agonies of fear lest any evidence of his share in the plot should reach the Cardinal. Guiche, who met with a cordial reception, produced all the arguments with which he had been briefed to persuade 'Monsieur' to return to Court. But the Prince was too frightened even to consider the matter; he poured out his usual torrent of easy eloquence, protesting that he was Richelieu's humble servant and the King's most devoted subject, but leave Blois he

[1] Montrésor, *Mémoires*.

would not. Indeed Antoine as it happened was lucky to leave Blois himself, for whilst 'Monsieur' was apparently full of deference and flattery, what he was really considering was the possibility of imprisoning Antoine and threatening to murder him if the Cardinal took any steps to attack Blois.

CHAPTER III

★

EIGHTEEN years had now passed since Guiche left home to try his luck in the capital, years during which, so far as we know, he had never revisited Gascony, and at Bidache members of the family who can have been only names to him were growing up. Notably his half-brothers Henri and Philibert. Philibert at fifteen was already an original; was to retain that character for the next sixty years; was to be one of the most talked of men in France and was by his unique and inexhaustible fund of impudence to make for himself a niche in the best society.

> *Il peut revenir un Condé,*
> *Il peut revenir un Turenne,*
> *Un Comte de Gramont en vain est demandé;*
> *La Nature auroit trop de peine*

as St Evremond was to sing of him. Whether Guiche and the Chevalier de Gramont as he now was, had ever met before 1636 is uncertain, but in this year they got to know each other when Philibert, a theological student at Pau, was sent to Paris in the vacation to acquire a society polish under the eye of Guiche.

Never had there been more unpromising material for the priesthood, thought Society, and no one agreed more heartily with this verdict than Philibert himself. He had all the family determination to arrive, and even less than the usual family allowance of scruples; now or never, he decided, was the time to rebel against his fate, and the manner of his revolt was characteristic. He had himself presented at Court, dressed in riding boots, spurs, buff belt and sword, over which he wore a short cassock.[1] Even the melancholy Louis XIII laughed at his masquerade, and Philibert's father, realizing that his son had effectively closed the door to Church preferment by his escapade, consented to his abandoning his theological studies –

[1] Hamilton, *Memoirs*.

which by the way cannot have proceeded very far, for years later, having accidentally heard the Lord's Prayer, he remarked on the excellence of its style and asked who had written it. Free of the hated cassock, Philibert, with his elder brother Henri, Comte de Toulongeon, now entered the Académie Royale, which was half a military academy and half a select finishing school. There the Gramont brothers had the good luck to be classmates of no less a person than Louis de Bourbon, Duc d'Enghien, afterwards famous as the Great Condé; and being Gramonts, they did not fail to cultivate the acquaintance, though the friendship which sprang up between them was to have embarrassing results in years to come.

Their sisters too were apparently living in Paris at this time, probably being educated at a fashionable convent; at any rate in a position to exercise the family talent for cultivating useful friendships; for 'Mademoiselle'[1] tells us that in 1634, when she herself was seven, the Gramont girls, Suzanne and Anne, were amongst her favourite playmates. In 1637 Richelieu gave Antoine a further mark of his confidence by posting him to serve under La Valette in Flanders where the main French effort was to be made. And if the results of the campaign were not all that had been hoped for, Antoine at least succeeded in keeping himself in the public eye; winning a small victory over the Spaniards under Don Juan de Vinero and clearing the French lines of communication to Maubeuge. For this he was handsomely rewarded, being made King's Lieutenant of Normandy and Governor of Rouen, both well-paid posts for which he drew the salaries whilst performing the duties by deputy.[2]

Having put his men into winter quarters, Guiche returned to Paris, there to pick up the latest Court and family news; and for once he must have found the latter the more interesting, for whilst he had been at the front his wife had borne him a son, Armand, of whom we shall be seeing a good deal presently.

[1] MONTPENSIER, Anne Marie Louise de Bourbon, Duchesse de, 1627–1693, whose Court title was 'Mademoiselle'; only daughter of 'Monsieur' by his first wife; a leading rebel during the Fronde, and was exiled at its close; about 1671 married secretly the Comte de Lauzun.

[2] Gramont, *Mémoires*.

Nothing much else seemed to have happened except that Toulongeon had passed out of the Académie with an ensign's commission.

Guiche had by now a well-earned reputation as a debauched man about town, and it must have been with reluctance that he took the mission assigned to him this winter by Richelieu, which was to reopen negotiations with 'Monsieur', who was still lurking at Blois, where he was acting as a rallying point for the Cardinal's numerous enemies. Antoine knew his 'Monsieur' better now than he had done in 1636, and it was with weariness and disillusionment that he and his colleague Chavigny[1] prepared once more to endure a flood of inconclusive eloquence. 'They had much trouble in persuading "Monsieur" to submit to the King's will' says Montglat, though it is difficult to see in what 'Monsieur's' submission consisted. For as always when he was surrounded by stronger characters than his own, his attitude had hardened; he no longer posed to Guiche as the Cardinal's humble servant, but on the contrary, 'showed open suspicion of him and attacked his two deputies, whom he accused of being spies'. Antoine was a happy man when the time came for him to abandon the dreary little Court of Blois for the wine and women of Paris.

In 1638 he was sent to the Italian front, much to his dissatisfaction; for Italy, though fighting went on there year after year, was starved of men and material, a front on which Richelieu exerted just sufficient pressure to create a diversion for Spain. Certainly no theatre in which an ambitious junior could find the opportunity for which he craved. But he had been sent out to Italy merely as a stopgap to command between the death of Créqui and the arrival of his successor. On his return Antoine realized that his star was at last in the ascendant; in August he received one of the big prizes in the gift of the Crown, the command of the French Guards, and with it the Governorship of Lorraine. With his new dignities he could raise his eyes to the top of the hill. It was no longer a case of looking downward

[1] Chavigny, Léon Bouthillier, 1st Comte de, 1608–1652, a man much in the confidence of Richelieu, who was suspected of being his father; he was constantly in and out of favour from 1643 to 1652.

to estimate the distance he had climbed, but of an upward glance to measure the length of the journey to the summit.

In February 1639 Antoine was sent to the Northern front to attempt the relief of Château-Cambresis, and Bussy-Rabutin went with him as his second-in-command. The latter's description of the affair shows the informal nature of military assignments at the time; they being regarded in the light of social rather than professional engagements:

> I heard that Château-Cambresis was besieged . . . and that Guiche . . . was ordered to its succour. As he was a friend of mine . . . I went with him, but on reaching St Quentin we heard that the enemy had raised the siege; so Guiche returned to Court after giving me a thousand thanks for the proof of friendship I had given him in accompanying him.[1]

No doubt the two enjoyed their trip, for they had tastes in common; both were fashionable wits and Bussy, though as a soldier he never got beyond the level of competence, filled a larger place in the public eye as a man of the world than did the future Maréchal de Gramont. Antoine must have been proud of his company.

In April Guiche, promoted temporarily to Lieutenant-General, was again sent to Italy to deputize for La Valette who had managed to get himself blockaded in Turin; but his fate did not concern Antoine, whose orders were to throw himself into Pignerol, the French outpost in Italy, and hold it at all costs. The Spaniards, however, whose conduct showed a considerable lack of initiative, did not lay siege to either Turin or Pignerol, and when both sides fell back on a languid war of manœuvre Antoine was recalled to France with orders to proceed to Mouzon, there to assume command of the troops detailed to escort Louis XIII to Grenoble where he had arranged to meet his sister, the Duchess of Savoy. Disguised as a mere family visit, the interview was really dictated by the necessities of Richelieu's foreign policy, Louis being briefed to persuade the Duchess that she could maintain her Regency only by giving herself wholeheartedly to the French cause. Richelieu, who

[1] Bussy-Rabutin, *Mémoires*.

apparently thought it not worth while to wear the mask with her, 'spoke a little more boldly than the respect which he owed the King's sister should have allowed . . . reproaching her with her personal conduct'.[1] With justice, if not with tact. Christine of Savoy, who had married the late Duke Victor Amadeus in 1619, was now a domineering bully of thirty-one, whose name had been coupled with that of many men, and whose people had challenged the legitimacy of her three-year-old son, Duke Victor Emmanuel II. At the moment she was struggling to preserve her son's Duchy intact in the face of heavy pressure from Austria, and so had to swallow Richelieu's insults; 'she dare not take offence . . . for all her hopes depended upon the Cardinal'. And Louis emerged from the interview, with France accepted as the 'protector' of Savoy.

To Guiche the journey must have presented itself as a tedious ceremonial duty whose sole advantage was that it brought him closer to Richelieu. Possibly on the road he may have been thinking more of domestic matters than of French policy, for in this year his last child, Cathérine Charlotte, was born, and she, like her brothers, must be educated to play her part in the general scheme for the family advancement. Armand, we may remember, had been born in 1637, and in 1638 his wife had presented Guiche with another son, Antoine Charles, who had received the ill-omened title of Comte de Louvigny, in abeyance since the death of that black sheep Roger in 1629.

1640 was an important year in Antoine's life, for with his appointment to command the cavalry of the crack Army of Flanders he definitely emerged from the rank and file of subaltern generals, and with any luck the ball was now at his feet. And hardly had he arrived at the front when he had the signal honour of being recalled to Paris to confer with Richelieu on the practicability of the siege of Arras. As a result of his advice Antoine went back to Flanders to act as second-in-command to Châtillon,[2] where he at once exhibited the in-

[1] Montglat, *Mémoires*.

[2] CHATILLON, Gaspard de Coligny, Maréchal de, 1584–1646, grandson of the famous Huguenot leader Admiral de Coligny; accused of 'selling out' to the Court in 1622 for a Marshal's bâton.

corrigible vanity and indiscipline of his caste. Châtillon forbids him to make one of those reckless, showy charges so dear to a Gascon's heart. ' "Monsieur!" ' shouted Guiche in a fury, 'you insult me by such an order, I shall complain to the King.' Perhaps he carried out his threat and was duly snubbed by Louis XIII, who was something of a soldier; at any rate it is significant that he afterwards admitted himself to be wrong; and even more so that he makes no mention of the episode in his memoirs. He shows to better advantage at Bapaume, where he not only broke Bucquoy's cavalry[1] but showed his typical adroitness in escaping from an awkward situation: [2]

> The Comte de Guiche charged with his regiment... and found himself mixed up with the enemy regiment which he had failed to rout... Then Guiche showed his presence of mind; unobtrusively getting rid of his white scarf (the French distinguishing emblem) he placed himself in the front rank of the enemy regiment which was about to charge Guiche's own regiment... and Rouville, commanding in his absence, recognised and rescued him.

But all this was of less importance to Antoine than the friendship which the campaign enabled him to establish with the Duc d'Enghien, now on the threshold of his great career. The two cannot have met as strangers, for Antoine's half-brothers had been Enghien's companions at the Académie and had no doubt presented their already distinguished brother to the young Duke; but this was the first occasion when the pair had a chance to take stock of each other. Though Enghien was only nineteen whilst Antoine was thirty-six, the disparity of age formed no obstacle to the growth of a real intimacy; for on the one hand Enghien had all the precocious maturity of seventeenth-century royalty, whilst on the other there never was a man so skilled as Guiche in bridging the gap of years between himself and those whose friendship he thought of value to him. Enghien,

[1] Bucquoy, — de Longueval, 2nd Comte de, Spanish General, commanded 'Banner of Hainault' Cavalry Brigade 1640; killed in action in Sicily 1676.

[2] Rostand in his *Cyrano de Bergerac* makes an effective use of this incident.

we are told, enjoyed Antoine's wit and good humour, and took no exception to his morals; which suggests that the elder man's method of putting himself on a friendly footing with the younger was not perhaps one of the nicest delicacy. It was not everyone who could get on with Enghien, even if he was accepted on his own terms; for the mocking arrogance which was to remain his most striking characteristic was already apparent. Like all his generation he had learnt to suffer Richelieu's despotic control of every detail of his life with impotent fury; and he never forgot the supreme humiliation of being forced into marriage with a connection of Richelieu's;[1] which he was unmanly enough to avenge by a lifelong hatred of his unfortunate wife, herself as much a victim of Richelieu's tyranny as he was. We get a clearer picture of him in externals than of most of his contemporaries, for practically everybody tells us that he looked like an eagle; a very shabby eagle, for his slovenliness at Court was notorious. He was a well-educated man, not only by the standards of his rank but absolutely; and there were few subjects from theology downwards on which he could not hold his own. Like all the Condés he could be the best of good company when he wanted to charm; and he could also behave with a brutal arrogance which many were not prepared to endure even from the First Prince of the Blood. In his savage, open, and imprudent contempt for all civilians he resembled a Prussian officer of the nineteenth century rather than a French prince of the seventeenth.

He had one ambition to which he sacrificed everything, and that was to force his way into the innermost ring of the international military hierarchy. In his early twenties he was to be successful in this beyond his wildest dreams, and his triumph ruined an already unstable character. Circumstances were there-

[1] CONDE, Claire Clémence de Maillé-Brezé, Princesse de, 1628–1694, daughter of Urbain de Maillé-Brezé, Marshal of France, brother-in-law of Richelieu; married Enghien 1641; something mysterious happened in 1671 which 'changed her husband's cold dislike of her to vindictive anger', and she was imprisoned by him at Châteauroux in Berri, where she spent the rest of her life. In 1686 Louis XIV granted Condé's dying request that his wife should never be set free.

after to throw him into civil war with no asset but his military fame, and with the fatal liability of a character whose innate imperiousness had been exalted to the point of madness by the homage rendered to the hero who had broken the power of Spain. As a politician he was pitiable; involved in the spider's web of half-lights, nuances, hints, compromises, secret bargains, the world of the Fronde in fact, he behaved as we should have expected him to do. He made enemies on every side and lost most of his friends; confronted with that close corporation of lawyers, the Paris Parlement, he raged against those 'square hats', those devils, those rascals for whom hanging was too good, with all the brutality of a vindictive child in an uncontrollable passion.

He is seen at his best in the field in command of an army. His arrogance was there bridled by the fact that he was subject to the criticism of his peers, men who like himself belonged to that inner ring to which birth neither gave nor denied admission. It is easy to understand the passionate admiration with which he was regarded by his own subordinates and by the rank and file; for whilst other Generals ordered attacks, Condé led them. If not a great General, he was at least a great fighter; if there was a frontal attack to be made, against odds and over difficult ground, no better commander for the task than Condé, who would lead attack after attack in person until the position was taken; and who never forgot even a private soldier who had distinguished himself under his command. One regrets for his reputation that he did not die before the civil war with his great name untarnished.

But Guiche had other preoccupations in 1640 than ingratiating himself with Enghien; his father was still alive, which meant that Antoine was an embarrassed man, and now as always he relied upon the dice box for a substantial portion of his income. One would like to be able to record that he showed at the card table that bland, ironic good humour which he normally displayed, but in fact he behaved like the majority of his contemporaries. Arnauld served under him this year, and gives a picture of him over the cards, 'swearing and cursing in his usual manner'. 'My trouble is,' said Guiche, 'that when I lose, I have no friend to box my ears.' 'That is what you need,' said Arnauld, 'but nothing would induce me to be that obliging friend.' A story not worth repeating except for the fact that it was widely circulated as an example of the outspoken way in which Arnauld behaved towards 'the great'; which shows how high Guiche had already climbed in public estimation by 1640.

Antoine's winter leave was largely taken up with what he describes as 'a trifling affair'. His former tutor had a relation in Paris, the Abbé de Croisilles, a priest. This Abbé, being short of cash, had ingratiated himself with the widow of a Paris lawyer, whom he always visited dressed as a layman, and to whom he represented himself as being a Councillor of State with great prospects. But the widow, though charmed with his attentions, refused to disburse, and the Abbé in desperation at last offered marriage. The 'wedding' was duly solemnized by Croisilles' valet, whom he had dressed up in his own vestments for the occasion. All went well for a year, then the secret leaked out, and the enterprising Abbé was arrested. But Croisilles still had a trump up his sleeve. He was related to Mademoiselle Paulet, known in Society as The Lioness on account of her tawny golden hair, a woman who occupied a unique position in the fashionable world. She had had many lovers, but was admitted to the Hôtel de Rambouillet, and there on her first visit was met by a flower-crowned choir of girls who presented her with the keys of the house, while the toy cannon on the roof fired a salvo of welcome. In her later years not only had she graduated as a famous blue-stocking, but she was everywhere received with the respect due to a woman who had slept with Henri IV. In Henri's lifetime this fact had aroused little interest, but the best-loved of the Bourbons had now been dead for thirty years, and few were left who could boast of his subjection.

The Lioness took up her kinsman's case warmly, and appealed to Guiche to use his influence with Richelieu to secure lenient treatment for Croisilles; and it is a significant illustration of the extent of Antoine's influence that Richelieu, who had meant to hang the Abbé, agreed that he should be imprisoned for life in a monastery. But this did not satisfy Mademoiselle Paulet, who actually talked the cautious Antoine and three of his friends into promising to liberate the Abbé by force. Guiche however, once out of reach of the tears and eloquence of Mademoiselle Paulet, began to reflect, and the more he reflected the less he liked the idea. Ultimately he decided to ascertain what view Richelieu would take of the matter, and very lucky it was for him that he did so. 'You have shown your usual good sense in telling me this,' said the Cardinal, 'for if you had attempted such a thing I should never have seen you again.' A hundred times in later life, as Guiche tells us himself, he was to stand amazed at his own stupidity in contemplating an outrage which could have brought him no benefit and might have cost him his head.

When the military postings for 1641 were announced, Antoine regarded his own with mixed feelings; true, he had an independent command for the first time, that of the Army of Champagne. But it was an open secret that the whole French effort was to be made in Flanders, whilst in Champagne Guiche would stand on the defensive; and no doubt he was grateful when at the last moment Richelieu changed his mind and sent him to the main theatre as second-in-command to La Meilleraye.[1] Characteristically, he managed to draw the pay of the lapsed appointment in addition to that due to him as Meilleraye's lieutenant.

This year Guiche was again one of the council which met under Richelieu to settle the details of the forthcoming campaign; at which it was decided that France should begin operations with the siege of Aire. This involved Guiche in some of the toughest fighting which had yet come his way; and it was not until after forty-nine days of fierce struggle that Aire surrendered and its garrison marched out with the Honours of War – 'Colours flying, bullet in mouth, and with two pieces of artillery'. Antoine's own conduct during the siege was much admired and in September another opportunity came his way; Brezé[2] was recalled from Flanders and his command was given

[1] LA MEILLERAYE, Charles de La Porte, Maréchal and 1st Duc de, 1602–1664; first cousin of Richelieu's, made Marshal, 1639; Duke and Peer, 1663; a man of some merit, but an indifferent soldier.

[2] BREZÉ, Urbain de Maillé, Marquis and Maréchal de, 1597–1650, married Richelieu's younger sister; made Marshal 1632, and Governor of Catalonia, 1641; entirely under the thumb of his mistress, who was the wife of one of his valets – 'a bluff, brusque, indifferent man, noted for his pride and obstinacy'.

to Guiche, who lost no time in exploiting his promotion, for on the day of his appointment he laid siege to Bapaume, which he took on the 20 September. Two days later he received a visit from La Meilleraye, who brought him a parcel from Louis XIII; at the sight of it Antoine's heart must have dropped a beat, for there could be no doubt about the contents of that cylindrical package which he had seen so often in his day-dreams. It was the bâton of a Marshal of France.

Here we should have expected an exuberant passage in the memoirs, calling attention to the fact that the honour had been earned by his own unaided merit; but the receipt of the most coveted distinction in the kingdom seems to have struck him dumb, and he merely records the fact without comment. Or perhaps, in his insatiable Gascon way, he had no sooner got it than he was already reaching out for the only two remaining honours within the grasp of a subject, the blue ribbon of the St Esprit and a Peerage. La Meilleraye, 'much inconvenienced by gout', or in other words seeing no prospect of dislodging the Spaniards from their position, now went on leave whilst Guiche remained as commander-in-chief in Flanders; but nothing of importance happened in the brief remainder of the campaigning season.

1642 was an unlucky year for the new Marshal, and his memoirs are full of a vehement self-justification which shows that the recollection of his failure rankled for the rest of his life. He was given command of the Army of Champagne, which, in concert with the Army of Picardy, was to stand on the defensive whilst Richelieu and Louis XIII drove south to support the revolt in Catalonia. The Champagne defensive was bungled from the start, and after sundry manœuvres Guiche found himself at Honnecourt on the Scheldt facing a Spanish army which outnumbered his own by nearly three to one. Worse still, he was caught with his cavalry out at forage, his commissariat wagons loading at St Quentin, and his artillery horses away on ammunition convoy. The enemy was so close that a retreat would have been suicidal, and Antoine had to stand and fight. The result was inevitable; outfought, outnumbered, nearly surrounded, he was lucky to bring off as much of his army as he did, and he himself admits that the battle was a complete Spanish victory. Harder to bear than the defeat was the reaction to it of the Parisians, who said openly that Antoine had orders from his patron Richelieu to lose a battle in order to provoke a crisis which would affirm the Cardinal's position as the indispensable man. It seems in the highest degree unlikely however that Guiche, even to please Richelieu, would have agreed to expose himself to such a loss of reputation in the eyes of his professional peers. But he would have been wiser not to emphasise so strongly the wonderful reception he was given by the King on his return, whilst carefully omitting all reference to the mockery of the pamphleteers, whose nickname 'Marshal Lampoon' he took a long time to live down.

From the Cardinal he got neither criticism nor praise, for Richelieu's reign of terror was drawing swiftly to its close; and indeed Guiche was barely in time to see his patron die. For Guiche, Richelieu seems to have felt some real affection; on his death-bed he kissed him tenderly, said calmly that the hour had struck when they must part; that in him Antoine was losing such a friend as he would never find again; and then begged him to withdraw, as it did not become a man such as he to let his feelings overcome him in his last hour.

Richelieu died as calmly and as coldly as he had lived; to his confessor, who called upon him to forgive his enemies, he made the astounding reply that as he had never had any, the question did not arise; and when his niece told him that a holy Carmelite had prophesied his recovery, he asked her not to talk nonsense.[1] He died on 4 December in his fifty-seventh year, and in the universal rejoicing which followed no one was more prominent than Louis XIII, who saw himself King at last; little knowing that he was to be in his tomb within six months.

Antoine could not join in the great sigh of relief which went up all over France; on the contrary, the loss of the man to whom he owed his fortune shocks him into an unwonted sobriety:

> The instant he was dead he was forgotten; and this man who, eight days earlier was master of the world, was now no

[1] Bonneau-Avenant, *La Duchesse d'Aiguillon.*

more than the dust; which is a valuable lesson to the wise man not to be anxious for the things of this world, which are but smoke and vanity.

But Guiche soon forgot such sentiments in the comfort which was at hand. Louis XIII 'consoled him with an inexpressible kindness for his great loss, assuring him that he would be as good a friend to him as the late Cardinal, and that as a first proof of his sincerity he was appointing the Comte de Guiche to serve under him in the next campaign'.

Thus reassured, Guiche plunged into the delights of winter leave in Paris, where he and Toulongeon, nicknamed 'The Prince of Love', were rivals for the affections of Marion de l'Orme; but neither of them seems to have been successful.

A curious woman this Marion, for whose favours the two Gramonts contended in vain. Now thirty-one, she had started in life with a fortune of some £9,000 and could have made a good marriage, but she had deliberately chosen to be a courtesan. First, because she was extremely lascivious, and second, because the freedom of such a career appealed to her irresistibly. She was pretty, not very clever, played the theorbo, sang well, and spent her mornings sitting with her feet in a tub of water to prevent her nose getting red. Of her innumerable lovers she said that only six or seven had really satisfied her; and one of them tells us that she had the most beautiful body in all France. She poisoned herself in 1650 by taking an overdose of antimony to procure an abortion, and by her own directions her corpse lay in state for twenty-four hours, wearing a virgin's crown.[1]

Ninon de l'Enclos seems also to have refused Guiche about this time. Was Antoine's much advertised debauchery perhaps after all only part of the façade which he had built up for himself? His ill-success with Ninon must have been specially galling to him, for she held a place in French society which was unique; whilst Marion was merely a courtesan, Ninon was both a courtesan and an institution; she had many lovers, but she also maintained a salon where fashionable France, particularly the sceptics and the atheists, met to exchange news and scandal; and

[1] Tallemant des Réaux, *Historiettes.*

at these gatherings she insisted on the observance of the strictest decorum. Her house was a finishing school for young nobles, whose fathers, and even whose mothers, sent them there to acquire social polish in one of the politest societies in Paris. Some few who came as pupils stayed as lovers, and all sighed for possession of the mistress of the house; for though Ninon was no beauty, she had that mysterious something which all men found irresistible. She was, as we have said, an institution, knew it, and allowed herself liberties which no Duchess would have dared to take. In 1651 the priest of her parish denounced her to the Court for eating meat in Lent, the evidence being that one of his curates had been hit by a beef bone thrown at him out of Ninon's dining-room window. Left to herself the Queen would probably have taken no action, but she was pestered by the devout party at Court into sending Ninon a *Lettre de Cachet* ordering her into a religious house. No particular one was named and Ninon, noticing this, wrote to Anne saying that as Her Majesty had been so good as to give her the choice, she craved leave to enter the Grey Friars, who looked to her the lustiest fraternity in Paris. When the Queen could speak for laughter she said, 'Fie! the rogue. Let her go where she likes'. And Ninon continued to live at home unmolested. In her own lifetime she became a legend, for she lived on until 1705, surrounded by friends to the last. Perhaps the only famous man in France with whom she had not at least a nodding acquaintance was the most famous of them all, Louis XIV. But even Louis was not outside her sphere of influence; if a sense of decorum on his part prevented their ever meeting, he was at least very inquisitive about her, and at more than one moment when his own love affairs were exciting general interest, he is reported to have asked, 'What does Ninon say about it?'

Guiche's annoyance at his failure with Marion de l'Orme cannot have been lessened by the subsequent discovery that where he had been rebuffed, his youngest brother Philibert had succeeded.

It appears that Marion had given Philibert an appointment for the night at her house, but late in the afternoon he received a note from her with the classic excuse; she was prostrated with a headache, she was terribly disappointed, but... 'She was as capricious as the Devil,' says Philibert, 'and this headache appeared to me very suspicious.' Consequently he set off after dark to reconnoitre the house of his mistress in the Marais. Sure enough, on entering the street in which she lived, he overtook a cloaked man who turned out to be his chief rival, the Duc de Brissac,[1] whose inopportune presence he disposed of with his usual impudence and ingenuity; 'My dear friend,' said Philibert, 'you must do me a service; I have an appointment here with a girl, but only to fix a date. Just lend me your cloak a minute and walk my horse about a little'. And before Brissac quite knew what had happened, he was cloakless in a dark street, holding a strange horse, and looking with indignation after the vanishing Philibert; who, running down one side of the street, came up the other in the shadows and entered Marion's house, where he found the lady, 'lying on a couch in the most charming déshabille imaginable'. Marion expostulated, Philibert was firm. 'I know why you are so anxious to get rid of me,' he said, 'you are terrified in case Brissac should walk in on us. He won't, he is otherwise employed; take a peep at him.' This was too much for Marion, who burst out laughing – 'My dear, you are too amiable and eccentric not to be forgiven; we'll let Brissac go on exercising that horse for a while'.[2]

In the spring of 1643 Philibert set out to serve his first campaign under Prince Thomas of Savoy in Piedmont. Before making his military début, he had turned his attention to other subjects as well as love; and had equipped himself for his career by learning 'that which gives the finishing stroke to a young fellow's education and makes him a gentleman, namely all sorts of games both at cards and dice'. His equipage was modest, a family servant called Brinon being sent with him in the triple capacity of governor, equerry, and *valet de chambre*; a man

[1] BRISSAC, François Louis de Cossé, 3rd Duc de, 1626–1661; spent vast sums on Marion de l'Orme, and was so jealous that he hired the house opposite hers and kept spies on duty there day and night. He was credited with having got a separation from his wife by deliberately contracting and communicating to her an objectionable complaint.

[2] Hamilton, *Memoirs*.

according to Philibert 'more surly than an old ape... perhaps the only Gascon who ever possessed so much gravity and ill-humour'. But Philibert's opinion is not unbiassed, for at the second post house he and Brinon had a violent quarrel about the purse of four hundred louis which had been entrusted, not to the Chevalier but to the valet. Brinon in the end surrendered the purse with a reluctance which was well justified, for that night at Lyons Philibert lost the whole sum at play to a Swiss merchant 'as round as a ball, with a ruff and a high crowned hat'. However, the faithful Brinon turned out to have a reserve fund by means of which Philibert managed to reach Piedmont, where an extraordinary run of luck at cards enabled him and his friend Matha[1] to live luxuriously and entertain the commander-in-chief in a way which made him dissatisfied with his own table. But luck of course changed and the precious pair disagreed as to the course to be pursued in their extremity; the Chevalier was for increasing expenses on credit, Matha for cutting their losses. 'Have you no sentiments of honour,' said the indignant Philibert, 'where is the dignity of France?' 'And where is the credit?' replied the sulky Matha. However, Philibert was not long in retrieving the position by cheating a Piedmontese Count out of 1,500 pistoles[2] at cards. And, the campaign being over, he went off to spend his winter leave in Turin where, according to his biographer, he was brilliantly successful amongst the ladies of the Court of Savoy.[3]

Probably because his defeat at Honnecourt was still fresh in the public mind, Guiche was allotted a secondary role in 1643, that of commanding in Arras, where one of his duties was to collect information regarding troop movements in the Spanish army and transmit it to Enghien, commander-in-chief of the Northern Army. After Enghien reached the front in April Antoine was in constant touch with him, in letters which contain a curious blend of military report and social gossip. How, asks Guiche, is his younger brother Toulongeon doing, and is

[1] Matha, Charles de Bourdeille, 4th Comte de, a witty talker, notorious for his profligacy and impiety. He died in 1674.

[2] A Spanish gold coin, worth about sixteen shillings.

[3] Hamilton, *Memoirs*.

he cutting much of a dash on that new charger of which he is so proud? Indeed Antoine shows up better as a gossip than as a source of military information, for it is evident that he completely failed to penetrate the designs of the Spaniards, thinking that his own fortress of Arras was their first objective; and in his memoirs he asserts that only his own vigorous measures baffled the Spanish plans. The 19 May was the most important date for France in the whole of the war. Enghien, who was determined to fight, had manœuvred himself into a position in which a pitched battle was unavoidable; and the result was the French victory of Rocroi which made Enghien the most famous General in Europe and ended the military predominance of Spain.

CHAPTER IV

★

THROUGHOUT the spring of 1643 Louis XIII was slowly but obviously dying, and the event was looked forward to impatiently by all France. To the courtiers he had been a broken reed, and since the death of Richelieu he had been regarded as an unwanted appendix to the history of the Cardinal's reign. During the early months of the year a courtier arriving at the Louvre could read at a glance what was the latest news of the King's health; if all faces were glum, then His Majesty had taken a turn for the better; if everyone was cheerful, he was sinking. The end came on the 14 May, five days before the resounding victory of Rocroi, the first of the great triumphs of the Siècle Louis Quatorze; and though the new King was not yet five, the stream of adulation on which he was to be borne for the next seventy years began to flow. Some indeed asserted that Louis XIII had been granted a vision of the glories destined for his son, and had been divinely inspired to appoint Enghien as the instrument 'to wreathe his cradle with laurels'. Guiche, with his usual talent for being in the right place at the right moment, had managed to reach the Louvre forty-eight hours before the death of Louis XIII, and was well placed to unravel the confused situation which followed. The dead man had left a will by which his consort, Anne of Austria, whom he both loathed and distrusted, would have been deprived of all real power; but on the 18 May, four days after his death, the Parlement annulled the will and confirmed Anne in the full traditional powers of a Regent. Freed from the tyranny under which they had so long suffered, Anne and her courtiers resembled nothing so much as a pack of children released from school; favours were scattered broadcast, regardless of the state of the finances, and one courtier remarked that the French language was reduced to five words – 'The Queen is so kind'. In the joyous bewilderment of the liberation almost any political settlement was possible, and it behoved men like Guiche to read the riddle correctly; once more he was at a cross-roads, and the attainment of his ambitions depended upon his taking the right turning.

What were the choices?

There was to begin with Anne herself, who had been so relegated to the background for nearly thirty years that she was something of an unknown quantity. As the languorous, beautiful, and passionate Infanta of Spain she had for reasons of State been thrust into the arms of the peevish, emasculate little Louis XIII when they were both fifteen years old; but when Anne was already a woman, whilst Louis was still a child. In the best of circumstances the union could hardly have been a happy one, and circumstances from the outset fought against Anne. Or rather Anne rebelled against circumstances. She was every inch a Hapsburg, and her immense pride was at once up in arms against the arrogance of her mother-in-law, who attempted to domineer over her as she did over Louis; the King took his mother's side, Anne refused to humble herself, and when in 1622 Anne miscarried through her own carelessness, their relations permanently worsened. Louis, goaded on by his mother and Richelieu, adopted towards his wife an unwavering policy of cold cruelty which was probably his reaction against the tormenting knowledge of his own insufficiency as a husband; and when in 1625 Buckingham arrived in France, matters reached a crisis. This is not the place to retell the story of Anne's one great romance; her most intimate friend says that the Queen acted very indiscreetly; and Anne herself many years later said of Buckingham, 'I loved him, but he was never my lover'.[1] And the two statements appear to be the basic facts behind a sensational story. But a less suspicious husband than Louis XIII might reasonably have shown indignation at the scandal, and the King went so far as to threaten divorce.

Anne's dealings with Richelieu were equally unhappy, and harder to disentangle; according to one contemporary the Minister had the audacity to make love to the Queen, and hinted that so long as she remained childless she was in perpetual danger of repudiation; so he, for the welfare of the State, was prepared

[1] Motteville, *Mémoires*.

to make good the King's apparent inability to supply France with a Dauphin. It is certainly true that Richelieu suddenly developed a deep and lasting hate for Anne which seems too vindictive to have been produced by her semi-treasonous correspondence with her brother, Philip IV, but might well have been engendered by mortified vanity. Be this as it may, he did everything in his power to perpetuate and exacerbate the division between husband and wife; and from 1630 until Richelieu's death in 1642, Anne was in disgrace, and the victim of constant humiliations.

The Anne who emerged to rule France in 1643 was a still handsome woman of forty-two, with lovely eyes, hands, and hair, a majestic figure, and a modicum of good sense; able to read and write, but very averse to doing either; quite uneducated and totally ignorant of affairs. But if she had no formal knowledge, her precarious situation during the lifetime of her husband had given her a shrewd grasp of human nature, and of the art of using her charm to sway those whom she met. She was still ready for 'honest gallantry' of the elaborate Spanish type, and managed to combine what in a lesser woman might have been called flirtatiousness with a sincere devotion to the externals of religion; a trait which she was to pass on to her sons. Her most pleasing characteristic was her charity, which was not confined to alms-giving; for she was never happier than when she could slip away from the Louvre in disguise to distribute food and comforts to the sick in the Paris hospitals. Under an exterior of lethargic good-nature there slumbered a formidable temper, whose unexpected presence startled her Council when she became Regent; and her servants soon learnt to take cover at the sound of 'the sharp and piercing soprano' to which her voice rose whenever she encountered opposition or contradiction. Anne being what she was, it was obvious that she must now lean heavily on some man of experience, and the burning question for Guiche was, on whom? It was a case where nothing was to be gained by attempting to ingratiate himself with the Queen; for with her he had always been careful to keep on as good terms as was possible without arousing the anger of Richelieu. What he had to do was to ingratiate himself with whoever succeeded in ingratiating himself with Anne. At first it seemed as if the Regent inclined to the Bishop of Beauvais, her Almoner, a worthy, pious, and utterly incapable man. Tersely described by de Retz as 'the most idiotic idiot I ever met', his political sagacity may be gauged from his conduct at an early meeting of the Council of Regency, where he laid it down that if the Dutch wished to remain the allies of France, orders must be sent them that they must all enter the Roman Catholic Church immediately. Clearly, thought Guiche, there was no need to waste time in thinking about the Bishop of Beauvais.

Then there was the Duc de Beaufort, towards whom Anne was showing a marked graciousness, and to whose keeping she had entrusted the little King and his brother on the day of Louis XIII's death. Beaufort, whose father, the first Duc de Vendôme, was a bastard of Henri IV's by Gabrielle d'Estrées, was a showy, vain, floridly good-looking man of twenty-seven, arrogant, utterly lacking in either capacity or discretion, with almost no brains, and famous for his malapropisms. He would have been a negligible figure but for his birth, and for an even more important asset, namely that he was the idol of the Paris mob, spoke the language of the slums, set up as the people's friend, and could raise a serious riot in the capital at a nod. He was at the head of a group of young men as incapable and conceited as himself, whose airs had earned them the nickname of *Les Importans*, and whose insolence was speedily to disgust the Regent; for Beaufort, like many a cleverer man, had never dreamt of the stubborn Spanish pride and readiness to take offence which smouldered under Anne's normally placid exterior. But even whilst Beaufort was still in favour Guiche had realized that he was not the stuff of which Prime Ministers are made, and that the Queen's choice must fall elsewhere.

There remained Cardinal Mazarin, and Antoine decided to back the red again. A decision probably not uninfluenced by the fact that while Beaufort and the Bishop were unknown to him, Mazarin was an old acquaintance; for they had served together in Italy a dozen years earlier. In the nick of time Guiche offered his services to him, and on 18 May, four days after Louis XIII's death, Mazarin was appointed Prime Minister.

> Guiche . . . speedily pleased him [Mazarin] . . . Guiche loved the Cardinal tenderly, and the Cardinal reciprocated the sentiment; he could not do without him, and gave him all his confidence, which state of affairs continued without a break until the Cardinal's death.

To anyone who knows Mazarin it seems highly unlikely that he ever gave 'all his confidence' to anyone, and had he done so, very improbable that the recipient would have been a soldier; but he was an adept at pretending to put all his cards on the table, and by a judicious show of confidence he won the loyal support of Antoine throughout the vicissitudes of his troubled reign.

In foreign policy King Mazarin was to follow closely in the footsteps of King Richelieu, and like his predecessor, Mazarin was to become the absolute ruler of France. But here all resemblance between the two Cardinals ends; in origin, temperament, and method of governing, they were poles apart. Richelieu was a Frenchman, sprung from the squirearchy, Mazarin a Sicilian whose father had risen to be major-domo to the House of Colonna. Mazarin had accompanied the young Colonna to the university as valet and fellow-student, had served with the Papal army, then got a footing in the world of diplomacy, and had turned his insinuating talents to such good account that in 1634, at the age of thirty-two, he had been appointed Vice-Legate at Avignon. His duties there brought him into occasional contact with Richelieu, who, struck by his ability, persuaded him in 1639 to settle in France as his Private Secretary; and in this post he so distinguished himself that the dying Richelieu recommended him to Louis XIII as his successor. Recommended him too to Anne of Austria with an insolent brutality which even he did not often dare to employ – 'You will like him, Madame; he greatly resembles the late Duke of Buckingham'. On the day after Richelieu's death Mazarin was admitted to the Council of State, and was now Prime Minister of France.

But this good-looking, charming, supple Italian was far too clever a man to presume on his great promotion; with exquisite adroitness he affected to regard himself as a mere stop-gap; it was not for such a man as he to look for even the humblest office in the forthcoming administration; the Queen had done him too much honour in permitting him to call himself Prime Minister whilst she looked about her for an adviser worthy of her own greatness and that of France; the desire nearest his heart was to be allowed to return to his native Italy to solace the declining years of his aged parents. But day by day he kept on hinting to the Queen in his fluent Spanish that they were both strangers in a strange land, and that he might be of use to her; had not a mouse once helped a lion?[1] His success was both complete and permanent. Anne fell in love with him, and remained in love with him for the rest of his life; whether they married is a still unsolved problem, and one which will probably remain insoluble. There is a considerable body of presumptive evidence that they did, and as Mazarin never took Orders there was no bar to wedlock. One thing is certain, that the footing on which the two stood gave Mazarin an unassailable position, and it was in their failure to appreciate the fact that Anne would go to any lengths to prevent the expulsion of Mazarin from France that the Frondeurs were to make their biggest miscalculation. But Mazarin, who was not in love with Anne and was never quite sure of her, did not see his position through the Queen's eyes; for he was a man who knew men thoroughly, seeing them without bitterness and without illusions. He knew that he had not a friend in France except the Queen, and with all his charm he was never able to make one, for he was false right through. His every word and act were calculated. And he was completely aware that even those who, like Guiche, served him loyally, were actuated by the purest self-interest. By his own family he was detested, and with reason; no man can act a part from morning to night without resting occasionally, and it was his family that saw the real man. In the family circle the stage Mazarin, suave, smiling, deferential, was replaced by a brutal, ill-tempered, and selfish tyrant. 'Thank God he is dead at last', said his nephew on hearing the news. But if Mazarin could not win friends he could at least buy allies, and once he was firmly in the saddle he proceeded to do so. By promises if possible, but

[1] Fédern, *Mazarin.*

to those who made themselves sufficiently dangerous he would grant favours lavishly, and sometimes even cash. Never was there a man so devoid of idealism. And he had other assets; he was utterly lacking in any moral sense, and without any feeling of dignity; there was no humiliation which he would not undergo with a smile, provided that in enduring it he saw a profit for himself; and he showed wonderful skill in disuniting enemies and biding his time – 'Time and I against the world', he used to say.

What most repels us in him is his avarice, coupled with his incessant praise of his own disinterestedness. As his velvet grip on France tightened, he gradually came to absorb the whole revenue of the State, which was mixed with his private fortune in a confusion which was both calculated and inextricable; as a contemporary says, he managed France as if it had been a private gentleman's estate of which he was the dishonest steward. Everything he touched turned to gold, and at the height of his career he grasped at a ten-pound tip as eagerly as if he had still been the starveling Captain of Papal Infantry. Turn to what business you will in France, and there is Mazarin skimming the cream for his personal benefit; under various aliases he was a gold-broker, foreign exchange speculator, sugar merchant, a wholesale dealer in soap, titles, whale oil, and government posts. Again under aliases he was a big shipowner, and the chief victualling contractor to the French army. And the beauty of these multifarious transactions from Mazarin's point of view was that any commercial competition with him was impossible; firstly because he exempted himself, and himself only, from all Customs dues; and secondly because settlement of Mazarin's little bills was a first charge on the exhausted exchequer.[1] When we remember that he also held estates and benefices all over France, and had the finest collection of jewelry and objets d'art in Europe, we begin to get some idea of Mazarin's wealth; we are no longer surprised to find that in 1658, for instance, his legitimate income was about £75,000, and to that handsome figure his not so legitimate income added a further £200,000. And the reader will remember that I am

[1] *Ibid.*

translating, not into the money values of today but those of 1914.

But though in domestic policy Mazarin was merely a clever opportunist who made no effort to deal with the financial chaos which he had inherited from Richelieu, he had considerable merits as a Foreign Minister. He thoroughly understood the European chess-board, and throughout his reign worked with remarkable skill and energy for what in the language of his time was called 'the glory of France'; to him belongs the chief credit for the Peace of Westphalia and the Peace of the Pyrenees.

Early in the summer Guiche, having made his pact with Mazarin, was rewarded by being sent to serve under Enghien; and it is interesting to notice how rapidly Antoine is advancing in self-esteem. A few years ago how proud he would have been to serve under a Prince of the Blood; but in 1643 he feels it necessary to give us a long parenthesis in which he is at pains to show that in consenting to serve under Enghien he is doing nothing derogatory to his own rank of Marshal of France.

The meeting between the two men was cordial, and strengthened the friendship which already existed:

> The Duc d'Enghien showed great pleasure at being given Guiche, whose wit and cheerfulness were very agreeable to him, and who admired the reputation which he had acquired. Their union was perfect from the start, and lasted during all the campaigns which they served together . . . at Paris [that winter] the Duke usually dined and supped with Guiche every day. Which delighted the Maréchal, who had conceived a warm friendship for him, with all the esteem which his great and rare qualities deserved.

Antoine's father was not forgotten in the flood of honours which Anne in the first enjoyment of her freedom poured out so lavishly on all France; he was made a Brevet-Duc. Guiche must have viewed this award without enthusiasm; a Brevet-Dukedom was merely a Court distinction, tenable for the life of the holder only, and not carrying with it a Peerage. So far from being of any service to Antoine it was a source of lively misgivings as calculated to encourage his father to spend money which the son felt he could lay out to much better advantage himself in a few years time. It was a disgruntled Guiche who strove to forget the unsatisfactory nature of the Gramont prize in the Court lottery by plunging into the debauchery and excitement of the gayest winter Paris had known for thirty years.

In 1644 France mobilised three armies. The Rhine Army, commanded by Turenne, the Army of Picardy under 'Monsieur', and the Army of Champagne under Enghien, with Antoine as his second-in-command. Enghien concentrated at Verdun on 10 May; 'we took the field without any definite objective', says Guiche truly, for Enghien's only orders were to stand by to reinforce either 'Monsieur' or Turenne as the situation dictated. From the outset it was obvious to everybody that the Army of Picardy was the weak link in the French chain; why 'Monsieur' should have taken it into his head to command an army we do not know; possibly out of envy of the growing fame of his cousin Enghien. He had never shown the slightest military ability; but being a Son of France, his whim must be gratified, even at the risk of a grave setback to the French plans. As expected, he proved useless, though lavishly supplied with men and money, and in June Enghien was ordered north in the hope that he would save such little prestige as 'Monsieur' still retained. But whilst Enghien was on the march he received disquieting news direct from Turenne, and on the 21st set off at top speed to his assistance at Fribourg. On 2 August at Brisach he learnt that Fribourg had fallen to the enemy five days earlier. For Guiche, Enghien's decision to effect a junction with Turenne instead of with 'Monsieur' was lucky, for the Duke, being a Prince of the Blood, became Generalissimo of the combined armies whilst Antoine succeeded him in command of the Army of Champagne; Turenne of course continuing to command the Rhine Army.

On 2 August Enghien held a council of war composed of his two army commanders and d'Erlach, the Governor of Brisach, to discuss the Fribourg problem. Erlach, who knew the ground, advocated working round the enemy's rear through the valley of the Petersthal, and was backed up by Guiche, because if the manœuvre succeeded, the enemy would either be forced to fight at a disadvantage or else be starved out whilst standing on the defensive. But Enghien disagreed; hit the enemy hard where he was strongest, he said; and his vote carried the day. Early on 3 August Enghien and his staff went forward to reconnoitre the enemy position. And even Enghien hesitated when the full nature of the task became apparent; a steep spur of the Black Forest, the Schonberg, ran down to touch at right angles the Brisach-Fribourg road, which was the only possible line of approach for the French; and Mercy,[1] the enemy commander, not only held the Schonberg but had improved an immensely strong natural position by every known device of field engineering; and where the slope ran down to the plain, had entrenched himself across the road. Enghien knew however that there was a practicable defile to the southward of the Schonberg; and although Mercy had doubtless guarded the point where it opened into the plain, the position might be forced; and if forced at the moment when the Schonberg fell, Mercy would be obliged to make a dangerous retreat. Enghien at once ordered Turenne to march his army through the defile whilst he himself attacked the Schonberg, seconded by Guiche.

At five o'clock Enghien's troops attacked, led by Espenan,[2] for Guiche had, with difficulty, persuaded the Generalissimo that it was unseemly for him to lead the opening attack in person. Espenan and his men did all that could be expected of them, but the position, held by some of the best infantry in Europe, proved impregnable, and the broken French were drawing off when Enghien and Guiche scrambled up the hill and put themselves at their head. Here was the sort of situation for which Enghien was supremely fitted, for he knew his countrymen as few Bourbons did; what troops, however disheartened, could refuse to follow a Prince of the Blood who was the first to scale the enemy barricades? And let us not forget that Guiche was by his side; Enghien stole the limelight, but did nothing that day which Antoine did not do also; and both

[1] Mercy, Franz, Field Marshal Baron von, an Austrian, defeated the French at Marienthal, 1645; one of the best Generals in Europe.

[2] Espenan, Roger de Boussolts, Comte d', soldier of fortune, began in the ranks, and had risen to Major-General by 1637; a brave man, but an incompetent general.

were still in the forefront of the battle when late in the evening the French broke into the last Bavarian redoubt. And there they slept, lulled by the distant roar of artillery from Turenne's battle to the south-west, and indifferent to the torrents of rain which fell all night. An officer seeking Enghien at midnight found him and Guiche fast asleep in their cloaks on an improvised mattress of enemy dead.

In the grey dawn of 4 August Mercy, seeing that he was getting the worst of his battle with Turenne, withdrew to a new position closer to Fribourg; it was the Schonberg over again, magnificent defensive ground, on the Josephsberg with his right flank blocking the valley between the hill and the town. But with this important difference, that there was no getting round the rear of the Josephsberg, and if Enghien took the offensive he must stake everything on the success of a frontal attack. But for the moment even Enghien had had enough, and for twenty-four hours his exhausted army lay unmolested in the abandoned Austrian camp, but without shelter from the downpour which turned the plain into a marsh.

On the 5th Enghien, leaving Guiche to contain the Imperial right wing in the Petersthal, attacked with left, right, and centre; all three attacks were to reach the summit of the Josephberg simultaneously, and Espenan on the left, who had the most difficult ground, was to advance first; d'Aumont,[1] on the right, was not to attack until he knew from the sound of firing that d'Espenan had contacted the enemy; the centre attack was a feint. But d'Espenan suddenly decided to divert his force to the capture of a redoubt at the foot of the hill, and d'Aumont, hearing the resultant blaze of musketry, assumed that d'Espenan had reached the summit; so he in his turn advanced, unaware that he was attacking the whole position single-handed. By the time Enghien arrived on the scene the inevitable had happened and the wreckage of d'Aumont's infantry was stumbling down the hillside strewn with its own dead. All that Enghien could do was to take command himself, call up his reserves, and renew the attack; but even his courage and energy could not retrieve

[1] AUMONT, Charles de Villequier, Marquis d', 1606–1644, Lieut.-General, 1637; died of wounds, Landau, 1644 'as became a gentleman of high estate'.

the situation. Guiche, watching from his post on the left, could at last endure it no longer, and turning over his command to Palluau[1] he galloped across the French front to join Enghien, by whose side he remained for the rest of the day. It was late in the evening when he managed to persuade Enghien that to continue attacks in which the flower of the French infantry was withering away, was murder; already many regiments had lost all their officers, and the number of 'volunteers' who had fallen was enormous. Sullenly the remnants of the French foot descended the corpse-strewn hillside in the twilight, even now not admitting defeat; for France had lost neither colours nor guns, and had so handled Mercy that he was unable to counter-attack. Full casualty lists were never published, but in dead alone the losses of the two armies amounted to nine thousand, and the heavier death roll was that of the French. From 5 August to 9 August the worn-out French army lay in the stifling heat of Fribourg plain, licking its wounds amidst the putrefying dead, with a plague list which was going up by leaps and bounds. But Mercy and his Bavarians were in a still worse plight, for in addition to heat and plague, they were short of food as well; which prompted Enghien on the 9th to try to cut Mercy's communications and thus force him to a decisive engagement before he could escape from an untenable position. The Black Forest south of Fribourg was roughly an equilateral triangle whose base ran from Fribourg to Langendenzling and whose apex was the Abbey of St Peter at the head of the eastern side of the triangle; this side, the Petersthal, a river valley, was held by Mercy, and the similar valley on the western side, the Glotterthal, was open to the French. Whichever army secured the Abbey held both valleys at their junction and closed the road to the south, Mercy's only line of retreat. At dawn on the 9th the French advance guard under Rosen[2] marched down the

[1] Palluau, Philippe de, 1st Marquis, Maréchal de Clérembault, 1653; died 1665; 'He owed his bâton to his epigrams and his agreeable conversation rather than to his feats of war.'

[2] Rosen, Reinhold von, Livonian adventurer, known to the French troops as 'the old rose'; entered the French service, 1639; Lieut.-General, 1647; died 1667.

Glotterthal to cut off Mercy at St Peter's; but Mercy was not caught napping; 'one could imagine', says Guiche, 'that he was a silent and invisible member of our Council of War'. And scarcely had Rosen got on the march before Mercy was racing down the Petersthal. It was a dead heat; on the morning of the 10th, as Mercy reached the junction, there on the left was Rosen debouching from the Glotterthal. An indecisive skirmish followed, and Mercy had rather the better of it, for though he lost many cannon and all his baggage, Rosen was unable to pin him to the ground and when Enghien came up he had to be content with plundering the enemy baggage train.[1]

At Court news of the fall of Fribourg was expected, but Enghien was no Louis XIV to be diverted from a strategic prize by a showy conquest of little permanent value. Disregarding expostulations, he bullied Mazarin into sending reinforcements and then moved south into the heart of enemy country to besiege Philipsburg, the key to the middle Rhine. Even his own officers heard the decision with uneasiness; the end of the campaigning season was near, the army was tired, full of recruits, and Philipsburg nearly two hundred miles away. But with Enghien in command there was no opposition and the march was accomplished. 'Long and painful', says Guiche, but 'the gaiety of the generals, the affability of the Prince [Enghien] with every officer and soldier, the high esteem in which he was held amongst them, smoothed over all difficulties, and no one showed the least reluctance to do what was required of him'.

On the 25 August the French army arrived before Philipsburg after a twelve-days march; and such a march as we now find it difficult to picture. Here were no disciplined columns with supplies awaiting them at prearranged points, none of the complicated second-line machinery of Marlborough's age. There were no uniforms; no two men would be dressed alike; and no unit would be marching in formation. Let us imagine a disorderly mob of twelve thousand stubble-bearded tramps with muskets on their shoulders and their toes out of their boots, pouring along a rutted cart track, their rags fluttering in the breeze and no knowledge of where their next meal was to come

[1] Godley, *The Great Condé.*

from; generals in their coaches, junior officers on horseback endeavouring without much success to keep some sort of coherence in the marching columns. Behind the troops would follow the enormous tail of grooms, valets, baggage wagons, canteen women, camp followers and so forth; the wagons piled high with ammunition, bedding, oddments, and the cuirasses of the cavalry. For cuirasses were never worn on the line of march, and indeed rarely in action. The usual French explanation is that the cavalry scorned the protection which the cuirass afforded. But without being cynical, one must attach some weight to a contemporary who attributes the reluctance of his fellow officers to wearing it to the fact that the wadding with which it was lined was always crawling with vermin. We can imagine what this must have meant on a hot summer day, and small wonder if even that generation, hard-bitten though it was in every sense of the word, refused to endure the torment.

Behind the tail came yet another detachment, the hurrying looters who had been left behind in the last village and were now trying to rejoin their units. And to the modern soldier this rabble would have looked odder than anything which had preceded it; here is a man who, as he trots along, clashes with the pots and pans hung from his bandolier; here another, bent under the weight of a sackful of household goods; and there a third, who has a couple of squawking hens hanging head downwards from his saddle. Over all, thick dust which exasperates the troops, not so much because it is thirst-provoking, but because it gives early warning to the inhabitants of the next village that the time has come to escape to the woods with what effects they can carry.

Enghien's plan of getting control of the middle Rhine whilst Mercy was in no state to take the field proved brilliantly successful; after a thirteen-days siege he took Philipsburg, and then swept the enemy out of the Rhine country before putting his troops into winter quarters. Antoine was not with him in the closing stages of the campaign. Philipsburg had hardly fallen when he received a message from Paris that his father had died in the last days of August, and Guiche was now the 3rd Comte de Gramont. His father had done nothing for him since the distant days when he had grudgingly provided him with enough money for those Paris suppers of dry bread, eaten by the light of the stinking lantern; he had refused to pay a penny towards Guiche's ransom when he was a sick prisoner in Italy; and we have no evidence that father and son had met or even corresponded in the twenty-six years which had passed since Antoine left home. It is hardly surprising that Antoine expresses not even a perfunctory regret at his loss, but, having recorded the fact without comment, hastens to tell us that Mazarin gave him all the dead man's offices and governments. Gramont, as we must now learn to call him, knowing the risk of delay in snatching offices, hurried to Paris, took the oath of fidelity for his new posts, and went down to Gascony to take possession and pick up any loose cash, jewelry or other trifles which his father had left behind him. He says nothing of his sensations at revisiting his old home after an absence of nearly thirty years, and probably felt nothing but annoyance at having to make such an uncomfortable journey so late in the season.

The family credit was high this autumn. Gramont himself, on the testimony of Enghien, had done brilliantly in the field, Philibert had behaved creditably, and Toulongeon was one of the inner ring at the Condé country house, Chantilly, where Enghien was being fêted and flattered to the top of his bent. And very pleasant autumn leave at Chantilly must have been in the last years of that fashion for comparative simplicity, which was so soon to give place to the tedious magnificence of Louis XIV. Gramont and Toulongeon, with their host and a crowd of gay young officers, *Les Demoiseaux de Chantilly*, would spend their days strolling with some of the prettiest girls in France through glades in which fountains played day and night; behaving 'gallantly' after the manner which they had all learnt at the Hôtel de Rambouillet, exchanging tender verses, dancing on the lawns to the music of Enghien's fiddlers; sometimes hunting in the neighbouring forest; of an evening, amateur theatricals, or perhaps a set debate on 'true delicacy', 'the real and the false love' or some similar topic; and another night would be devoted to the reading and criticism of a new poem or the captious dissection of a sermon.

But Gramont had too many irons in the fire to allow of his paying lengthy visits to Chantilly; he was, we are told, 'agreeable to the Queen', and his first task was to make such an impression that his absence would leave a blank in her day.

Anne ordinarily woke between ten and eleven, said a prayer, and then admitted the Courtiers of both sexes to her bedroom; and after their dismissal she would have an intimate chat with personal friends, amongst whom Gramont is particularly mentioned. After half an hour or so the men were turned out, Anne said a second prayer, and then breakfasted 'with an excellent appetite' on soup and cutlets. Then she prepared herself for the day; 'the pleasure of seeing her dress and do her hair with her own lovely hands', says Madame de Motteville, 'was unsurpassable'. Having dressed, she heard Mass and then turned reluctantly to the business of government; though as early as 1644 she had already discharged so much of her work on to Mazarin that on two days a week she was able to shut herself up in her own rooms, 'seeing only familiar friends, and those people who did not bore her'. Next came dinner with her children, after which she dozed over a devotional book and then 'held her circle', that is to say, was at home to those ladies of the Court who were entitled to visit her; or else she would slip off to a convent, more often than not to the Carmelites of Val-de-Grâce, in gossiping with whom she spent some of the happiest hours of her life. On her return there would be a gathering of the royal family, with Mazarin a member of the party, after which she and Mazarin would spend an hour or so together in her private room. Then she would emerge, bid the Court good night, and open her room to 'a few men, and four or five women'; and Gramont was one of the few men who was always welcome at this hour. This intimate company dismissed, the Queen went to her Oratory for an hour and reappeared at eleven for supper, after which she and her women went into her bedroom where there was 'a gay and free chat' lasting until midnight or one in the morning. Easy, uneventful days, enlivened by carriage exercise, gambling, a play in the Court theatre, and Anne's incognito excursions to the hospitals, she and a favourite lady dressed as maidservants.

CHAPTER V

★

1645 opened disastrously for France with the rout of Turenne by Mercy at Marienthal on 5 May. The French were forced back into Hesse-Cassel, there to await the arrival of Enghien and Gramont with the army of Champagne. On 2 July Enghien joined Turenne near Mannheim, where 'we found everything in a very bad state', and from where Gramont was sent out to sweep the enemy out of Wimpfen lower down the Rhine, and in French territory. Gramont accomplished his task 'with great celerity, though the work was not easy'; and having taken and garrisoned Wimpfen he crossed the Rhine 'with the first troops he could lay his hands upon' to rejoin Enghien, with whom he marched east to lay siege to Rothenburg on the Tauber. The town fell in forty-eight hours, and Enghien then turned south towards Nordlingen in the hope of forcing Mercy to battle at that place; and on the night of 2 August the French and Imperialists were marching on parallel lines for Nordlingen, separated from each other by a couple of small rivers enclosing the forest of Oetlingen. Mercy won the race, and when on 3 August Enghien entered the plain of Nordlingen, he found that not only had Mercy reached the goal first, but that he was already entrenching himself at Allerheim, with his centre on the village and his flanks on steeply rising ground. Furthermore, to east and west of the Imperial front were streams running through marshes which secured him from any danger of having his flanks turned. Gramont says it was perhaps the strongest defensive position which he ever saw.

But Enghien lost no time in deciding that Mercy must be attacked before he could turn Allerheim and the high ground east and west of it into an impregnable fortress. The French army deployed for battle in the conventional three division formation, Turenne on the left with the Weimar cavalry,

Marsin[1] commanding the infantry of the centre, and Gramont commanding the mixed force of the right, facing the celebrated Jean de Wirth.[2] Marsin was to open the battle with an attack on the village of Allerheim, for even Enghien realised that to engage his flanks under the cross-fire from Allerheim and the troops on the hills would be calamitous. Until evening, wave after wave of French infantry, usually led by Enghien in person, broke on the impregnable church of Allerheim, and the story of the battle might have been very different had not Mercy, with victory in sight, been killed by a musket ball. Allerheim was still untaken, but with Mercy's death the life went out of the Bavarian defence, and Enghien seized the opportunity to make a supreme effort with Turenne's cavalry. It was successful. Gleen's cavalry, though led by the Imperial Cuirassiers, was routed, and before midnight the garrison of Allerheim had surrendered; the remnants of Mercy's beaten army withdrew towards Donauworth on the Danube, fifteen miles from the field of battle.

And what of Gramont? Early in the day he had sent some officers to reconnoitre a defile which crossed his front diagonally from the Nordlingen road on his right to the centre of Wirth's position; and these officers, after a perfuntory glance, had reported it impassable for cavalry. Gramont had accepted their report unquestioningly, with the result that when the struggle for Allerheim was at its hottest and Gramont's wing had been greatly weakened to support the centre, he saw to his horror that not a hundred yards away Wirth's cavalry was bearing down upon him as it emerged from the 'impassable' ravine.[3] Before anything could be done, the Bavarians were in the middle of Gramont's force. Panic set in, the whole of Antoine's cavalry took flight and did not draw bridle until they had put five miles between themselves and the enemy. Antoine himself, attempting

[1] Marsin, Jean Gaspard Ferdinand, Comte de, a Belgian noble who had been a soldier since he was fourteen; entered French army, 1638, became a naturalized Frenchman, 1651; an intimate friend of Enghien.

[2] 'Wirth', Jean de, really Jan van Wert, a Netherlands adventurer, and one of the best cavalry commanders of his day.

[3] Montglat, *Mémoires:* Godley, *The Great Condé.*

to hold the enemy horse with two infantry battalions, was surrounded and taken prisoner; was lucky to be alive, for he now had his first escape on what was to prove one of the most dangerous nights of his life. 'I was in the hands of four horsemen who were unable to agree on which one of them had taken me; and were on the point of compromising the matter by killing me', when a Bavarian officer appeared in the nick of time. But this was only a beginning; as he was being taken from the field he and his escort stumbled upon Mercy's page, a lad of fifteen, who, on hearing that the prisoner was a Marshal of France, plucked one of Gramont's pistols out of the holster and fired point blank at him, luckily without effect. It was Gramont who saved the boy's life by his pleas, for 'the Germans are pitiless towards such actions'. Late at night Gramont reached the Rhine crossing, where the escort found the confusion so great that all attempt to get the prisoner to Donauworth was abandoned, and he was put into a house on the river bank to await daylight. Not without further peril, for Mercy's body lay outside the house in a cart, and stragglers of the beaten army more than once considered breaking in upon Gramont and murdering him in reprisal for the death of their general; indeed so threatening became their attitude that Gramont's destination was changed from Donauworth to Ingolstadt on the orders of Jean de Wirth, who had heard of his danger.[1] The sight of Mercy's corpse made an impression on Gramont which he was to remember all his life:

> This man, who commanded the armies of the Empire with such absolute authority, and five or six hours earlier had been so feared throughout Germany, now lay naked, with his belly to the moon, in the miserable cart of a vivandière, having for his only guards a couple of the lowest prostitutes.

Next day Antoine left for Ingolstadt, and with him went the dead Mercy – 'which did not at all please me after what I had already endured'. But in his mercurial way he soon rids himself of all memory of his unpleasant journey in his eagerness to give us full details of his flattering reception at Ingolstadt:

[1] Gramont, *Mémoires*.

Never was a man more surprised than when he saw the people surround him on all sides, throw flowers at him, and pay him a thousand compliments, for all the world as if he had been the Emperor's General returning in triumph. In the evening the Town Commandant put him in a hostelry with a guard where he entertained the Magistrates to supper; and the Maréchal having drunk with them all night, was hailed as their best friend and loaded with presents, so much were they charmed by his gracious and polite manners.

And there were even more flattering attentions to follow:

Two days later the Elector of Bavaria sent the Sieur Kittner, his Prime Minister, with a very obliging letter, and an order to the Town Commandant not only to release him from the castle, but to give him full liberty on parole in the city. And to render him everywhere the honours due to one of his birth and merit... This gentlemanlike conduct on the part of the Elector was followed by the gift of all sorts of enamel gilt boxes filled with sweetmeats which the Electress sent to the Maréchal, together with a white scarf having a golden border.

It sounds charming, but it must not be regarded as typical of the treatment accorded to prisoners in Germany. Let us see what happened to Pointis of the French Guards, taken prisoner in this same campaign:

When we drew near to Augsburg we were ordered to dismount, and were led in groups into the town in a triumphal procession. I had to drink this cup and many others which I had not expected when I surrendered on the guarantee that I would receive the treatment of a person of quality... We were put in cellars, with straw for bedding, and where the only light was that which came through the air vents, or to put it bluntly we were shut up in dungeons in order to draw a fat ransom from us... We lived on charity, sending the poor prisoners out into the town to beg for us... there were worthy women in the town who brought us bread and beer which they let down by ropes through the air vents.[1]

[1] Pointis, *Mémoires*.

A few days later Gramont heard the news that he was to be exchanged for Gleen, and Kittner in bringing it also brought an invitation, or rather a command, from the Elector that Gramont must visit Munich before leaving Bavaria. Antoine, who by the way nowhere shows the least uneasiness about his disastrous conduct at Nordlingen, nor any undue haste in returning to duty, accepted the invitation and was flattered to the top of his bent at Munich; he was 'superbly lodged', the Elector's officers 'treated him splendidly', and on his first night there was 'a long and lively supper where so many healths were drunk that all the guests and the Master of Ceremonies finished up dead drunk under the table. This is the fashion in Germany, and one must take it in good part'.[1]

It strikes us as an unfortunate preliminary to the five-hours diplomatic talk which Gramont had with the Elector on the following morning, but he seems to have emerged from the ordeal with credit; and to have been not in the least abashed at airing his views before one of the most important men in Europe. Since 1642 the Elector had been toying with the idea of a separate peace between Bavaria and France, and hence the splendid reception which Antoine attributed solely to his own personal merit. At the audience Maximilian broke it to Gramont that he was anxious for peace with France, and could think of no better intermediary than the Maréchal to break the ice with Mazarin; Gramont of course undertook the Elector's commission, and departed very well pleased with himself and his share in the talk; for as he says, not entirely without truth, his 'dexterously drawn sketch' was the seed which grew into the Treaty of Munster.

Next day Gramont was reconducted to Donauworth, passing the Bavarian camp on his way, where 'all the General officers came out to meet him with such demonstrations of honour and respect as they would have shown to the Elector himself'. And on the following day he rejoined Enghien at the siege of Dinkelsbuhl, where his welcome, in spite of Nordlingen, was all that he could desire:

[1] Gramont, *Mémoires.*

Although it was a dark night the Duc d'Enghien left the trenches to come out a league along the road to meet the Maréchal de Gramont, whom he received with unbelievable demonstrations of joy.

Dinkelsbuhl having fallen on 24 August, Enghien set out to besiege Heilbronn, some sixty miles distant; but to the alarm of Turenne and Gramont he arrived before that place in a litter, suffering from fever and delirium. What was to be done? Enghien himself, in an interval of sanity, implored Gramont to get him to Philipsburg, the nearest town where he could obtain treatment; but unfortunately Philipsburg was forty miles away, and the intervening country was thick with enemy troops. 'It was a tricky business and called for much consideration', says Gramont, but in the end he himself offered to get the Duke to Philipsburg if he was given a thousand picked horse as escort. Turenne agreed and Gramont was lucky; Enghien was rushed through the danger zone at the utmost speed of a horse litter, and Gramont returned in triumph to Heilbronn where his first care was to notify Mazarin of the service which he had rendered the State. The rest of the campaign was unfortunate, through no fault of Turenne's or Gramont's. Mazarin refused reinforcements, and consequently Turenne, now weaker than the Imperialists, had to raise the siege of Heilbronn and cross the Neckar at Wimpfen. Though the river was high, Antoine coaxed the troops to swim it by sending into the water first, two troopers whom he had brought to the optimistic stage of drunkenness with judicious doses of brandy. There were no casualties, except that 'a monk and a lady of his acquaintance' were drowned when the baggage was crossing. From the Neckar to Philipsburg on the Rhine was a race between Turenne and the Archduke Leopold; and Turenne won it with nothing to spare. But his troubles were not yet over, for his army was cramped and hungry, forage was scarce, and he was on the wrong side of the Rhine with only six boats out of which to build a bridge. The crossing, a perilous operation, took forty-eight hours, but the enemy was in no condition to pursue, and with surprisingly few casualties the French retreated to Landau, where Gramont received orders to return to Court after putting the troops into winter quarters.

Court life was full of excitement this winter. Late in the autumn the Queen returned from Fontainebleau, sated with the view of 'those horrible solitudes', and settled down with a sigh of relief in Paris, the only place outside Spain where she found life tolerable. But she had scarcely arrived when she had to intervene to stifle a first-class scandal. One evening Enghien, a guest at a crowded entertainment given by 'Monsieur' was accidentally jostled by an *Exempt*[1] of 'Monsieur's' guards; and he reacted with the hurt vanity of a school bully by snatching the man's bâton of office and breaking it over his ears. No one of course objected to Enghien's beating the *Exempt*, but to do so in the presence of a Son of France was an outrage. However, the matter was smoothed over by the Queen's insistence that Enghien should offer a personal apology to 'Monsieur', and by her orders to 'Monsieur' that he should accept it when tendered.[2] Next came the still greater excitement of the reception of the Polish Embassy sent to demand the hand of Marie de Gonzague[3] for King Ladislas IV. To the novelty-loving French Courtiers the solemn entry of these curiously dressed barbarians from the frontiers of civilisation had something of the thrill of a circus procession; in their 'Turkish vests of red and yellow there was', says Madame de Motteville, 'something of that old-time magnificence which the Persians inherited from the Medes . . .'. But closer contact with the romantic strangers was disillusioning; they were filthily dirty, even by French standards, 'wore no linen, slept between furs instead of sheets, and were so greasy that they turned one's stomach'.

The French plan of campaign for 1646 was, briefly, to hit the Spaniard in Flanders where it would hurt him most. 'Monsieur'

[1] An *Exempt* was the senior non-commissioned officer of a regiment; an *exempt* in the Guards was the officer usually sent to serve a *lettre de cachet*.

[2] Motteville, *Mémoires*.

[3] POLAND, Queen of, 1612–1667, daughter of the Duke of Mantua; Richelieu attempted to seduce her, 1633; twice Queen of Poland, for when Ladislas IV died in 1649, she married his successor; 'Was a woman of keen and commanding intelligence.'

was to command, supported by Enghien, who had with him Gramont. It is a little surprising that Enghien should have consented to serve, even nominally, under such a general, but the fact was that he was sick of the German front, and realised that if victories were gained in Flanders, no one but Court poets and the *Gazette* would give the credit to 'Monsieur'; and no doubt similar reasons induced Gramont to serve under Enghien. Probably also they expected that it would be easy to dictate to anyone so malleable as 'Monsieur'. But they had forgotten his favourite, La Rivière,[1] who was perhaps the biggest coward in all France. Enghien's plan was to provoke a general action, but at the Council of War he could make no headway against 'Monsieur', who had been worked into a state of offended dignity by La Rivière's perfectly true insinuation that Enghien intended to make him a figurehead; nor had 'Monsieur', who was himself a good deal of a coward, been unmoved by the Abbé's entreaties to him to guard his precious life which was so much more valuable to France than any victorious pitched battle. So Enghien, in tears of rage, was forced to undertake a subordinate role in a siege of Courtrai. The town was invested on 14 June, and on the 29th the Spaniards surrendered with the Honours of War; easily earned in this case:

> One of the hostages [from Courtrai] drew Gramont aside after the capitulation was signed and told him as a great secret that they had been forced to surrender because they were out of powder... to which the Maréchal replied that the sole reason why the Duc d'Orléans had agreed to the terms proposed by the Spaniards was that he was out of both powder and ball, and did not see where he was going to get either.

The hostage, says Gramont, 'looked sheepish'.

In the meantime Mazarin was hard at work bargaining with the Prince of Orange[2] for his more energetic participation in

[1] Rivière, Louis Barbier, Abbé de La, son of a day labourer, entered 'Monsieur's' household, 1633; though disgraced and exiled in 1650, was made Duke-Bishop of Langres, 1655; a clever, well-educated man, but greedy, untrustworthy, and a mischief maker.

[2] Orange, Henri Frederic de Nassau, Prince of, died 1647.

the war; for the Dutch fleet was the only weapon with which France could strike at the great Spanish coast fortresses of Gravelines and Ostend, seeing that her own ships were all operating in the Mediterranean. Ultimately a bargain was struck; France was to send six thousand men to stiffen the Dutch army, and this joint force was to co-operate with the Dutch fleet in an offensive against Spain's coast fortresses.

Gramont was the unlucky man selected to lead the treaty force into Holland. To effect the junction was difficult, for the Spaniards had got the flank of Antoine's obvious line of march; and indeed he admits that only the lethargy of the enemy enabled him to win through without fighting a dangerous battle. Elated by his escape, Gramont marched into Holland with plans for no less an exploit than a combined naval and military operation against the great fortress of Antwerp; only to have his hopes shattered by his first interview with Orange:

> Gramont tried to get down to business, but he [Orange] took him by the hand, and having led him very rapidly round the room twice without speaking a word, asked him if he would care to dance the Coranto with him. Adding that now or never was the moment to do it . . . The Maréchal, seeing the state of affairs, danced the Coranto as well as he could, then made his bow to the Prince and left.

Mazarin's plan had collapsed because apparently no one in France knew that the Prince of Orange was a lunatic. In the seventeenth century it was considered ill-bred to notice the eccentricities of the great; a French Duke, believing himself a carnation, could spend his winters in a hothouse and in the spring have himself buried up to his knees in a flowerbed, without being thought incapable of managing his affairs; and all over Europe were ruling princes who, but for their rank, would have been in a madhouse. In Florence the Grand Duke[1] would not sleep with his wife because he believed that copulation produced fatal injuries, and spent his day traversing a gallery, at each end of which was a thermometer and a heap of nightcaps;

[1] TUSCANY, Ferdinand II de Medici, Grand Duke of, 1610–1670.

if during the journey the mercury had risen, he put on a lighter cap, if it had fallen he changed into a thicker one.[1]

All hopes of the great enterprise against Antwerp having vanished, Antoine was reduced to coaxing the mad Prince into making a show of taking the offensive, and in pinning down as large enemy forces as possible so as to relieve the pressure on Enghien, who, having at last disgusted 'Monsieur' into quitting the army, had laid siege to Dunkirk. By working on the Prince's vanity Gramont even managed to get a little fighting out of the Dutch element in the joint army. But it was up-hill work; once when he had persuaded Orange to join in a promising adventure, the Prince at the last moment abandoned him to besiege 'a château which looked more like a pigeon loft than a strong place'. And 'after this great exploit he again proposed to me that we should dance the Coranto'.

However, his troubles were nearly ended, for Mazarin had realized that the Dutch were about to betray France by making a separate peace with Spain. If Gramont was not to be trapped in a neutral country, it was high time that he got out, and he received orders to bring his corps back to France.

But it was one thing for Mazarin to order, another for Antoine to obey. Mazarin had directed that the cavalry return by sea, and the officers concerned refused flatly; they were land animals, quite prepared to fight their way home, but entrust their lives to seafaring *canaille* they would not. And Gramont had to agree, somewhat cheered by the fact that the mad Prince promised him an escort of two thousand Dutch horse to the frontier; 'delighted', says Antoine, 'at the prospect of ridding himself of this devil of a man [Gramont] who every day proposed some new scheme which the Prince had no desire to be mixed up with'. So the infantry went home in the cavalry transports, and Gramont with the cavalry set out by land; completing the journey in nine days, a feat upon which he was deservedly complimented. From Sedan Antoine himself set out for Paris, 'the King having ordered him to return immediately'.

He was not long in picking up the current news; Enghien had

[1] Arnauld, l'Abbé d', *Mémoires*.

had a grenade explode in his face at Mardyck, without doing him any damage; the Prince of Wales had taken refuge at the French Court, and 'Mademoiselle' was convinced that he was dying of love for her;[1] and Harcourt, commander-in-chief in Spain, had been forced to raise the siege of Lerida. No doubt Gramont heard this with concealed satisfaction, for it was rarely that a French Marshal was prostrated by the news of a professional rival's misfortunes. And it was this setback which had caused Antoine's recall to Paris, for Enghien and he had been selected to retrieve French prestige in Spain, and there was to be a consultation on ways and means. Another interesting event was the death in December of Enghien's father, the 3rd Prince de Condé; a man so little regretted that even charitable Madame de Motteville remarks with a smile that the Queen's formal visit to the widowed Princess was 'rather for the purpose of rejoicing with her than for offering condolences'.

To Enghien his father's death was a source of unqualified satisfaction; it made him head of one of the most powerful Houses in the kingdom, the last brake on his actions had been removed, and there rose before him the dazzling vision of ousting Mazarin and becoming the *de facto* King of France. Already a national hero, to what might he not aspire? Small wonder that Anne and Mazarin viewed his overwhelming position with uneasiness. But for the moment smiles and honey were the order of the day, especially when Mazarin made his proposal in Council; why should not 'M. Le Prince', as Condé was now called, go to Spain with the title of Viceroy of Catalonia, and there restore the situation? Condé accepted the assignment, and Mazarin reflected that if the Prince suffered a check in the peninsula, he for one would shed no tears; it would make Condé a good deal easier to handle if he returned to Court with his tail between his legs.

At the end of March Gramont left for the Spanish front, and at Gironne received an urgent message from Condé summoning him to a conference at Barcelona to discuss the siege of Lerida; for the famous virgin fortress, before which La Motte-Houdan-

[1] Montpensier, *Mémoires*.

court[1] had failed in 1644 and Harcourt in the previous year, was an irresistible magnet for France's hitherto unbeaten General.

On 11 May Condé and Gramont arrived at Lerida, perched on a cliff overlooking the valley of the Segre, and at first all went well. The Spaniards, characteristically, had neglected to demolish Harcourt's lines of circumvallation, the Spanish army had not yet taken the field, and Condé's chief engineer 'proved to him mathematically that the place was worth nothing at all'.[2] On 13 May the town was invested, Condé taking the left sector and Gramont the right. Both Generals were a little above themselves:

> The Prince, covered with glory and elated with the campaigns of Rocroi, Nordlingen, and Fribourg, to insult the place and the Governor, ordered the trenches to be mounted at noonday by his own regiment, at the head of which marched four and twenty fiddlers, as if it had been a wedding.

And Gramont amused himself by writing witty letters to Mazarin about the Spanish defence; letters whose despatch he lived to regret. Don Gregorio Brito, commanding in Lerida, watched Condé's fanfaronnades with a grim smile; the Prince was disposed to jest, Don Gregorio would carry on the joke; and he began that very night:

> We were all in high spirits, our violins playing soft airs . . . and were joking about the poor Governor and his fortifications . . . when we heard an ominous cry of 'Alerte!' . . . followed by a discharge of cannon and musketry and this discharge by a vigorous sally which, after having levelled our earthworks, pursued us as far as our Main Guard. The next day Brito sent a trumpet with a present of ice and fruit to the Prince, humbly beseeching His Highness to excuse his not returning his serenade as unfortunately he had no violins; but that if the music of last night was not disagreeable to him,

[1] MOTTE-HOUDANCOURT, Philippe, Duc de Cardonne, Maréchal de La, 1605–1657, served from 1622 to 1652; 'a simple gentleman of Picardy who rose to the highest position open to him, entirely by his own merit'.

[2] Bussy-Rabutin, *Mémoires*.

he would endeavour to continue it as long as His Highness did him the honour to stay before Lerida.[1]

Condé, so intolerable at Court, so tolerant in the field, was the first to admit that the Don had the best of the laugh; Lerida was obviously not to be taken with violins, and he and Gramont, laying aside all gasconnade, settled down to do their utmost. It was a period of heart-breaking toil, savage counter-attacks by the Spaniards, constant heavy casualties, and macabre diversion which told eloquently of nerves strained to the breaking point. Bussy-Rabutin was asked to dinner one evening by La Vallière,[2] at the head of Gramont's trench, which was in the ruins of a church... 'we had violins, and while they played Brabantane (Lieutenant of the Condé Life Guard), being at a loss for adventure, lifted the lid of a tomb in which was a whole corpse in a shroud. He brought it over to us, and Bretache... taking the corpse's other hand, they proceeded to dance with it to the music'.

'We had a real good debauch', continues Bussy, and goes on to say that in the middle of dinner La Vallière was killed by a bullet:

> We finished dinner as if nothing had happened... except for Jumeaux . . . who ran off to ask 'M. Le Prince' for the Governorship of Fleix, vacant owing to the death of La Vallière.

But try as Condé and Gramont might, facts were too stubborn for them, virgin Lerida remained inviolable; no longer was Condé's string band heard in the trenches, and its silence was underlined for the Prince by the continued attentions of Don Gregorio, who every day sent him a present and a courteous message. Disease and desertion were playing havoc with the French army, and by the middle of June the trenches were manned by three hundred men each instead of twelve hundred as at first. Condé was too good a soldier not to know when he

[1] *Ibid.*

[2] Vallière, François La Baume Le Blanc, Chevalier de La, 1613–1647, uncle of Louise de La Vallière, the famous mistress of Louis XIV.

was beaten, and on 17 June he communicated his decision to raise the siege:

> The surprise of Gramont was extreme . . . knowing as he did the high and proud character of the Prince . . . the Maréchal praised and approved the Prince's decision, which was the wisest he could have taken.

In November Condé and Gramont put their troops into winter quarters and set out for home. With them went Philibert, who observes that they returned 'not overladen with laurels . . . we did nothing but joke with one another during the march, and 'M. le Prince' was the first to ridicule the siege . . . We made up some of those lampoons on Lerida which were sung all over France, in order to prevent others more severe; however we gained nothing by it, for notwithstanding we treated ourselves freely in our own ballads, others were composed in Paris in which we were ten times more severely handled'.[1]

It was a poor homecoming for Gramont who had long basked in the reflected light of Condé's glory; and if in the past he had felt any annoyance at the way in which his chief monopolized the limelight, he was no doubt only too anxious to let him have it all to himself in the winter of 1647.

At Court, the first exciting event of the season had been the arrival of three nieces and a nephew of Mazarin on 11 September; ostensibly on a mere visit, but actually, as everyone knew, in order that the Minister might dower them handsomely at the expense of France.[2] On the whole the children made a good impression, but within two months all interest in them was temporarily eclipsed by the news that Louis XIV had caught smallpox. The Queen shut herself up with her son, and all girls with any pretensions to beauty fled the Court; rather making a mountain out of a molehill, thought Madame de Motteville, for 'after all, it is an illness which is common among children'. But in fact the King was seriously ill, and more than once his life was despaired of.

The illness focused the Court's attention on a King who had

[1] Hamilton, *Memoirs.*

[2] Perey, *Roman du Grand Roi.*

hitherto been merely one of the children constantly underfoot about the palace, distinguished only from his playmates in that you raised your hat on catching sight of him. But now far-seeing Courtiers like Gramont began to speculate on what manner of King this child was to be; it was for instance noticed that even at play, no one had ever seen him laugh. 'In my opinion', says Madame de Motteville, 'those who had the honour to approach him told him too often that he was the master; in his childish quarrels with his brother, the Queen always insisted that the King must be obeyed, and it seemed that she herself wished to respect the King as much as she loved him.' Soon after Louis' recovery the Court got its first glimpse of the coming Grand Monarque whose 'terrifying majesty' was to awe everyone who ever met him; he delivered a public and stinging rebuke to the Duc de Joyeuse,[1] who arrived a few minutes late for some Court ceremony. The incident must have given Gramont food for serious reflection, for it was urgent that he got an early and accurate picture of the King's character. His eldest son, Armand, had already made a successful début at Court as one of Louis' playmates, for he was a member of the King's company of child-soldiers who drilled in the palace gardens, attacking and defending the model fortress which had been built there for them. Gramont saw that his son had made a promising start, but the situation had its difficulties; Guiche, from the altitude of ten years, patronized the King of nine, and thought him 'a stupid'. He was to revise his views and to regret the frankness with which he had exposed them, as his father had foreseen. To the seven-year-old Duc d'Anjou, Louis' brother, Armand was of course a hero, and he was to retain his ascendancy over the younger prince for many years to come; which was to have an important influence on both their lives.

In this year Gramont's half-sister Suzanne[2] married under peculiar and rather mortifying circumstances; her great-aunt, the Marquise de Montpezat, a childless widow, had made Suzanne

[1] Joyeuse, Louis de Lorraine, Duc de, 1622–1654, second son of the 4th Duc de Guise, and Grand Chamberlain of France.

[2] St Chaumont, Suzanne Charlotte de Gramont, Marquise de, 1627?–1688.

her heiress on condition that the girl married one of her late husband's nephews, and by the time Suzanne was of marriageable age, there were thirteen of them eligible. Madame de Montpezat's executors accordingly offered the girl to the Montpezat clan, but each in turn, except the cadet, declined the offer; much to the surprise of society, for Suzanne, in addition to being rich, with influential connections, was 'well-made and kindly'. It would have been as well for Suzanne had the last of the nephews followed the example of his elders, for Melchior Mitte, Marquis de St Chaumont, who married her was 'a very eccentric man'; which seems a charitable way of describing one who, in addition to being almost insane, 'gave his wife a terrible wedding present; he poxed her thoroughly'.[1]

It was with considerable relief that Gramont learned early in 1648 that he would not return to Spain, that grave of military reputations; Condé, who had been sulking at Dijon whilst the laughter over Lerida died down, was summoned north to command the army of Flanders, and chose Gramont as his second-in-command. Both men were glad to set out for this always popular theatre of war, and glad also to turn their backs on Paris; for the days now seemed far distant when all France had said, 'The Queen is so kind'. Taxation was approaching the limits of endurance, there was scarcity in several provinces, and even in Paris could be heard the mutterings of an approaching storm. The explanation was simple; France then, as throughout the reign, had not a national income sufficient to maintain a tolerable standard of living at home whilst simultaneously pursuing an aggressive policy abroad. And faced with the choice between conflicting demands on an overdrawn treasury, her rulers unhesitatingly chose Guns before Butter; or rather before bread. To Condé, Gramont, Turenne, even to Mazarin, the idea that the 'glory of France' should be sacrificed for the benefit of a hungry peasantry would have seemed fantastic; the *noblesse* died by the sword in their hundreds every year for that glory, and why should not the peasant contribute his quota by dying of hunger? But all the same, the suppression of civil disturbance was an inglorious business, and Gramont was glad to evade it.

[1] Tallemant des Réaux, *Historiettes*.

The strategic objective of 1648 was to clear the enemy out of the area between the River Lys and the sea, but no tactical plan had been agreed upon when Condé reached the front in April. However, shortly after his arrival at Arras, he received orders that Rantzau's[1] scheme for the siege of Ypres had been adopted. Condé was not optimistic about the Rantzau plan for taking the town by assault; his own army must cover a siege if the assault failed, and Gramont reported that the only route open to Condé would be a road with dykes on either side; and furthermore, that the Lys could not be crossed without exposing the French flank. Palluau too was protesting against the plan because whilst Ypres was being attacked, his own citadel of Courtrai might fall – as actually happened on 22 May, three days after Ypres was invested. It was a serious setback, in no way compensated for by the fall of Ypres on the 28th; though the manner of the town's surrender furnished Gramont with a much needed laugh:

> The man they sent to surrender [Ypres] was a Walloon Lieutenant-Colonel, one of the most ridiculous personages one could find in a day's march; he kept on assuring us in the strongest terms that the officers and the soldiers had been dying to surrender from the start, but that those wretches the inhabitants, would not permit it . . . and only today at the entreaty of the whole garrison, had they allowed him to do so.

Courtrai once lost, the value of Ypres was small; plans had to be recast, and Rantzau produced a scheme for an attack on Ostend which both Condé and Gramont thought 'chimerical'. Condé indeed washed his hands of it, thus earning a snub from Mazarin, for Rantzau was authorized to carry out the Ostend attack independently. But he vindicated Condé's judgement by failing with heavy losses; 'Rantzau's plan', says Gramont, 'looked splendid on paper . . . so easy, except perhaps for one trifling snag, which was that it depended on filling up with brushwood a tidal canal which carried sea-going ships'.

[1] Rantzau, Josias, Maréchal de, soldier of fortune from Holstein, entered French service 1635, and became a Maréchal, 1645; 'his health and temper were always uncertain, partly from wounds and partly from drink'.

It was not until mid-August that Condé's chance came at last; on the 17th news reached him that the enemy, 18,000 strong, was making for Lens, and on the following morning the whole French army, some 16,000, set out under Gramont for La Bassée. In the evening Condé, who had spent the whole day in reconnoitring the Imperial army outside Lens, rejoined his men and drew up his battle orders. Condé himself would command the right wing, Châtillon the centre, and Gramont the left, consisting of sixteen squadrons and two infantry battalions.

At dawn on the 19th the French army set out on its five-mile march to Lens, and on entering the plain found that the enemy had shifted his position during the night. The Archduke's army was no longer on the plain proper, but withdrawn into the rising ground under Lens, its right flank resting on the town and two-thirds of its front protected by a marsh. Archduke Leopold, though superior in numbers, was evidently taking no chances. Nor was Condé; if the Archduke hoped to entice him into attacking uphill as at Fribourg, he was doomed to disappointment; but could the enemy be coaxed into the plain? Condé thought it worth trying, and as soon as it was light on the 20th, he began to withdraw, ostentatiously exposing his right flank to the enemy. And the Archduke, though apparently contemplating no general advance, sent out his cavalry to harass Condé's right wing which had, as the army moved into column, become the rearguard. More troops gradually came into action on either side, the rearguard action was insensibly developing into the pitched battle which Condé desired, when suddenly his own cavalry, seized with a baseless panic, broke and fled. The rout was apparently Condé's own fault, he having left too wide a gap between his rearguard and his main body. But his manœuvre was so far successful, that the Archduke, seeing the confusion in the French ranks, and being assured that 'to attack and to defeat the French was one and the same thing', yielded to temptation and issued orders to join battle all along the line. At eight o'clock the Austro-Spanish army descended into the plain, the French advancing to meet them; at a distance of thirty yards, both sides halted; the enemy opened fire; the French replied; Condé's sword flashed over his head, and a moment later the battle had begun.

Gramont, always a great believer in his own rhetoric, had found time before the clash to deliver 'a short and pathetic discourse' to his men; 'all the infantry gave cries of joy and threw their hats in the air; the cavalry drew their swords and all the trumpets gave a fanfare'. After which they advanced 'in such silence that in the whole wing no one could be heard talking except myself'. To Gramont fell the ugly task of tackling Bucquoy's Spanish Cuirassiers, and it was 'more of a duel than a battle'. In the Spanish army cuirassiers were armed with muskets, and 'their fire was so close and so terrible that one would have said that hell was opening'. Practically every French squadron leader was killed or wounded, but before the enemy could reload Gramont's horse had charged home. The struggle was short, fierce, and decisive, the enemy right was broken, and Gramont, leaving the pursuit to his juniors, galloped over to the left wing to see how Condé fared. The victory here and in the centre had been as complete as his own on the left; the whole enemy army was fleeing in disorder, hotly pursued by the French cavalry. The battle had lasted three hours.[1]

Condé, who had led ten charges in person, rode up to Gramont, sword in hand, and attempted to embrace him; but, 'our horses, hitherto as quiet as mules, attacked each other so furiously that they came within an ace of putting their masters into greater danger than they had encountered all day'.

It was Condé's most complete victory since Rocroi; many of the Imperial generals were taken in the rout, 3,000 enemy were dead, 5,000 prisoners or wounded, and the Archduke had lost his pontoons, baggage, and 38 guns; the French losses in killed, wounded, and missing, were about 1,500. But rejoicing in the French camp was soon silenced by ominous news from Paris, where things were going from bad to worse; there was scarcely a province in which disaffection was not widespread, a section of the nobility was showing signs of revolt, and the Parlement appeared to be setting up as the champion of the discontented mob. When in due course orders arrived for Gramont to make

[1] Godley, *The Great Condé*.

his best speed for the capital, bringing with him the French and Swiss Guards, the Gendarmerie, and the Light Horse, no one could mistake the significance of that call for the pick of the French army. The Civil War had begun.

CHAPTER VI

★

THE Civil War is not of much importance in Gramont's life. Quite uninterested in its causes, he regarded it as mere sound and fury, an exasperating interruption in that assault on Olympus to which his life was dedicated. His aims could not be furthered by neutrality, nor even by blind adherence to that party which showed the best prospects of being victorious. But unlike so many of his fellows, Antoine contemplated nothing so crude as offering his services to the highest bidder; he understood that one party must have his consistent support. Consistent but not provocative; support of such value as would entitle him to share the fruits of victory without making an irreparable breach with political opponents whose friendship would be of value to him when the war was over. A problem of no little delicacy, whose solution left him no time to consider the larger issues involved.

Thus it would be irrelevant to enter largely into the history of the Fronde, and here it suffices to say that it began as a movement to restore the constitution which Richelieu had destroyed, headed by the Paris Parlement, aided by the higher bourgeoisie, and supported by the unprivileged who could no longer endure the miseries inflicted upon them by arbitrary and excessive taxation.

The trouble started on 13 May 1648 when a new tax which struck at the lawyers, brought about a meeting of the Parlement and the Sovereign Courts. At this it was decided to demand from the Crown:

i. The abolition of Intendants
ii. Reduction of taxation
iii. Recognition of the principle of no taxation without the consent of the Parlement
iv. Admission of the illegality of imprisonment without trial and subsequent conviction of a crime.

Mazarin retorted by attempting to extract a forced loan from the Parlement, was worsted, and had to dismiss the Superintendent of Finances. On 20 August Condé won the battle of Lens, and Queen Anne determined that under cover of the victory parade she would teach the Parisians a lesson which they would long remember. On the 26th the King went in state to Nôtre Dame to return thanks for the victory, and whilst the *Te Deum* was in progress, the three most important Parlementary opponents of the Crown were arrested. It was a capital blunder; so far from overawing Parlement and people the result was that within a few hours the streets were barricaded, the mob surrounded the palace, and the lives of Royalists were not safe outside the Louvre. For two days anarchy reigned, and on the 28th Anne capitulated; the three members were released, the barricades disappeared, and on the surface life in Paris returned to normality. But all parties realized that this was a mere breathing space, a gathering of strength for a decisive battle.[1]

In Flanders Gramont pondered upon the news from Paris, but not for long. He had seen too many revolts against the Royal authority to entertain any sanguine hopes of the latest one; lawyers, bourgeois, and the mob he regarded with the amused contempt of his class and profession; loyalty had paid him handsomely in the past, and he decided that he must drive the best bargain he could with the Court.

Condé regarded the problem rather differently; headstrong, intoxicated with his own prestige, full of grandiose dreams, he hesitated over his course of action. Ultimately he yielded to the persuasions of Gramont and decided for the Crown; and Gramont, having thereby done the Court a notable service, showed no diffidence in letting Mazarin understand its importance. The arguments with which he had won over Condé were characteristic; the Parlement, he said, if not checked would gradually acquire complete authority; next, it would start interfering in military matters; and after that, it would attack the privileged classes. To Condé, Gramont's last argument was both alarming and convincing; for if the *noblesse* was to be attacked,

[1] Retz, *Mémoires*.

might not these scoundrels next turn their attentions to the Princes of the Blood? No punishment which he and his army could inflict would be adequate for their mere contemplation of such an outrage. Antoine had not invented his arguments; 'on the whole', says the Frondeur Rochefoucauld,[1] 'it was a tolerably true picture'. On 18 September Condé was given an overwhelming reception at Court; Anne, 'in tears, assured him tenderly that she regarded him as a third son'; Mazarin promised that for the rest of his days he would have no other ambition but to comply with all the wishes of 'M. le Prince'; and Louis, kissing him, said that on his dear cousin alone depended the salvation of the State.

Condé secured, Mazarin's most dangerous enemy was the future Cardinal de Retz,[2] known at this time as the Coadjutor. A younger son, conscripted into the priesthood, and now at the age of thirty-four waiting impatiently to step into the shoes of his uncle the Archbishop of Paris, Retz was a born demagogue, delighting in mischief for mischief's sake, proud of his power over the Paris mob, his ambition to be master of the puppet show with all France as his puppets. Like Mazarin, he realized the vital necessity of securing Condé's support, and was prepared to use every means to detach the Prince from the Court.

Had Condé possessed even rudimentary political ability and a modicum of tact, he could in 1648 have become *de facto* King of France; but, insolent, arrogant, unbending, he made enemies unnecessarily, quarrelled improvidently with potential friends, and within a twelvemonth became the best hated man in the kingdom. But for the moment Mazarin had won him, and was now straining every nerve to win further military support; for even Condé could not fight without lieutenants. Of these Gramont was much the most efficient, and he had decided to throw in his lot with the Royalists. But he affected indecision,

[1] ROCHEFOUCAULD, Francois VI, 2nd Duc de La, 1613–1680, author of the *Maximes*, 'dark, dignified, suave and melancholy, the perfect embodiment of the *honnête homme*'.

[2] RETZ, Jean Paul François de Gondi, Cardinal de, 1614–1679, brother of the 3rd Duc de Retz, nephew of the Archbishop of Paris.

and had his reward; Mazarin, too anxious to pay him in his usual coin of flattery, caused Louis XIV to make him a Duke in November. Antoine had at last reached the top of the ladder.

1648 closed in an uneasy truce, a Parliamentary victory, for by the Declaration of St Germain on 22 October Anne had been forced to make important concessions to the popular side; but everyone realized that she would adhere to her promises for just as long as it would take to collect the troops and money needed for a drastic attempt to restore absolutism.

1649 opened with what was rather a Court conspiracy than a *coup d'état;* the Royal family and Mazarin were to be smuggled out of Paris to St Germain, and once they were clear Condé was to blockade the capital, cutting off all foodstuffs, particularly the Parisians' bread which came in daily from Gonesse; to Gramont fell the task of getting the King out of Paris on 5 January, and Madame de Motteville has given us the best account of how he did it:

> I went to the Queen in the evening ... and found her in her little room watching the King at play, and apparently thinking of nothing else ... Madame de La Tremouille, who was sitting beside her, whispered to me very softly, 'It is rumoured that the Queen is leaving Paris tonight' ... I shrugged my shoulders at an idea which seemed to me chimerical ... The Queen seemed livelier than usual. The Princes and the Minister [Mazarin] paid their respects, but did not stop, as they were going to supper with the Maréchal de Gramont, who always entertained splendidly on this night [Twelfth Night eve] ... To amuse the King, the Queen cut the cake and got the bean herself ... We [i.e. the Ladies-in-Waiting] supped as usual in the wardrobe room on the remnants of the Queen's supper ... and so well deceived were we all that we laughed heartily with the Queen at those who had spread the rumour that she was leaving Paris that night.[1]

But shortly after midnight Madame de Motteville began to suspect that something unusual was in the air. Why should

[1] Motteville, *Mémoires.*

the Queen send for Beringhen[1] and why should she, who never explained her actions to anyone, tell her Ladies that she had summoned him about an affair of charity? Suspicion deepened with the arrival of Mademoiselle de Beaumont from the Hôtel de Gramont, where she had received a strong hint from the Maréchal that the air of Paris was unhealthy, and that it was time to try a change. Let us hear Madame de Motteville further:

> Maréchal de Villeroi[2]... let the King sleep till three o'clock, then got him up, and also the little 'Monsieur', and put them into the carriage which was waiting for them at the garden gate. The Queen went with the King and 'Monsieur' ... They came down by the secret staircase which runs from the King's room to the garden... and all having arrived at the Cours-la-Reine, the Queen halted there to await the arrival of the rest of the Royal family... I, like everyone else, was now informed of the Queen's departure; and one of my friends came banging on my door to say that he had a coach and six ready for me... but I did not go, feeling that it would all be very uncomfortable.[3]

Madame de Motteville thereby showed her usual good sense, for it was all very uncomfortable. At St Germain, as at all summer residences of that day, the rooms had been dismantled for the winter and the windows taken out; there was a hard frost; and there was an acute shortage of food.[4] But for all this Gramont was not to blame; any preparations to render St Germain habitable would have been reported to Retz, whose spies were efficient and ubiquitous, and if Retz had heard in time of the proposed flight he would certainly have raised the Paris mob to prevent it.

[1] Beringhen, Henri, 2nd Marquis de, 1603–1692, Valet-de-Chambre to Anne 1642, First Equerry of France, 1645; as such he was responsible for ordering carriages for a royal journey, and hence Madame de Motteville's suspicions of his interview with the Queen.

[2] Villeroi, Nicolas de Neufville, 1st Maréchal and 1st Duc de, 1598–1685, Maréchal, and also governor to Louis XIV, 1646; Duke and Peer, 1663.

[3] Motteville, *Mémoires*.

[4] Montpensier, *Mémoires*.

In the capital the news was received with a consternation which swiftly changed to anger. The Parlement made open preparations for civil war and launched a personal attack upon Mazarin; on 8 January he was banished, and on the 25th his property was confiscated and auctioned to aid the rebel war chest. On the 13th the Bastille, which had no garrison except its handful of warders, surrendered after a farcical siege, and the civil war was fairly under way.

But the Fronde already had within itself the seeds of its own destruction; to raise a citizen army was easy enough, but how was it to be officered? Only by nobles, and a sufficient number of them must be bribed or flattered into joining the rebel cause. It was easily done; with that levity and irresponsibility which characterized them, a considerable minority of the *noblesse* decided that to fight outwards from Paris would be more amusing than to loaf about on blockade duty with the Royal army; and a stream of deserters left St Germain, including the Prince de Conti,[1] who was appointed 'Generalissimo of the Army for the release of the King'.

This recruitment of the *noblesse* by the Parlement fatally altered the character of what had begun as a constitutional struggle for a legitimate objective; control of the movement passed to the noble officers, who were utterly lacking in patriotism, political common-sense, or even coherence. Those who were not fighting for mere love of excitement were fighting for their own selfish ends, and were as suspicious of each other as the Parlement was of Retz' mob and as both were of the *noblesse*; all three groups were unstably held together only by their common hatred of Mazarin; and whilst Parlement wanted reform and the mob easier living conditions, the *noblesse* wanted the restoration and perpetuation of anarchy.

Condé set about the blockade with his usual savage energy, and within a week he had succeeded in almost stopping the entry of food into Paris. Gramont, serving as his second-in-command,

[1] CONTI, Armand de Bourbon, 2nd Prince de, 1629–1666, was delicate and a hunchback; after a dissipated youth he married one of Mazarin's nieces, became pious, and a model husband. Between 1636 and 1641 he was a class-fellow of Molière's at the Collège de Clermont.

held St Cloud and Meudun, from where he observed the situation with the bland irony of the professional called upon to make war against civilians. On 10 February he found himself in action for the first time since the trouble started; the previous evening Beaufort had left Paris to meet and escort a food convoy coming up from Etampes, and Gramont attacked him with a force of about 4,000 men, which included at least one battalion of the French Guard. Not for the first time in his career did Gramont regret his witticisms about an enemy; for his encounter with Beaufort was one of the most deplorable fiascos of the war. Not of course that he was beaten by Beaufort, but the fact remained that the citizen soldiers ran their convoy into Paris under the nose of a Marshal of France.

Of serious fighting in the first Fronde there was practically none; the defeat of Charenton, which destroyed the only professional units in the rebel army, completed the Parisians' disgust with the war into which they had entered so light-heartedly. To plenty had succeeded shortage, to shortage famine. In spite of the utmost efforts of Retz, Conti, and Beaufort, the Parlement insisted on opening *pourparlers* with the Court, to which Gramont escorted the deputies during February. Neither party being strong enough to dictate terms, the atmosphere was conciliatory, and it was agreed that formal conferences should assemble 'in a place which was not suspect'. The deputation summoned to meet the Officers of the Crown at Rueil on 4 March was again escorted by Gramont to its destination, this time with his own company of *Gendarmerie*; and there on the 11th was signed a treaty, which on 1 April became the Peace of St Germain. It was a compromise, satisfying no one, and leaving Beaufort and Retz free to keep sedition alive in Paris; but it was peace of a sort, and was hailed with relief by all except the 'malcontents'.

Anne showed no haste in returning to the capital, and it was not until 18 August that the King made his state entry, receiving a rapturous welcome; there were even a few shouts of *Vive le Cardinal!* but these Mazarin had paid for in hard cash, and was much annoyed at the bad value he got for his money. Mazarin had emerged as victor in the struggle, but only at a price; Condé was the real winner, the absolute master of France, and to the Cardinal he behaved with an insolence which even Mazarin found hard to endure. His only consolation was that Condé was making fresh enemies every day, and that if given enough rope, he was sure to hang himself.

Perhaps during the autumn of 1649 Condé suffered from a nervous breakdown, for only on that supposition is his conduct explicable; for instance, at a Council meeting in September, the Prince asked for the Government of Pont de l'Arche, and Mazarin flatly refused it; whereupon Condé flipped him on the nose, said 'Goodbye, Mars!' and went off without taking leave of the Queen. During the next few weeks he drove Royalists and Frondeurs nearly mad by his constant changes of front before finally coming down on the side of the Fronde; then a couple of days later he signed a treaty with the Court whereby Mazarin resigned virtually all his powers into Condé's hands – an apparently final *volte-face* which was as inexplicable as what preceded it.[1]

To the superficial observer it appeared that Condé had won, but Mazarin knew better. Condé had alienated both Fronde and Parlement; better still, he had personally insulted the Queen by ordering her to cancel the well-deserved exile to which she had just sentenced an ass, the young Marquis de Jarzé,[2] who had had the impudence to attempt to make love to her; and she was not the woman to forget such a humiliation. Furthermore, the Prince was steadily estranging his remaining noble supporters by his intolerable arrogance. 'Time and I, time and I', said Mazarin gleefully, rubbing his hands together. At last Condé brought matters to a crisis by arranging a clandestine marriage for the young Duc de Richelieu, in defiance of the Queen.[3] Was Condé to be allowed to rule France or was he not? Decidedly not, said Anne, and measures were taken for his arrest, together with that of his brother Conti, and his brother-in-law, the Duc de Longue-

[1] Rochefoucauld, *Mémoires*.

[2] Jarzé, Réné du Plessis de La Roche-Pichemer, 1st Marquis de, 1620?–1672, entered the army 1637, and became one of the group of young officers surrounding Condé. Good-looking, quarrelsome, brainless, and conceited.

[3] Montpensier, *Mémoires*.

ville.[1] Condé, though warned of what was impending, and advised that it was unsafe for the three princes to visit Court at the same time, laughed at his informants; with the result that all three were arrested at the Louvre on 18 January and hustled off to Vincennes without the slightest disturbance, and to the great relief of all France.

To Gramont it was a stunning blow, and he burst into tears on hearing of it; not only had he lost the chief architect of his career, but he himself had become suspect. He had always been prominently identified with the Condé interest, and Mazarin, having netted the big fish, was now turning his attention to the smaller fry, amongst whom Gramont was easily the most important. True, Antoine had assured the Queen of his loyalty, but what were promises worth in these times? His half-brother Philibert, having participated actively in the rebellion, had, on learning of Condé's arrest, deserted to the Spaniards. No wonder Mazarin felt dubious about the Gramonts; and he was in fact going to arrest Antoine when Laigues[2] guaranteed his loyalty.[3]

The arrests raised Mazarin's credit considerably, and brought about an alliance between the Court and the 'old Fronde'; but these gains were offset by the outbreak of a second and more disastrous phase of the civil war. Condé still had many partisans, chiefly competent soldiers, who with the skilled support of professional mischief-makers now proceeded to raise the provinces and levy what they were pleased to call 'His Majesty's Army for the release of the Princes'. On 10 April Condé's wife escaped from house arrest at Montrond with her little son, the Duc d'Enghien,[4] made her way to Bordeaux, and there talked the city into declaring for the rebels. It was a notable coup, but

[1] LONGUEVILLE, Henri II d'Orléans, 2nd Duc de, descended from the famous 'Bastard of Orléans'; in 1642 he married Condé's sister, Anne Geneviève, Mlle de Bourbon; he was 'feeble, irresolute, and distrustful'.

[2] LAIGUES, Geoffroi, Baron de, 1614–1679, served in Guards, 1644–8, and in 1649 became an ardent Frondeur. His mistress, the Duchesse de Chevreuse, married him in 1657.

[3] Fédern, *Mazarin*.

[4] ENGHIEN, Henri Jules de Bourbon, Duc d', 1643–1709, inherited his mother's insanity; succeeded his father as 5th Prince de Condé, 1686.

Gramont struck a telling counter-blow; on 20 April the rebels had signed a treaty with Spain, and Spanish aid could only reach Bordeaux through Bayonne. Antoine had hoped to slip through Bordeaux unrecognized; but in the nick of time he received warning from a friend that the Frondeurs had the whole plan for his murder in Bordeaux cut and dried. In consequence he made a considerable detour, but reached Bayonne in time to cut the rebel land communications with Spain and instal his brother Toulongeon as Governor.

Toulongeon was and always had been a friend of Condé's, but he declined urbanely to desert the royal cause. From Bordeaux 'Madame La Princesse' wooed him in vain with appeals to their old friendship; but Toulongeon merely shrugged his shoulders, sent back a verbal message that he saw no sense in putting his head in a noose, and advised her to make peace with the Court at once. She fared no better with Gramont, now in his Government of Béarn where he had gone to sulk because Mazarin had refused him a benefice; Antoine's reply was in writing, and more flowery than that of his brother, but it was an uncompromising refusal to join the rebels; and though throughout the year he did make some ineffectual efforts to persuade the Queen to release the Princes, he also reported to Mazarin the efforts which 'Madame La Princesse' was making to seduce Toulongeon, and sent the Prime Minister copies of his own correspondence with her. 'His (i.e. Gramont's) fidelity is unshakable', notes Mazarin in his *Carnets*.

In Paris sympathy for the Princes was gradually spreading; people forgot Condé's behaviour and remembered only his victories; plans for the escape of the three became so frequent that in November Mazarin had them transferred to the citadel of Hâvre. Gramont, who had returned to Court, felt that without tainting his own loyalty, he could now work for the liberation of his friend. Mazarin was perfectly ready to listen, and was lavish in vague promises which Antoine seems to have tried to take at their face value. Mazarin, says Retz, fooled Gramont from morning to night. It may have been so, but it sounds to me very unlike Gramont. Later Gramont tried to enlist 'Monsieur' on Condé's behalf; and failed, for 'Monsieur' as usual agreed with the last speaker, who at this time was generally Retz. All Antoine could get out of 'Monsieur' was that he wished the Princes to be set at liberty by the Court, and not by a civil war. But matters moved a step further when on 30 December Parlement demanded that the prisoners be either tried or released; and two days later the Princess-Palatine[1] united 'Monsieur', the Old, and the New Frondes in a league for the release of the Princes.

Gramont, though in sympathy with the objects of this league, did not join it, for almost every member was in bad odour at Court; hence Retz' sarcasm when Gramont was at Mazarin's request negotiating with the Princes at Hâvre to get them to give surety for their good conduct if released. Mazarin, says Retz, had no intention of liberating them on any terms, and 'the poor Maréchal, with the best intentions in the world, played the most ridiculous role for which any gentleman of his quality was ever cast'. If Retz is correct, then Mazarin made an impulsive *volte-face;* on the 2 February Antoine is sent off on a bogus mission to Hâvre, Mazarin merely pretending that he is about to set the Princes free – but on the 6th, Mazarin leaves for Hâvre himself, with the Royal warrant for the release of the three prisoners. Surely Gramont's mission was perfectly genuine, and through him Mazarin had meant to find out how much the Princes would bid for their liberty; but events moved too quickly for the Cardinal, and on the 6th or 7th he saw that public opinion had shifted so decisively to the Princes' side that his only chance of preventing his own downfall was to go to Hâvre himself and persuade them that they owed their liberty to him alone; which he did, by-passing Gramont whose instructions were now out of date.

As the prisoners and Gramont were sitting down to dinner on the 13th, Mazarin in person entered the room and announced

[1] PALATINE, Anne de Gonzague, Princess-, 1616–1684, daughter of Charles I, Duke of Mantua; tricked into a sham marriage with Duc de Guise, 1640; married Edward of Bavaria, Prince-Palatine, 1645; 'very gallant', and marriage made no difference to her way of life; 'she inherited the talent for intrigue for which her family had for generations been noted, and she well knew how to turn it to account'.

that the Queen had set them free unconditionally. Condé received the news gravely, and invited Mazarin to join them at table; and the meal was eaten, says Madame de Motteville, 'as if they were all on the best of terms with each other. The comedy of Vanity Fair so decreed. And every actor present was a star'.[1] But when Condé was stepping into Gramont's carriage after dinner, he apparently found it impossible to play his part any longer; Mazarin bowed to the ground; Condé, giving him the curtest of nods, flung himself into the coach and with a burst of laughter, told the coachman to whip up. All that Mazarin had gained by his endeavour to pose as the liberator of the Princes was personal humiliation and the contempt of France; and he was not slow to realize that he had made the country too hot to hold him. Prudent as always, he had 'inadvertently' packed the Crown jewels in his carriage before leaving Paris; so there was nothing to prevent him seeking a healthier climate. He vanished unobtrusively, and when next the Court heard of him, he was in the Electorate of Cologne, which he had reached after an alarming journey round north-eastern France.

Gramont was now engaged in the dangerous and exhausting occupation of walking the tightrope. Here was Condé, once more at liberty, and formally reconciled to the Court; but was the reconciliation likely to endure? Antoine dared not show coolness to Condé; if the Prince was acting in good faith, he would undoubtedly be restored to his army command, and Gramont's chance of further employment would depend on his being on the old intimate terms with him when the time came to select generals for the next campaign. But equally, he dared not jeopardize his position with the Queen; the groups that had united to liberate Condé were all Frondeur at heart, and the Prince was heavily in their debt; they would not be shy about pressing for repayment, and their idea of settling was more than likely to take the form of insisting on the Prince leading a new revolt; and should Antoine be caught on Condé's side when this happened, he would be ruined. Then there was Mazarin, who was by no means the spent rocket that the public imagined, but was governing France from Cologne as despotically as if

[1] Motteville, *Mémoires*.

he were still in Paris; was, as we now know and as Gramont suspected, exchanging love letters as well as governmental correspondence with Anne. Gramont had done well out of Mazarin, and hoped to do better if, as seemed likely, the Cardinal managed to return; and if, when he arrived, the Queen complained to him of Antoine's lack of zeal, he was ruined as surely as if he had supported a rebellious Condé. After much anxious consideration Gramont decided that his only course was to try to maintain the existing peace, incline as much as he dared to the Court side, and continue on cordial but non-committal terms with 'M. le Prince'.

Once more Condé fumbled his chance; he had learnt nothing since the first Fronde, and merely repeated his old blunders on a more disastrous scale. All the old arrogance, insolence, political ineptitude and irresolution reappeared; especially irresolution. With exasperation the Frondeurs watched Condé throw away his second and last chance of governing the Kingdom; it would, says Rochefoucauld, have been easy for him to get Parlement to transfer the Regency from Anne to 'Monsieur' and relegate the Queen to a convent; deprived of the Queen's support, Mazarin's prospects of returning to France were hopeless; and 'Monsieur', the feeblest Prince of his day, would have become the cloak under which Condé ruled France. But whilst Condé was missing chances, the Court had no chances to miss. Retz was determined that there was to be no second flight of the King, and the Royal family were virtually prisoners in the Louvre. All Anne's hopes were centred, firstly on a split in the enemy camp, and secondly in playing for time until Louis attained his majority on 7 September; and she and Mazarin found in Condé himself their best ally. One of the conditions agreed upon between Condé and the Frondeurs as the price of their work for his release was that his brother Conti should marry Mademoiselle de Chevreuse,[1] whose mother was a leading rebel. But on 3 April Condé broke the match with a brutality which deeply shocked a society trained to regard cowardice and impoliteness as the only unforgivable sins; he let it be known that his reason was

[1] Chevreuse, Charlotte Marie de Lorraine, Mlle de, 1627–1652, a granddaughter of the 3rd Duc de Guise; died unmarried.

that the young lady bore a dubious reputation. Society could scarcely believe its ears. There was nothing at all dubious about the reputation of Mademoiselle de Chevreuse; all the world knew that she was the mistress of Cardinal de Retz; but that Condé should have called attention to the fact was felt by even lenient critics to put him outside the pale. Retz was furious, Madame de Chevreuse more furious still, and the formidable Princess-Palatine, who had made the match, was the angriest of them all. The immediate result was that Madame de Chevreuse offered her services to the Court; Retz, having urged Condé to head a revolt in the capital, and having received the scornful answer that he, Retz, was better fitted for a battle with chamber pots in the Paris gutters than the First Prince of the Blood, followed Madame de Chevreuse's example. Condé was once more isolated, and the Queen fell to considering his rearrest; but Condé, who had no wish to revisit Hâvre, retired to his castle of St Maur, never sleeping in Paris, though often visiting it.

Early in July the Court felt itself strong enough to attempt an arrest, and had it not been for Gramont, Condé might have been taken on the road between St Maur and Paris. But Lionne,[1] who was one of the first to hear of the scheme, was anxious to step into Mazarin's shoes; and he realized that so long as Condé was at liberty there could be no return for the ex-Premier. He therefore betrayed the plot to Gramont; who, though too wary to hold any direct communication with St Maur, passed the news on to Condé's devoted friend Chavigny. Matters were in this state when on 7 July Antoine arrived at St Maur, charged by the Queen to invite Condé to return to Court and to assure him in her name that he could do so in perfect safety. It was a mortifying experience for Gramont; his old chief refused him a private interview and told him curtly to deliver his message in the presence of witnesses; and having heard it, said that the Queen's word was not a security in which he felt inclined to put any great trust. Probably Antoine, knowing the secret intentions of the Court, did not press the matter very hard; but he was

[1] LIONNE, Hugues de, 1611–1671, brilliant diplomatist, Minister of Foreign Affairs, 1663; his successes included Treaty of Munster, 1648, League of the Rhine, 1657, and Treaty of Aix-la-Chapelle, 1668.

wounded by 'the haughtiness and rudeness' of his reception. However, he managed to put a good face on it when he returned to Court, where he delighted everyone with a farcical account of the 'meeting of the Estates of the League' at St Maur. Unwilling to fight either for or against Condé, Gramont was now clever enough to get himself sent south to levy troops for a projected siege of Bordeaux; a duty which he thought was not likely to bring him into personal collision with the Prince.

This was practically Gramont's last appearance in the Second Fronde, and we may therefore deal with the rest of the story very briefly. Late in the autumn Condé, who had retired to Montrond, there raised the standard of revolt, signed a treaty with Spain, and plunged his country once more into the horrors of civil war. But he had mis-timed his rebellion. The King had attained his majority, and there were many Frenchmen, notably Turenne, who had no objection to fighting a Regency but refused to draw their swords against a King of France. And Condé was not the man to lead rebels; he had made his name as a leader of disciplined troops, with all the resources of the State behind him, and no man knew less than he did how to conciliate the Squire Westerns who formed the bulk of his new command. When he cursed them for their failure to accomplish the impossible they merely returned to their manors, taking their peasant soldiers with them.

On the 16 November Anne felt strong enough to recall Mazarin, who needed much persuasion. Timidity and greed were at war in him, but greed won, and he started to travel slowly west under the escort of eight regiments which he had raised 'at his own charges'. But after he rejoined the Court on 28 January 1652, his first act was to make the Treasury reimburse him in full for his eight regiments.

On the 7 April Condé defeated the Royalists under Turenne at Bléneau, and then, with inconceivable folly, abandoned his army in the field to plunge into the whirlpool of intrigue in Paris, hoping to secure by negotiation the peace terms which he had failed to obtain by force of arms. This was to challenge Mazarin on his own ground, and the result was a foregone conclusion. The Cardinal 'opened an abyss of negotiations' before the exasperated Prince, and from the security of his headquarters with the wandering Court watched him embroil himself again with the Parisians. Towards the end of June Condé rejoined his army which he had brought up to the suburbs of Paris, and on 2 July he was trapped under the walls of the city by Turenne. The result was the desperate battle of the Porte St Antoine in which the rebels were saved from annihilation only by the action of 'Mademoiselle', who insisted on the gate being opened to Condé, and who covered his retreat by turning the guns of the Bastille on the Royal army.

Paris paid dearly for the admission of its 'liberators'. On the 4 July, almost certainly with Condé's connivance, perhaps at his instigation, the Hôtel de Ville was sacked; several members of the Parlement who were thought to be favourable to the Court, and many of the wealthier bourgeoisie were shot down by officers of the Condé Regiment disguised as civilians, and others were taken as hostages. Anarchy reigned unchecked in the capital until the 14 October when Condé, recognizing the hopelessness of trying to swim against the Royalist current any longer, left the city. On the 21st the King entered Paris, exiling 'Monsieur' on his arrival; on the 22nd the leading Frondeurs, including 'Mademoiselle', were banished, and an amnesty was published for the remainder; Condé fled to the Spanish Netherlands, and with the capture and imprisonment of Retz on 19 December, the civil war in the north finished. But it was not until 13 July 1653, when Bordeaux surrendered to the King, that the last embers of revolt were quenched. But we must turn back to see how the other Gramonts had been faring.

In 1652 Gramont's elder son, Armand, Comte de Guiche, whom we last met as one of the King's child-friends, appeared in society, and made a favourable impression on Condé, at whose various houses he was a welcome visitor. 'M. de Guiche', writes the Prince to Antoine, 'is full of intelligence, is exactly like you to look at, and I think you will be completely satisfied with him.' In October, when he had smallpox, the society weekly *La Muze Historique*, gravely deplored the damage done to his 'beautifully modelled features and his lovely roses and cream complexion'.

Guiche's uncle Philibert was also in Paris for part of this year;

tired of the civil war, tired of the Spaniards, and even more tired of Condé, he had now attached himself to 'Monsieur', though he seems to have had more dealings with 'Monsieur's' high-spirited daughter 'Mademoiselle' than with 'Monsieur' himself; and on 27 March he helped her to break into Orléans in the hope of raising the city for the rebels. But Philibert was out of his element; he enjoyed a pitched battle well enough, but could not tolerate the discomforts of campaigning with a scarecrow army; and flattering the Orléans bourgeoisie was only a shade less tedious than wandering about France with an extemporized regiment. With relief he returned to Paris, and there settled down to the formidable task of trying to cheat Mazarin at cards; which was fair enough, seeing that Mazarin was as notorious a sharper as Philibert himself; 'address was reciprocally employed', as Hamilton puts it in describing these games.

If Philibert succeeded in robbing Mazarin it profited him little, for on one of his expeditions to the country in this year, highwaymen relieved him of some £2,000 in gold. One can well believe that he returned to Paris 'full of anger, rage, and oaths'; for like all men of his stamp, nothing shocked him so much as dishonesty on the part of others. But it may have been Mazarin who robbed Philibert, for in 1653 he set himself to annoy the Cardinal by making open love to his niece, the Duchesse de Mercoeur;[1] hopelessly as he well knew, for the Duchesse was as virtuous as her sisters were vicious, and was deeply in love with her husband. But Philibert's antics drew down considerable ill-natured ridicule on Mazarin, which was no doubt the object of the whole manœuvre.

1654 opened with the trial of Condé for High Treason; a farce which merely drew the attention of Europe to the impotent rage of the French Court. For Condé, now commanding for Spain in Flanders, was as unassailable as the Emperor of China.

[1] MERCOEUR, Laure Victoire Mancini, Duchesse de, whose engagement to the Duc de Beaufort's elder brother Mercoeur Condé had insisted upon breaking in 1649; Mercoeur, who was in love with her, followed her to Mazarin's retreat, Bruhl, and there married her, 1651; she died in childbirth aged twenty-one, 'much regretted by the whole Court'.

Gramont, summoned as a Peer to act as one of the judges, obeyed with reluctance, and at the commencement of the trial on 19 January made a last effort to preserve his neutrality. He left his seat and appealed to Louis, who was presiding in person, to discharge him on the ground that he was related to 'M. le Prince'; but the King was inexorable, and ordered him to resume his place.

It was not Gramont's lucky year, for as soon as the trial was over he fell foul of 'Mademoiselle'. She, we may remember, had been exiled, but on the conventional plea of ill-health was loitering at St Fargeau in Normandy instead of immuring herself in the Royal abbey of Fontevrault as ordered. Antoine, whilst paying his respects to 'Monsieur', urged him to order his daughter into the convent at once, saying that 'when such men as the King had had the horses put in the carriage, they drove to their destination'. 'Monsieur' in writing to his daughter of course represented himself as being merely the mouthpiece of Gramont, and 'Mademoiselle' was justly indignant at Antoine's interference; and quite unmollified by her Equerry's assurance that Gramont had spoken only in jest. But by the time this leaked out, Antoine was at the opposite end of the Kingdom, reporting to the Court that Retz, who had escaped from prison, was now out of the King's clutches and living at St Sebastian on the north coast of Spain. In this year Gramont's daughter Charlotte, now a beautiful girl of fifteen, made her début at Court, attracting much notice when she appeared in the Royal ballet of *Psyche* on the 24 February.[1]

The Peace of Westphalia, signed on 24 October 1648, had ended the Thirty Years War but had not brought Europe peace. France and Spain still fought on in a war to which no end was yet foreseeable. The chief event of the 1654 campaign was the siege of Arras by Condé, and his defeat by Turenne on the 24 August; and there we find Philibert, now serving as a 'volunteer', that is to say a gentleman without a commission, ready to make himself generally useful. And a very troublesome volunteer he proved to be. He was, he tells us complacently,

[1] Loret, *La Muze Historique*.

received with open arms by the Marquis d'Humières[1] at daybreak. d'Humières, who had been on trench duty all night, can hardly have found the dawn much brightened by Philibert's opening remark: 'Well, opinion at Court will be that if you beat "M. Le Prince" you will have done nothing more than your duty, and that if you are beaten by him, you will be dubbed madmen for attacking'. 'Very comforting', replied d'Humières dryly. After which exchange Philibert cantered off to see what was doing in the front line; and not content with this, went over to the enemy outposts where he received a hearty welcome:

> Many people ... on both sides ... assembled together with the greatest eagerness; so that the two armies, without design, without truce, and without fraud, were going to join in conversation if by chance M. de Turenne had not perceived it from a distance. The sight surprised him. He hastened that way ... and sent an aide-de-camp to recall the officers of his army and to acquaint the Chevalier de Gramont with his impatience to see him.

What Turenne said to Philibert we do not know, but Hamilton reports that he mentioned details of his impending attack, and that on the following morning the Chevalier set out to have a chat with Condé. Having cheered the Prince up with the assurance that if he was taken prisoner he would infallibly be hanged, he then proceeded to betray Turenne's plans; and the astonishing thing is that no one saw anything blameworthy in Philibert's conduct, which was apparently regarded as being just one of those little services which one gentleman is expected to render another.

However, in spite of his inside information Condé was decisively beaten, and Philibert must in some way have distinguished himself, for to him was given the coveted assignment of riding post to Court with the news of Turenne's victory. And in the execution of the task he showed typical Gascon cunning:

[1] HUMIERES, Louis de Crévent, 4th Marquis, Maréchal, 1st Duc d', 1628–94, created Marshal 1668, Knight of the St Esprit, 1688, and Duke and Peer, 1690; 'a good Courtier and a bad General'.

> He [Philibert] had to prepare against greedy and officious Courtiers who on such occasions post themselves in the avenues in order to cheat the poor messenger out of his news ... Therefore he hired two horsemen at Bapaume ... and ... ordered them to ride on before, to appear very terrified, and to tell everyone ... that all was lost; that the Chevalier de Gramont had stopped at Bapaume, having no great inclination to be the messenger of ill-news; and that enemy troopers were spread all over the country ... Everything succeeded to his wish; the horsemen were intercepted ... Peronne [where the Court was] was already in consternation ... when the Chevalier de Gramont arrived. Nothing so much enhances the value of good news as when a false alarm of bad has preceded it.

It was a brilliant day for Philibert, clouded only by the behaviour of Mazarin, who affected to regard the victory as a trifling affair in order to avoid paying the gratuity which custom decreed should be given to the officer detailed to carry the news. But if Philibert was done out of his money, he at least took a revenge which must have given him great pleasure; surrounded by buzzing Courtiers eager for further details, he enlarged upon his gracious reception by the King and Queen – 'But faith, M. Le Cardinal received the news as if he had gained no more by it than by the death of old Pietro Mazarini, his father'.

CHAPTER VII

★

1655 found Gramont's eighteen-year-old son in high favour, his daughter regarded as a promising debutante, and the barometer apparently set fair for the House of Gramont. Armand, now one of that intimate little circle admitted to the familiarity of the King and 'Madame La Comtesse'[1] this year introduced a fellow-Gascon at Court; a penniless careerist, the Comte de Puyguilhem, better known by his later title of Comte de Lauzun, under which name he was to make a good deal of noise in the world. Puyguilhem's grandmother had been a Gramont, sister of that Antoine II who had so ingeniously disposed of his first wife. To our way of thinking the bond was not a very close one, but it was unhesitatingly recognized by Gramont, who took the almost destitute Puyguilhem into his house where he was brought up with the Maréchal's children. And there for the moment let us leave him.[2]

Antoine, having been forced into appearing in Parlement as one of Condé's judges, could not without inconsistency now refuse to fight against him, and in this campaign he took the field against his old chief. It was a dull business, interesting to us only as showing that the friendship between Condé and Gramont remained unbroken by the strains which had been put upon it in the last seven years. The Prince returns three prisoners to Antoine with a note in which he says, 'I cannot bring myself to keep your prisoners. I am so unaccustomed to fighting you

[1] SOISSONS, Olympe Mancini, Comtesse de, 1639–1708, Court title 'Madame La Comtesse', came to France 1647, married Eugène de Savoie, Comte de Soissons, to whom she bore the famous Prince Eugène. Much admired by Louis XIV, but exiled 1665; suspected of poisoning her husband, 1672; implicated in poisoning scandal, 1680; and 1688, when she was living at Madrid. Died in Germany, 'in poverty and neglect, despised by everyone'.

[2] Sandars, *Lauzun*.

that I cannot bring myself to begin . . . I can never be other than your true friend and servant'.

Gramont acknowledges the courtesy 'with mingled joy and grief', and then passes on to lighter topics:

> Beef every day is not agreeable to those who are accustomed to partridges. . . . I seem to remember that we fared better in Catalonia, but much has changed since that time . . . When I reflect that I am within three leagues of you . . . without the possibility of seeing you . . . I am furious that this affair should be so long while life is so short.

The Gramonts were well represented this year; Guiche was serving his first campaign as captain of a troop of volunteers, and Gramont's brother, Toulongeon, now an old soldier, was also under the Maréchal's command. In battle Guiche showed himself a true child of his generation; one day, being engaged with the enemy, he caught sight of Condé, and instantly forgetting everything but that here was the man whom he regarded as his second father, he abandoned his troop and galloped into the enemy ranks to embrace him; and both sides admired the young man's action. Toulongeon, after a narrow escape from being blown up in the trenches, was taken prisoner; but returned to the French army the same day, having with the usual family adroitness persuaded his captors that he was a sub-lieutenant, and having paid the trifling ransom demanded for such a very junior officer.

Philibert does not appear to have served, but with the usual luck of his House he managed to bring the name of Gramont as prominently before the public as if he had been at the front. In mid-June when the King, the Queen, and the Duc d'Anjou, 'the little "Monsieur" ' as he was called, were crossing the bridge of La Fère in their coach, one of the leaders jumped the parapet, dragging the other after it, and it was touch and go whether the whole team would not be dragged into the river; Philibert, who happened to be passing, flung himself from his horse, drew his sword, cut the leader's traces, and helped the coachman and lacqueys to hold the frightened wheelers.[1] Louis never forgot it.

[1] Loret, *La Muze Historique*.

'The King', says St Simon writing many years later of Philibert, 'favoured and distinguished him throughout his life.'

It was during the season 1655–6 that Guiche, home from the front with something of a reputation, began to be noticed by the Press as the most prominent of the young seigneurs at Court; but in terms differing greatly from those which would be used by a society columnist today. In the account of the ball offered to the Duke of Mantua, Armand is 'the ravishing Comte de Guiche, whom Love and Nature have enriched with a thousand delicate charms'. In January a similar welcome was offered to the Duke of Modena, who was entertained magnificently by the Maréchal de Gramont at a banquet 'so noble and so gallant that a feast of Lucullus would have appeared ridiculous in comparison with it'. The Duke was, according to the newspapers at any rate, deeply impressed not only by the meal, but by 'the diversity of lustres, mirrors, lights, and the concert in four or five styles which accompanied this delicious repast'. Which may be true, though it seems unlikely that a twenty-seven-year-old prince would have much admiration to waste on mirrors in a room which contained Antoine's daughter Charlotte, now seventeen, who was making her way rapidly to the front rank at Court; and was perhaps already indulging in dazzling dreams of becoming Louis XIV's mistress. For she was every inch a careerist like the rest of her House; but on the whole she was to prove a disappointing family asset; for though she had in plenty 'the fascination peculiar to the Gramonts', she lacked that power of concentration, that single-minded tenacity of purpose, which alone could bring a man or a woman to the top at the Court of Louis XIV. Restless, erratic, debauched, unstable, and worst of all, a constant and indiscreet talker, her Court nickname is a thumb-nail sketch of Charlotte; she was called 'The Torrent', apparently as much for her impetuosity as for her flow of words. She died young, 'whilst undergoing treatment which should be a warning to all those tempted to imitate her debaucheries'; and she was very little regretted in the family.[1]

But in 1656 she was still the beautiful Mademoiselle de Gramont, a reigning toast in the world of fashion, with a

[1] Sévigné, *Lettres*.

glamorous future before her if she could only grasp her opportunities. But not without her own troubles already, particularly the presence at Court of her kinsman Puyguilhem; or Lauzun as we shall call him, though in fact he did not succeed to that title until 1660.

Lauzun was twenty-three, Charlotte seventeen, and they had grown up together as brother and sister; or so at least Gramont fondly imagined. But in fact there appears to be little doubt that before either of them appeared at Court, Charlotte was already Lauzun's mistress. Charlotte, with hitherto undreamt of possibilities opening before her, was anxious to end the liaison; it had been good fun while it lasted, but to continue it would be dangerous, and what could be more absurd than the idea of marriage between two Gascons, one penniless, the other absolutely dependent on her father? Kiss and part friends, argued Charlotte.

But Lauzun entirely declined to see matters in this light, and when hurt in his pride, could be a dangerous and vindictive enemy. Now a subaltern in the Regiment de Gramont, he was on the threshold of that career which, as his brother-in-law St Simon remarks, 'no other man would have dared to dream, much less to live'. With no assets except impudence and biting sarcasm, he was to become the confidant and rival in love of Louis XIV, to refuse the bâton of a Marshal of France, to insult the King to his face, and to marry a Grand-Daughter of France in defiance of Louis' prohibition. Then, when nearing forty, he was to crash as sensationally as he had climbed and to disappear into a prison from which he emerged as a forgotten and ruined man of fifty; only to carve out a new career for himself and die forty years later, immensely rich, a Duke and Peer, with the Orders of the Garter and the St Esprit. Spiteful, morose, capricious, and sarcastic, he was feared by Ministers, and even the King 'treated him with distinguished consideration'; and there must have been a strange fascination about him, for all the world knows the story of how 'Mademoiselle' fell madly in love with him and probably married him; he having with exquisite dexterity played the humble nobody until he forced the foolish woman to propose to him. Charlotte was to have much trouble with her Lauzun before she was at last able to cut free from the childish liaison with which she had so rashly encumbered herself.

In January 1657 Antoine was given the delicate mission of presiding at the Estates of Languedoc, at whose meetings the annual taxation of the province was assessed. The King chose the presiding officer, and this choice was always a matter for anxious deliberation; for much coaxing was needed before the province could be induced to contribute to the Exchequer as liberally as the King desired. Social qualifications, not financial expertise, were sought for in candidates; and where tact, affability, and magnificence were needed, there could be no better choice than Gramont, who steered the assembly to Mazarin's entire satisfaction.

April found him back in Paris, entertaining 'Monsieur'; a chastened 'Monsieur', recalled from exile only that he might see for himself that he was a survival from a vanished age, elderly, unfashionable, out-of-date in the nascent Court of Louis XIV. 'This great, good, and sensible Prince', says the reporter (surely with his tongue in his cheek?), 'could not have been more satisfied' with the entertainment offered him by Antoine, 'his excellent and charming wife, his dear son, his amiable daughter, and the renowned Chevalier de Gramont, valued in so many provinces'.

In 1657 the death of the Emperor Ferdinand III induced a feverish bout of diplomatic activity throughout Europe; for the Imperial Crown was elective not hereditary; and though already shrewd judges realized that a Hapsburg would always be the inevitable choice, an Imperial election was for the great powers a trial of strength, an assessment of national status in the field of power politics. This being a situation eminently congenial to Mazarin's tastes, he decided that the time was ripe for intensive French interference in German affairs. There was a certain grandeur about his plans which caught the imagination of the young Louis, who was never entirely to forget them. By the Peace of Westphalia in 1648 portions of Alsace had been given to France in full sovereignty. Now if only French Alsace could be converted into an Imperial fief for which Louis would do homage to the Emperor, the King of France would be entitled to a seat in the Diet; and that once obtained, Louis XIV, or at any rate his successor, might by dint of bribes, bullying, and propaganda be elected Emperor; in the last resort the Diet might find its meeting place surrounded with French armies 'to secure the freedom of the election'. But there was much hard spade work to be done before this state was reached, and obviously the first step was that Louis should be represented at Frankfort by an imposing Embassy supplied with some pretext for its presence in the town where the Diet met. And one was found; Louis had suddenly discovered that he must appeal to the Diet against sundry infractions of the Peace of Westphalia.[1]

It was not easy to choose a team whose members would possess between them all the qualities needed to ingratiate themselves with the Germans, 'a hard, boorish nation and, what is more, one that has no opinion of the French'. Ultimately Mazarin chose Gramont and Lionne; Antoine, suave, witty, the soul of good company, the perfect export model of a *grand seigneur*, was to exert his charm in social contacts, whilst Lionne, the hard-headed man of affairs, was to battle with his opposite numbers and organize the bribery of those whose rank made them ineligible to drink a bottle of wine with the Maréchal. For amongst Gramont's other assets for the work, he was one of the few Frenchmen who could drink level with a German; and without this useful accomplishment he might just as well have stayed at home. Though even Gramont shuddered at the task which lay before him; how was he to survive in a country where the Archbishop of Mayence[2] was eulogized for 'the sobriety of his repasts' on the strength of never drinking more than six pints of Rhine wine with his dinner?

But Antoine had other reasons for trying to evade the mission; he was, he said, in straitened circumstances, and the ruinous expense of the assignment would 'send him at full gallop to the poorhouse'. But Mazarin was inflexible, and Gramont had to

[1] Fédern, *Mazarin.*

[2] MAYENCE, Johann Philip von Schonborn, Elector of, 1605–1673, 'one of the most remarkable men in Germany. . . . He showed both patriotism and statesmanship in his efforts to save his country from the constant menace of foreign aggression'.

obey. Whereupon the Cardinal 'overwhelmed him with assurances of his tender affection', and promises of cartloads of gold; promises to which Antoine, who knew his Mazarin, listened with ill-concealed impatience.

Once briefed to detach Germany from the Spanish interest, Antoine turned to the more important question of preparing a train which would show up the uncouthness of the German boors amongst whom fate was about to cast him. And though he is considerate enough to spare us particulars of his magnificence, it is only because 'my equipage is still so famous that to repeat the details here would savour of Gasconade'.

One other passage he had with Mazarin before setting out. The French government had secured him a passport from the Spanish Commander-in-Chief Don Juan,[1] available for Frankfort where the Diet was to meet; but Antoine wanted one from Condé also, because 'he might easily find "M. Le Prince" in a mood in which he would show no great respect for the passport of Don Juan'. This Mazarin refused, knowing well that Louis would never forgive him for even hinting that his Ambassador should travel under the protection of a rebel subject; and Gramont, adroitly dropping the matter, quietly secured a passport from Condé by writing to him personally.

It was not until the third week in July that Antoine marched out of Paris in all his pomp; his exit made a Parisian holiday, and the papers give full details of the procession.[2] Outside Strasbourg he halted for a characteristic reason; he was anxious, before committing himself to an entrance, to make sure that he would obtain the honours due to his rank – 'knowing that these worthy gentlemen always pay the slightest compliments which they think they can get away with'. The Senate of Strasbourg said that a deputation of their number would meet M. le Maréchal outside the walls and there offer him wine, corn, and fish; but that they would not fire a salute. 'This did not please the

[1] JUAN, H. S. H. Don, of Austria, 1629–1679, son of Philip IV by the actress Maria Calderon, the only one of Philip's thirty-odd illegitimate children given princely rank. Served with distinction from 1647 to 1663. First Minister to his half-brother Charles II, 1676. Died unmarried.

[2] Loret, *La Muze Historique*.

Maréchal at all', who resolved to try the effect of what he described as 'a short and pathetic discourse': which turns out on investigation to have been an indignant complaint of the Senate's rudeness, and a refusal to enter the city, coupled with a promise that Louis XIV 'would not be long in finding occasion to deal with them according to their deserts'. We are hardly surprised to learn that 'this did not fail to produce a good effect', and Antoine was given his salvo of cannon, 'a thing which had never been done before except for the Elector-Palatine himself'.

Near Heidelberg the Ambassadors received from the Elector of Mayence the welcome news that they would be admitted into Frankfort, in spite of an earlier decision made at the instance of the King of Hungary that 'the gates should be shut on their noses'. The King of Hungary, by the way, being the eldest son of the late Emperor, and the strongest candidate for the Imperial Crown.

Six miles outside Heidelberg Antoine and Lionne were joined by 'the magnificent cortège of carriages and nobles' sent by the Elector-Palatine,[1] and in that town Gramont soon got down to business with his host; a man unique amongst the Princes of the Empire in preferring women to wine; also uncommonly hard to get the better of, but whose geographical position rendered it of vital importance to Louis XIV that he should be the ally of France. Gramont proved a match for him; he trusted Charles Louis just as far as Charles Louis trusted him, as we can see throughout negotiations which throw a vivid light on the corruption and cynicism of seventeenth-century *realpolitik*. After much haggling Gramont agreed to pay the Elector 60,000 crowns down, 50,000 on 1 January 1658, then 40,000 a year for three years, in return for his promise to sell his vote in the Diet to Louis XIV. And Gramont took good care to have the bargain in writing, signed by the Elector himself. For any Elector convicted of taking a bribe was liable to expulsion from the Electoral College, and therefore this invaluable paper could be used to

[1] PALATINE, Charles Louis I of Bavaria, Elector-, 1617–1680, son of the King of Bohemia, became Elector 1647 after many years in exile. He was the father of 'Monsieur's' second wife, known at the French Court as 'Madame-Palatine'.

blackmail Charles Louis into keeping his word. How far the precious pair trusted each other may be gauged from the arrangements for paying the bribe; 'owing to mutual distrust the money was deposited with the Swedish Plenipotentiary, who gave a written promise not to disburse it to the Elector-Palatine until he had received instructions in writing from the French Ambassadors'.

On Sunday 19 August Gramont and Lionne made a solemn entry into Frankfort with a train 'worthy of the representatives of a King of France'; and those who are interested in 'breast-harness covered in gold lace . . . Swiss in silver, with canes in their hands . . . thirty cooks magnificently mounted . . . the mules of M. le Maréchal in horse-cloths magnificently embroidered with his arms, the Ducal mantle and crossed bâtons in gold . . . ten pages marching two by two' and all the rest of it, should consult Coulanges,[1] who was in Antoine's suite and seems to have enjoyed the circus. Gramont himself 'was wearing a fire-coloured costume more magnificent than one can possibly imagine, with a mass of white plumes in his hat, and was mounted on a grey Spanish charger covered in fire-coloured ribbons, with a saddle of black velvet embroidered in gold lace . . . behind him were the Captain and the Lieutenant of his Guards . . . and his coach, heavily gilded, his arms painted on the doors, the interior lined with red velvet . . . and drawn by six splendid horses'.

Hardly had Gramont arrived when he heard that Turenne had taken Montmédy on 6 August so it was with an additional trump in his hand that he faced the Electoral College, whose members he summed up as 'wide-awake, supple, fertile in propositions, lovers of good cheer and good wine'. The Elector of Mayence caused him little uneasiness; for he had already shown a complete lack of hostility towards France, and a fortunate trifle soon helped to extinguish any warmth he may have felt for the Hapsburg faction. He was furious at being made the laughing stock of the College by the imbecility of a Spanish agent who had attempted to bribe him with two pairs of silk

[1] Coulanges, Christophe, Abbé de, 1607–1687, guardian and lifelong friend of Madame de Sévigné, frequently mentioned in her letters – 'to his continual care I owed the peace and repose of my life'.

stockings. Mayence was anxious that his cousin, the Elector of Trèves,[1] should meet Gramont, but the Frenchman saw no reason for putting himself out for him; Trèves was so placed geographically that he could not afford to offend Louis XIV, and therefore it would be sheer waste of money to buy him. Nor would Gramont dine with him, for drinking was the only thing in which the Elector excelled, and Antoine, whilst always ready to drink when duty called, saw no sense in getting drunk to oblige a brainless, uneducated, flat-nosed Archbishop whom he already had in his pocket.

The Elector of Cologne[2] was a very different proposition; incorruptible, firm, 'as civil as the pretensions of the House of Bavaria permit a man to be', he had never slept with a woman in his life, and was never seen drunk 'except on those occasions of ceremony when it was indispensably necessary to drink to excess'. Always open and frank, he let the Austrians know as soon as he arrived that they had nothing to hope for from him; and he and Gramont were on cordial terms, though they rarely met, and never except in the house of a third party; for Cologne had refused Gramont the honours which he claimed when visiting an Elector, with the result that neither could visit the other's lodgings.

Even the optimistic Gramont hesitated over devoting any attention to the Elector of Saxony,[3] for he thought it would be time thrown away; he being led by the nose by his councillors, all of whom were in the pay of the Court of Vienna. And Saxony had nothing about him which could induce the elegant Gramont to make his acquaintance except as a matter of business. For he was a man 'whose only care was to get drunk every day, which valuable accomplishment he had inherited from his father'. He could imagine no deadlier insult than to call an enemy a Calvinist, for 'he was an ardent Lutheran, and on the

[1] TRÈVES, Charles Gaspard von Leyen, Archbishop-Elector of, Archbishop in 1652, pensioner of Louis XIV from 1661, died 1676.

[2] COLOGNE, Maximilian Henry of Bavaria, Archbishop-Elector of, first cousin of the Elector of Bavaria, and 'practically a vassal of France'. Archbishop 1651, died 1688.

[3] SAXONY, John George II, Elector of, 1613–1680, became Elector 1656.

days on which he communicated he carried his respect for the Sacrament to such a point that he never got drunk in the morning'. But ultimately Gramont was prevailed upon to undergo a dinner with the Lutheran champion. 'The battlefield', as he calls it, was in the house of Prince von Furstenburg,[1] and his fellow-guests were the Electors of Mayence and Cologne. The dinner 'lasted from midday until nine at night, always with the constant din of cymbals and trumpets in our ears; we drank between two and three thousand healths' – and the proceedings closed with a Marshal of France, three Electors, and a Prince of the Empire performing country dances on the dinner table.

Mazarin, having spent the early autumn in considering the situation, had decided that French interests would best be served by the elevation of the Elector of Bavaria[2] to the Imperial Crown; and he was now working hard to attain this object, assisted by the Electress, an ambitious woman 'who was making her husband talk in a style which the Ambassadors at Frankfort recognized as being very different to his own'. Antoine doubted the possibility of the Electress imposing her pious, feeble, irresolute husband upon the College as Germany's Man of Destiny, but he determined to run over to Munich and sound Ferdinand for himself; for since 1645, when he had been a prisoner in Munich, he had kept up a correspondence with some of the leading Bavarians, and now was the moment to turn those friendships to account. Assured that Ferdinand would receive his visit with pleasure, Antoine set out for Munich, and there got to work with his accustomed energy to persuade the Elector to stand for the Crown; no easy task, for Ferdinand, sensible man, had said more than once that 'if the Crown were placed on his head, he would shake it off and let it roll at his feet'.[3] With Ferdinand Gramont felt that there was no danger of over-

[1] FURSTENBURG, Wilhelm Egon, Cardinal-Prince von, 1629–1704, 'one of the quickest brains of the age and the French master-key to Germany'. Bishop of Metz, 1663, of Strasbourg, 1682, Cardinal, 1686; Louis XIV installed him in his See of Cologne by armed intervention, 1688.

[2] BAVARIA, Ferdinand Marie, Elector of, 1636–1679, devoid of ambition, succeeded his father, 1651.

[3] Carlyle, *Frederick the Great*.

egging the pudding, so he began by saying that his visit was dictated solely by his passionate desire to elevate still higher the present grandeur of the House of Bavaria; and this being well received, 'the Maréchal put forward all his eloquence to flatter the Prince, praising his personal attractions, his sterling worth of character, and his wit'; all this to such good effect that it seemed for a moment that the Elector was prepared to stand. It is interesting to compare the shameless flattery of Antoine's harangue with his private estimate of this Prince Charming which follows on the four pages of soap and sugar from which we have taken a specimen; 'he was big, but with a bad figure, and far from good-looking... not entirely lacking in common-sense... devout, pious... and thinking himself as incapable of error as the Pope'.

Poor Gramont, it was all so much breath wasted, for Ferdinand, once relieved of the Frenchman's presence, reverted to his original decision to have nothing to do with the trouble-some and dangerous plan of thwarting the Hapsburgs.

Nor were the Maréchal's worries at an end, for on his return to Frankfort he 'found as refreshment after a long and tiresome journey', open war raging between Lionne and Mayence. It had come out that Mayence was making highly suspicious overtures to the Imperial candidate, the King of Hungary, and Lionne had hotly reproached him for his double dealing. Naturally Mayence wanted to be on the winning side, and Gramont was sufficiently alarmed at his attitude to call in the assistance of Mazarin. The Cardinal of course sent the Elector 'most obliging letters assuring him of the King's fullest confi-dence and friendship'; and what Gramont significantly describes as 'this apparent frankness' tipped the balance once more in the favour of France.

To Antoine fell the arduous task of sealing the reconciliation. In Germany, he tells us, a quarrel is never resolved without a drunken orgy, and this case proved no exception; the Elector gave a dinner to the French Embassy which lasted from noon until nine – apparently the usual dinner hours – and at the feast 'nothing was to be heard but protestations of true friendship'. However, on this occasion the French diplomatists got off very lightly; there was no country dancing on the table, nor did Gramont and Lionne find themselves underneath it when they awoke in the morning.

To Antoine, weighing up the problem, it was now clear that the casting vote in the election would be Brandenburg's,[1] and he bent all his energies to secure it; 'a pretty difficult enterprise ... but Gramont and Lionne followed the path marked out for them, though it was a thorny one ... to cut the story short, they gave a large sum of money to Brandenburg's Ambassadors ... money is a much more persuasive rhetorician at Frankfort than Cicero at Rome or Demosthenes at Athenes'.

But let us leave Antoine to his bribery, blackmail, and threats whilst we see what is doing in France.

Early in May Guiche's betrothal to Mademoiselle de Béthune was announced. Marguerite Louise Suzanne de Béthune, a daughter of the Duc de Sully, was fourteen, and the marriage had been arranged between the two fathers without asking the children's views; and as far as Guiche was concerned, the humiliation of being ordered to marry a schoolgirl rankled for the rest of his life. He could not refuse to obey his father, but he let it be seen from the outset that he disliked his child wife, and that he had no intention of relapsing into domesticity after his enforced marriage. The union was as unhappy as might have been expected, but this did not disturb the Maréchal de Gramont; for Mademoiselle de Béthune was very wealthy.[2]

Guiche, now twenty, was a typical Gramont, with a good figure, large intelligent black eyes, and a pale, well-modelled face; 'he was the best-looking and the best-shaped of all the young seigneurs, amiable, bold, full of grandeur and elevation of soul, but his vanity and his disdainful manner somewhat tarnished his several merits'. 'He was', says Madame de Sévigné, 'a hero of romance, bearing no resemblance to the ordinary run of men.' All his contemporaries agree that his manners were insolent and disdainful; no doubt a cultivated insolence, for he cannot have failed to observe how well that quality was serving

[1] BRANDENBURG, Frederick William of Hohenzollern, Elector of, 1620–1688.

[2] Montpensier, *Mémoires*.

his kinsman Lauzun and his uncle Philibert. This insolence he naturally reserved for his dealings with the other men of the Court, and with the women his technique was very different. In the boudoir he was, if the anachronism may be pardoned, the first of a long and successful line of Byronic heroes; he had what women call an 'interesting' face, and knew how to make full use of it. He was the man bowed down by some secret grief too poignant to be revealed, who sat gazing into space with vacant eyes, his beautiful head cupped in his left palm, whilst with his right hand he would pluck listlessly at the strings of a guitar; occasionally sighing heavily, or muttering a few low, meaningless words. And naturally all the women were only too anxious to ease the burden of his sorrows. He had invented a language peculiar to himself, 'a kind of deliberate distortion of wit in his expressions, and particularly in his letters ... it is almost impossible to understand his meaning. If he leaves memoirs, it will be necessary to have them translated into French'; thus Madame de Sévigné, who says elsewhere that she could only talk to him through an interpreter. But the involved style, the insolence, the disdain, the secret sorrows were a mere build-up behind which was the keen Gramont brain and the Gramont determination to arrive. His only sorrow was in fact the disconcerting youthfulness of his father, the Maréchal; for between the two men there was a certain friction. To Armand, M. le Maréchal was a man who had done good work in his time for the aggrandisement of their House, but who unfortunately failed to realize that his day was over; who, instead of taking to slippers and an armchair, persisted in hanging about the Court and giving his much better informed son unwanted and inept advice; smelling of the old Court, and even of the prehistoric days of Louis XIII. Whilst to Antoine, M. le Comte de Guiche was an impudent young cub who refused to be guided by one with a lifetime of Court experience, and worse still, urbanely declined to be a mere tool in his father's hands. But for the moment the Maréchal was pinned down at Frankfort, and Armand was free to plunge into the maze of Court intrigue and there play his cards without having his hand overlooked by his father.

Louis XIV was rapidly becoming a person with whom Mazarin had to reckon, or as one of the wits put it, the King was daily rising into greater favour at Court. No one yet realized the potentialities latent in the nineteen-year-old Louis, not even the Prime Minister, whose sole anxiety was to prevent the youth from falling into the hands of a clique which would 'govern' him in a manner hostile to the interests of Mazarin and the Queen. 'The Cardinal', we are told, 'could not let the King choose any friends without his permission.' And that permission would certainly not be forthcoming for a clique consisting of the Comtes de Soissons[1] and Guiche, Villequier[2] and the Abbé Fouquet,[3] though Mazarin was quite ready to play off this group against its rivals, the Prince de Marsillac[4] and the Comte de Vardes.[5] Anne held the same views as Mazarin; mainly because of her fear that Guiche would infect the King with the impiety of which he was at the moment making an ostentatious and rather ill-judged parade.

But Court intrigue in itself was not sufficient to fill the life of one who lived so intensely as did Guiche; he had a desire to be recognized as the great and irresistible lover, to outshine his friend and rival, the King himself. Why not take the first opportunity of cutting out Louis? To Guiche in the first flush of his young manhood and confident in his own powers of fascination, the project seemed to present no difficulty. He had, too, military

[1] SOISSONS, Eugène Maurice de Savoie, Comte de, 1633–1673, son of the Prince de Carignan, Colonel-General of the Swiss, 1657; generally supposed to be the original of Molière's Monsieur Jourdain in *Le Bourgeois Gentilhomme*.

[2] AUMONT, Antoine de Villequier, Maréchal and 1st Duc d', 1601–1669. Maréchal 1651, Duke and Peer, 1665.

[3] FOUQUET, Basile, Abbé, younger brother of the notorious Fouquet, and chief of Mazarin's secret police during the Fronde; a gangster who 'kept at his own expense some fifty or sixty gallows-birds', and maintained his bastards out of the funds of the diocese of Paris.

[4] ROCHEFOUCAULD, François VII, 3rd Duc de La, 1634–1714, son of the author of the *Maximes*, succeeded his father, 1680; 'always free in his speech with the King and on intimate terms with him'.

[5] VARDES, François René de Bec-Crespin, 3rd Marquis de, 1626?–1688; 'delicious and attractive worthlessness was his chosen role'.

ambitions, which were to be gratified before he was much older; in this year he was appointed Colonel-Designate of the French Guards, which his father commanded. To us the idea of a regiment having two Colonels seems strange, but it excited no more surprise amongst Guiche's contemporaries than we should feel today at finding a son the junior partner in his father's business.

When Guiche 'entered the lists of love', it was with the maximum of ostentation; a young man of fashion kept a mistress as a matter of course, and broke the tedium of that supposedly exciting hobby by casual intercourse with any girls about the Court who were 'not cruel'. It behoved a Gramont to do better than this, so Guiche, whilst not neglecting casual adventures, determined to keep two mistresses. One was not difficult to find; 'Guiche, young and beautiful, thought that the conquest of Madame d'Olonne would be both easy and honourable; and he resolved to win her'.[1]

Easy, yes; but it is difficult to understand why Bussy should describe such a conquest as 'honourable'. For Cathérine d'Angennes, Comtesse d'Olonne, was as common as a barber's chair. She had been a reigning beauty since 1650, when as Mademoiselle de La Loupe she had appeared at Court as a very young girl, and already, if rumour spoke true, the mistress of the Comte de Beuvron; afterwards of the Duc de Candale and of many others. And by the time she married Louis de La Tremouille, Comte d'Olonne, in 1652, she had acquired the significant nickname of Messalina. Ultimately her lack of 'cruelty' exceeded the limits of the permissible, even by the standards of the young Court of Louis XIV, and she was banished in 1658. For a second acquisition Armand turned his attention to Madame de Fiesque.[2] Here however he made little progress . . .'and all he succeeded in doing was to infuriate his uncle the Chevalier [Philibert]'. As well the affair might; for not only was Armand's

[1] Bussy-Rabutin, *Histoire Amoureuse des Gaules*.

[2] Fiesque, Gillonne d'Harcourt, Comtesse de, 1619–1699, daughter of the Marquis de Beuvron, married Comte de Fiesque, 1643; spent her whole life in quarrelling with 'Mademoiselle' and in becoming reconciled to her. 'She never passed the age of eighteen.'

groping for trout in a peculiar river a flagrant bit of poaching, but it exposed his uncle to the ridicule of the Court; which hugely enjoyed the spectacle of an uncle of thirty-six striving to defend his conquest against a nephew of twenty. The play ended with a slick, machine-made dénouement; Madame de Fiesque, worn out by the importunities of the two men, forbade either of them to appear in her presence.

Early in 1658 Gramont scored a diplomatic success. Prince Lobkowitz[1] claimed a seat in the College for his master, the King of Hungary, in his capacity as Elector of Bohemia. 'His arguments were good', admits Antoine; but the Frenchman successfully pleaded that Lobkowitz' admission would be contrary to precedent. Nor was Lobkowitz more successful in the trap which he set for Gramont by calling at the Maréchal's lodgings on his arrival. The only valid excuse for the presence of a French Embassy at Frankfort was to protest against Austrian infractions of the Peace of Westphalia; had Gramont accepted Lobkowitz' call, he would have had to return it; and the Austrian would have broadcast the assertion that the good relations between the Imperial and French delegations exposed the hollowness of Louis XIV's 'just grievances'.

The next important arrivals at Frankfort were the Spanish Ambassadors, Peneranda[2] and Las Fuentes;[3] 'their clothes were travel-stained from their long journey, and they were little admired', says Gramont, whilst of the ceremonial entry of the King of Hungary shortly after, he tells us that 'nothing could have been more lugubrious'.

Almost immediately proceedings were enlivened by a violent quarrel between Peneranda and Mayence, and this was of course all grist to the French mill:

[1] Lobkowitz, Wenceslas, Prince von, 'the only member of Leopold I's Council who rose above mediocrity'. Negotiated the secret treaty of 1668 whereby Louis XIV and the Emperor agreed to divide the lands of the Spanish Hapsburgs when that branch became extinct.

[2] Peneranda, Gaspard de Bracamonte de Guzman, 2nd Comte de, 1595–1676, 'the monarchy's most able servant', had been Plenipotentiary to Munster, 1645.

[3] Fuentes, Gaspard Tello de Guzman, Marquis de Las, advocated a policy of appeasement towards France.

His Spanish Excellency accompanied his harangue with some gestures to which the Elector was unaccustomed; he threw his hat on the floor, put his hand to the hilt of his sword, shouted and threatened until the Elector, tired of his impudence, remarked that he knew Peneranda had been President of the Indies; and that he had better leave the room and go back to Mexico and there talk to his Indians as he pleased.[1]

Nor did Peneranda's folly end there, for he made the additional blunder of spreading hostile gossip about the Elector – which Gramont used skilfully to exacerbate relations between the two.

The Spaniards struck back at the French, using the treaty of alliance between Catholic France and heretic England to represent Louis XIV as the destroyer of the Faith. But Mazarin flooded Germany with copies of a treaty which the Spaniards themselves had signed with the Protector a few years earlier. Peneranda declared this treaty a forgery; whereupon Gramont bet him twenty thousand crowns that he would place the original in the hands of the Electoral College within six weeks. And in the resultant laughter at the discomfiture of the Spaniard, the Anglo-French Treaty was forgotten. Another thorn in Gramont's side was the Papal Nuncio, Cardinal San Felice, 'who would have done better to drop the character of Nuncio and admit that he was the third Ambassador of Spain'. But on him too Gramont had his revenge; or rather on his master. Etiquette demanded that when an Ambassador called on the Nuncio, his complimentary speech should begin with a eulogy of the reigning Pope. How the Pope[2] enjoyed Antoine's we do not know; gravely the French Ambassador announced three actions whereby the Holy Father had rendered his Pontificate for ever illustrious; he had issued that great order so necessary to the repose of Christendom which forbade Cardinals to degrade their rank by wearing mourning for their parents; he had given instructions for the re-alignment of a street in Rome; and after

[1] Gramont, *Mémoires*.

[2] ALEXANDER VII, Fabio Chigi, Pope, 1599–1667, Secretary of State to Innocent X, Cardinal, 1654, and Pope, 1655. A vain, frivolous Pontiff, but upright and of irreproachable morals. Usually on bad terms with France.

prolonged and exhaustive research he had discovered the correct Latin word for *perruque*.

For the King of Hungary Gramont felt a good-natured contempt; 'He [the King] used to go incognito in a closed carriage to the garden of the Spanish Embassy, where he found supreme delectation in the noble game of bowls, a pastime entirely suitable for a Prince of twenty-two who expected to hear any minute that he had been chosen Emperor'. We find the explanation of this scorn in a remark of Philibert's: 'The game of bowls, which is in France the pastime of mechanics and servants only, is quite the contrary in England, where it is the exercise of gentlemen and requires both art and address'.

Gramont can at times give us a memorable picture; here is Leopold playing bowls with his friend, the Prince de Porcie, 'a man of limited intelligence'. It is raining hard, and the Emperor-Elect, his big Hapsburg mouth hanging open, complains that the rain is getting into it, and what shall he do? Porcie, 'having considered the matter in all its bearings', at last advises his master to shut it; which Leopold does, and finds himself 'much comforted'.

Entertainments were now the order of the day, and naturally Gramont was not behindhand in doing his share:

> He tried to do something out of the common for the friends of the King of France. So he had a large hall built in the garden of his lodgings where he gave a dinner to the Electors, Princes, and Counts of the Empire. He also built a theatre ... where a ballet was danced. The entertainment lasted from midday until ten at night. The Maréchal's house was meanwhile open to the bourgeoisie ... Barrels of wine were everywhere, and seasoned topers were posted by them to encourage people to drink; which they did with much joy. Trumpets and cymbals sounded on all sides, with shouts of 'Long live the King of France!' ... and this within forty paces of the lodgings of the King of Hungary.

After which Antoine concluded the account with a eulogy of himself, disguised as a moral:

It is this sort of thing that shows the difference between a courteous, approachable Ambassador, liberal when liberality is needed for the honour of his master, a man with an elevated soul who thoroughly understands the ways of the world... and one who lives in fear of upsetting his domestic budget.

But however great was Antoine's satisfaction at raising cheers for King Louis under the windows of King Leopold, it was Leopold who carried the day, and on 15 July he was declared Emperor. Only however on terms creditable to Mazarin and Gramont. For as the price of his election Leopold was forced to discontinue all support of the Spanish Hapsburgs in their conflict with France in Italy and the Netherlands; and thus peace was brought appreciably nearer.

Gramont also had the satisfaction of establishing the League of the Rhine, signed at Mayence on 15 August, which was a diplomatic triumph for France. By its terms the King of Sweden, the Electors of Bavaria, Cologne, Mayence, and Trèves, with the Duke of Brunswick, became the allies of Louis XIV; a shift in the balance of power in Germany which perpetuated that disunion which, from Louis' angle, was so desirable in the Empire. If the plan was Mazarin's, its successful execution was largely the work of Gramont, and this fact was freely recognized. 'His Majesty received him on his return as the man of all the world who had served him most usefully and zealously.'

CHAPTER VIII

★

BY THE spring of 1658 'the handsome, well-made, witty, agreeable Comte de Guiche' had elbowed his way into the front rank of Courtiers; high in the favour of Louis XIV, a privileged visitor at the Hôtel de Soissons, and dominating 'Monsieur' absolutely in virtue of the ascendancy which he had acquired over Philippe in the days when his three-years seniority had made a vast gulf between the two youngsters. Even had 'Monsieur' been normal, he would still have regarded Armand with the deference which eighteen shows to a married man of the world of twenty-one. But 'Monsieur', so far from being normal, was one of nature's mistakes; 'it was given to no woman', says Madame de Lafayette, 'to capture the heart of that Prince'. And so far from any effort being made to eradicate the marked tendency towards perversion which had been apparent in him since boyhood, it had actually been fostered by Mazarin, who well knew how dangerous a 'Son of France' could be to the State, and had no intention of allowing Philippe to become a second edition of his uncle Gaston. 'Monsieur' was encouraged to act the girl by his mother and her Prime Minister, and as he approached manhood he spent more and more of his time before his mirror in elaborate female costume, lost in admiration of his own charms. 'When I came to the Louvre', writes 'Mademoiselle' in this year, 'I found "Monsieur" dressed as a girl with fair hair.' And he managed to have all the vices of his adopted sex without any of the redeeming virtues; jealous, spiteful, vindictive, untruthful, a malicious gossip and trouble-maker, he was the most deplorable specimen produced by the House of Bourbon in the century. But he was not without merits; he had physical courage in plenty, and oddly enough was something of a general; a much better one than his brother. At the battle of Cassel in 1677 'he fought like a grenadier', and credit for the victory cannot be wholly ascribed to Luxembourg; 'Monsieur's' leadership and tactics in handling the French centre, which he commanded in person, were praised by those whose praise was worth having; and had Louis shown any generosity, Philippe's subsequent years might have been very different. But Louis found it intolerable that Philippe's victory had distracted attention from his own siege of St Omer, and 'Monsieur' was never allowed to serve again.

But to return to 1658.

It was in this winter that 'Monsieur' fell in love with Guiche; for Guiche were reserved his languishing glances and his tenderest sighs, for Guiche he paraded in his prettiest clothes, but all in vain. Armand was a normal man, and simply laughed at him. Indeed went further than laughter; his behaviour towards 'Monsieur' in public often astonishes us quite as much as it did his contemporaries. Here for example is 'Mademoiselle' reporting a Court ball:

> The Comte de Guiche was there, who pretended not to recognize us; he treated 'Monsieur' to a lot of teasing, and in dancing gave him kicks on the bottom. Which seemed to me tolerably familiar. I did not say a word, as I knew that that would displease 'Monsieur', who could find no fault with anything that Guiche did . . . I would have resented these familiarities strongly if I had been 'Monsieur'.

It was inevitable that Armand's reputation should suffer from his intimacy with 'Monsieur'; though the evidence for the prosecution is mere gossip. St Maurice, the Savoyard Ambassador, writes on 3 February 1670, 'The King has accused the Chevalier de Lorraine of the infamous crime of sodomy with the Comte de Guiche'.[1] But who else makes the same accusation? Only Visconti,[2] an Italian adventurer, who has his story from an unnamed and possibly a dismissed servant:

> The secretary told me that he had formerly been in the service of the Comte de Guiche, and that the Comte . . . had done great execution among the women, in spite of the fact

[1] St Maurice, *Lettres*, 1667–1670.

[2] Visconti, *Mémoires*, 1673–81.

that like most young Frenchmen, he had put his health in jeopardy by practising the Italian vice, particularly in the service of the pleasures of 'Monsieur'.

Possibly they may have confused Guiche with his brother Louvigny, who can be more plausibly suspected than Armand. Certainly Louvigny was in bad odour after the Vermandois'[1] scandal in 1683, and Bussy-Rabutin mentions him as one of the ring of perverts then exposed. But who would put much confidence in Bussy?

However, in 1658 Louvigny, like Armand, was still on the best of terms with Louis. As described by St Simon, Louvigny had a touch of uncle Philibert in his make-up:

> He was clever, with a handsome, manly face; owing to the distinguished position of his father he was admitted to a share in all the amusements of the King's younger days, and he always remained on familiar terms with him... He had no great reputation as regards play or money matters; in his governments of Béarn and Bayonne, people used to be careful of their purses with him.

In the spring Guiche served with the French Guards at the siege of Dunkirk, where through no fault of his own, his share in the operations was small; in an enemy sortie on 7 June, where 'he played his part well', he got a musket ball through his right hand and was forced to return to Paris; where 'Monsieur' visited him every day in bed, 'and the two opened their hearts to each other'. But the convalescent was soon to have a more important visitor than 'Monsieur'. Later in June Louis fell ill at Calais, and for several days the announcement of his death was hourly expected; to the horror of Mazarin, who seems to have lost his nerve completely. And with some excuse, for if 'Monsieur' were to become King, the best that Mazarin could hope for would be expulsion from France after the prince's favourites had stripped him of his ill-gotten wealth. Mazarin was never a

[1] Vermandois, Louis de Bourbon, Comte de, 1667–1683, son of Louis XIV by Louise de La Vallière, recognized in 1669; disgraced, 1682 'for things one does not know about and does not wish to'. ('Mademoiselle'.)

man who scorned to grovel where grovelling would serve his ends, and he showed no false shame in doing so in this crisis; 'he made large promises and paid visits to those who were much, or even a little in the good graces of "Monsieur", particularly to the Comte de Guiche, to whom he made advances which were revealed as coming from a base and feeble character'.[1] It was the most flattering situation in which Armand had yet found himself.

The long heart-to-heart talks with 'Monsieur', from which the bedridden Guiche was unable to escape, must have sickened him of his adorer, for his first thought on recovering health and liberty was to consider the possibility of ending the nuisance by giving 'Monsieur' a mistress. Only an incurable optimist could have entertained such an idea, and perhaps even Armand was not particularly surprised at its failure. Perhaps indeed he did not try very hard, for the lady he selected was his own mistress, Madame d'Olonne; and even had Philippe's tastes been normal, he might well have sought a less degrading adventure than to share 'Ardelise' with one of his own courtiers. For Armand seems to have had no idea of discontinuing his own relations with Madame d'Olonne; even whilst trying to ensnare 'Monsieur' he was gratifying his passion, and his taste for the bizarre, by visiting her apartments at night in the guise of a traveller in ladies' underwear; to the intense annoyance of the Prince de Marsillac, who had been trying to cut Guiche out for some time past.

But Marsillac's jealousy was nothing to Armand's when he discovered that Madame d'Olonne was 'betraying' him. Having come one day unannounced to her bedroom door, he heard a man's voice in the room, and promptly applied his eye to the keyhole; and there to his great indignation saw Madame d'Olonne 'caressing her husband for all the world as if he had been her lover'. As Guiche angrily confided to a friend afterwards, he had two legitimate grievances, firstly that Monsieur d'Olonne's conduct towards Madame was of a much tenderer nature than was seemly in a husband; and secondly that he

[1] Motteville, *Mémoires.*

should have been there at all by daylight, 'which has never been the time for husbands, but for lovers'.[1]

So far Guiche, in spite of his impudent treatment of 'Monsieur' and the exuberant publicity of his love affairs, had done nothing which even Anne and Mazarin were not prepared to accept with an indulgent shake of the head. But at Easter 1659 he found himself in a serious scrape. A party of courtiers, led by Bussy-Rabutin, left town for Bussy's country house, Roissy, where Holy Week was spent in a debauch which was to become famous. By the time the story got back to Court, the party had become an orgy rivalling those of Gilles de Rais; violation of the Sacrament, child rape, murder, highway robbery, kidnapping, abduction, there was nothing which was not believed of the roysterers. In fact it seems to have been a very ordinary debauch, which attracted attention largely owing to Armand's idiotic conduct when drunk. According to Bussy: 'I saw the Comte de Guiche come into the courtyard [at Roissy], leading a man by the bridle of his horse as if he were a prisoner of war, and Manicamp behind, with a postboy's whip to keep the man's horse moving. I ran out to see what was happening...'

And Bussy, having rescued the prisoner, got his story:

> The Comte de Guiche had stopped him on the highway, and having asked him who he was, and he having replied that he was Chantereau, the solicitor of M. le Cardinal, Guiche had replied, 'Ah! M. Chantereau, I'm glad to have met you, I've been looking for you for a long time; I'm very fond of chicane myself'.

And with that, Armand had arrested him and brought him to Roissy. Bussy smoothed down the enraged man of law with wine and flattery, but of course the story reached the Cardinal and lost nothing in the telling. Though no actual punishment was inflicted upon Guiche, he was out of favour for some time, and his father took the earliest opportunity to get him out of France.

In May Gramont again went south to preside at the Estates of Languedoc, leaving behind him in Paris rumours of an impending Franco-Spanish peace which was to be sealed by a

[1] Bussy-Rabutin, *Histoire Amoureuse des Gaules.*

marriage between the young King and the Infanta. On 4 June the diplomats had agreed in principle on the peace talks agenda, and in July Mazarin moved south to lead for France against the Spanish statesman, Don Luis de Haro.[1] By the 24th he had reached Bayonne, whence Gramont conducted him into his sovereignty of Bidache with an escort of five hundred horse, commanded by Guiche. Needless to say the Cardinal was magnificently entertained by 'this Maréchal almost without a rival in France in matters of politeness' to quote the newspapers; 'and five hundred flasks of wine were emptied; or so at least several Gascons told me', adds the reporter dryly.[2]

The first problem of the negotiators was to find a means whereby Mazarin, a Prince of the Church, could meet Don Luis, a Grandee of Spain, without either derogating from his dignity; and only a lucky accident of geography solved the problem. In the middle of the River Bidassoa, which here formed the frontier, was a valueless island which belonged to no one in particular. A hastily assembled delimitation commission awarded exactly half the island to each power; a pavilion was built upon it, which had been carefully sited by a joint board of French and Spanish engineers in such a way that half the structure was in each country; and finally a table was placed across the frontier in the pavilion, with identical armchairs at each end of it. It was a triumph of seventeen-century ingenuity.

Mazarin, holding the better cards, was able in August to warn Gramont to hold himself ready to proceed to Madrid to ask the hand of the Infanta for Louis XIV, and Antoine was delighted. He dreamt of outshining his own magnificence at Frankfort; but Mazarin, who had good reasons for getting Louis married at the earliest possible moment, would allow him only fifteen days for his preparations. 'The Maréchal submitted that it would be of infinite prejudice to the King's dignity if, after so long a war, his Ambassador should appear at Madrid without liveries, train, or suite . . . a figure of fun at a haughty

[1] Haro, Don Luis de, Duque del Carpio, 1598–1661, First Minister of Spain, 1643; 'was less corrupt than his predecessors, for there was now little or nothing left to seize'; by 1655, 'he was in all but the name, Vice-King.'

[2] Loret, *La Muze Historique*.

Court which thought itself above all others and which had not seen a Frenchman for years.' But Mazarin would not listen to him, and Antoine had to obtain what little he could by despatching courier after courier to Paris. His problem then was to make the best of a bad job. And Gascon ingenuity found the answer; he would broadcast the story that Louis' eagerness to possess the Infanta was such that the Ambassador had been sent off without even time to change out of his working clothes, so to speak. And after all, Antoine would have had ample time to prepare the great train whose absence he regretted so bitterly, for it was not until 4 October that he was permitted to leave the frontier town of Irun.

It was an odd country in which he now found himself. Spain then occupied a place in the popular imagination not unlike that held by China a hundred years ago; in that vast, treeless, waterless plateau, cut off from the world on three sides by the ocean, and on the fourth by an iron curtain of 'frightful' mountains, anything might be happening, and any story of Spanish manners brought back by hardy travellers was accepted without question in France; for only diplomatists and exiles visited Spain, and both classes disliked the experience heartily.[1] The Court of Louis XIV at its most glacial period was a Bohemian Liberty Hall compared with that of Spain, where every detail of palace routine had been established once and for all by Philip II (1556–1598), and where to propose the smallest departure from his ordinances was blasphemy; so that when Charles II's Queen, a headstrong lady, finally obtained leave to go to bed at half-past ten instead of half-past eight, old-fashioned Spaniards thought that civilization was collapsing. Probably the most irksome thing to the women of Spain was that there were no fashions; how could there be when Philip II had settled for all time the correct costume for ladies? 'Their clothes do abominably disfigure them', said foreigners, and the Queen of Spain

[1] My sources for this sketch of Spain are from the period 1679–81, twenty years later than the time of Gramont's Embassy, But as Spanish social life was apparently static between the death of Philip II, 1598, and the extinction of the Hapsburg line, 1700, it seems reasonable to assume that the Spain of 1679 was indistinguishable from that of 1659.

was even worse off in matters of dress than her ladies, for she alone in the whole Kingdom was forbidden to wear a mantilla, 'even when dying of cold'; Philip II had so ordained. In the 'dreadful life of the palace' the only indoor diversions seem to have been the nursery game of spillikins, which the King would play with the Queen for three or four hours on end, and an occasional comedy, 'than which there is nothing more detestable'. But the comedy was nevertheless popular with the courtiers; there was no need to watch, and it gave unusual facilities for converse with the Court ladies; conversations conducted in some sort of code on the hands and fingers. Men and women alike, if they had any pretensions to good looks, wore horn-rimmed spectacles, which in Spain were not for use, but were a beauty aid. All the women chewed; not gum or tobacco, but a special soft-baked, scented earthenware manufactured for the purpose.[1]

The ordinary outdoor amusement of the Royal family and upper classes was a carriage drive in a vehicle fitted with leather curtains which shut out all light, air, and view; for only women of easy virtue drove in uncurtained carriages. In summer the fashionable rendezvous was the dry bed of the Manzanares river, where the clumsy, stifling coaches jolted along in a thick fog of dust to admire the huge bridge; of which a visiting Frenchman, when asked by the King how he had liked it, replied that he wished His Majesty would sell the bridge and buy a river with the money. Occasionally there would be a bullfight, the sport of all classes, for which even the poorest would starve to buy a seat. But one free amusement out-did even the bullfight in popularity, namely the *auto-da-fé*, the periodical burning alive of a batch of Jews and heretics of both sexes; even well-bred Spaniards showed their surprise when foreign ladies refused their invitation to the performance.[2]

The King of Spain had of course his country seats; the Prado for example, where there were 'no woods, no garden, no fountains, and in the house no seats, benches, tables or beds . . . how the King amuses himself I do not know'. And there was Aran-

[1] Aulnoy, *Memoirs of the Present State of the Court and Council of Spain.*
[2] Villars, *Lettres.*

juez, the best of a dreary lot, but difficult for the Court to visit, Philip II having long since decreed that the journey must cost some £20,000, no more, no less; and as in normal years the King managed to collect about eleven per cent of his nominal income, he was not often in a position to find £20,000 for a breath of country air.

At dawn on 16 October Gramont and his suite left the little village of Mauden to cover the last mile of their long journey to Madrid, he and his followers mounted 'on the admirable and superbly decorated horses sent them by the King of Spain'. It was not merely an Embassy which Antoine led, it was also a family gathering; Guiche and Louvigny were with him, the former to give time for his Roissy performance to be forgotten at Court; also there, were Toulongeon and the Chevalier Philibert, the latter for some reason in an unwontedly subdued state; possibly bothered by his creditors, and glad of a seemly excuse to escape from Paris.

Antoine, keeping up the pretence of Louis' impatience to enjoy the Infanta, entered Madrid at a gallop and maintained that pace until he reached the palace; 'which hugely delighted the Spaniards, who had not lost the idea of old-time gallantry'. One would have liked to see the cortège, and particularly the Spanish escort of Master-Couriers, whose duty it was to play cornets during the solemn entry, and who had reckoned on the procession moving at a foot pace; in the circumstances it is hardly surprising that the unfortunate men 'made a noise like all the devils in hell'. But Antoine was very satisfied with his own performance, and so apparently was the mob – 'One may say that never was public rejoicing so complete . . . the manner of the Maréchal's entry appeared charming to everyone':

> The Maréchal could hardly climb the stairs [at the Royal palace], so great was the press; everybody ran to him; those who had already seen him wanted another look; men, and women too, caught him by the coat to make him turn round, and blocked the passages to make him stop and speak to them. As for me [Louvigny], I was captured by the street-walkers of Madrid, who, having torn off all my ribbons, looked as if

they were about to violate me in the street, which might very easily have happened had I not been rescued.

It was with difficulty that Gramont himself forced his way into the presence of Philip IV, who received him seated, and surrounded by the Grandees of Spain; though, as Antoine takes care to tell us, the King stood up to salute him and touched his hat to a Peer of France. The usual meaningless speeches of compliment were then exchanged, after which Gramont presented his suite; 'a fine-looking man', said Philip when Guiche made his bow; 'but', adds Louvigny, 'the King found me more to his taste, I having something about me more gracious than the Comte de Guiche'. Lastly the Maréchal's brothers were presented, and the King then closed the audience by saying to Gramont, 'You have a fine family; it is easy to see that the Gramonts were originally Spaniards'. 'And that', says Antoine, 'coming from a waxwork was a pretty long speech.'

From the audience chamber Gramont went to the apartments of the Queen, where he found her seated with her daughter, Marie Thérèse; and having been warned beforehand that to mention the word 'marriage' at a first interview would be thought highly indecent, he contented himself with handing the Princess a letter from her aunt, Anne of Austria. Having performed all these duties Gramont was at last free to go to his lodgings 'after a fatiguing and troublesome day'.

The following morning was spent in receiving visits of ceremony, and on the 18th the King paid the Maréchal a compliment with which he would gladly have dispensed; he sent his singers and musicians to give a three-hour concert in Gramont's lodgings; 'which', says Antoine, 'was all very well for Spaniards, who were accustomed to it, but diabolical for us French'.

Each day brought its ordeal. On the 19th the Admiral of Castille offered the Ambassador 'a superb and magnificent feast after the manner of Spain; that is to say an abominable and quite uneatable dinner. I saw seven hundred dishes served, all with the arms of the Admiral on them, and within, nothing but gilt and saffron; these were all carried off untouched, no one being able to tackle them'. A concert, 'which was not much better than the dinner', followed, and at midnight a comedy, 'which we had to admire, though there was nothing admirable about it'.

On the 20th Antoine had another audience of the King, at which Philip IV gave his formal consent to the marriage of the Infanta with Louis XIV, and in the evening the event was celebrated by another dreary Spanish comedy. But this time Gramont was better off than on the previous evening, for he was placed behind a screen so that he might sit without infringing Court etiquette; and, even more comforting, he was unable to see the stage. The next day was devoted to sightseeing at Aranjuez and the Escurial; Aranjuez with 'its fountains, terraced alleys, its trees ... and the beautiful River Tagus', the Frenchmen found 'admirable'. But as for the house, 'there is not a bourgeois about Paris who has not a more commodious one, more handsome, and better decorated'. The Escurial, says Antoine, does not bear detailed examination, but 'the *tout ensemble* is of surprising richness and magnificence'. The Prado 'has nothing of the air of a King's mansion', and the Casa del Campo is only 'some tiny gardens, badly kept, and a house which looked more like a tavern than anything else'.

On 22 October Gramont gave Louis XIV his first impressions of the bride to be:

> Those who know her admire her beauty and the gentleness of her character, but to tell the truth I can give Your Majesty very little information about her disposition, her only words to me being, at my first audience, an enquiry after the health of the Queen, and at the second, an assurance that she would always in all matters submit to the wishes of the Queen, her aunt. And I could not draw a single other remark from her.

To Anne, Gramont writes more cautiously, to Mazarin with greater freedom; but all three letters show very clearly that the Ambassador does not envy the King his bride, though 'the qualities of her body could not be more to my taste', as he confides to the Cardinal. There is a great deal more on this subject, all leading up to a compliment which he knows will be passed on – 'In fact, to cut a long story short, in her various beauties she exactly resembles our own Queen'.

It had been an interesting trip, but Antoine and his suite

heaved a sigh of relief when they crossed the border and rejoined the French Court, where tales of the fantastic land from which they had come found eager listeners; and where Gramont gave his considered opinion of his recent hosts: 'their vanity is beyond belief; and to tell the truth, in the long run it makes their company intolerable to those of any other nation'.[1]

Rhine wine and Spanish cookery appear to have played havoc with Antoine, who had to spend most of 1660 at Bidache, where in October he was seriously ill; and all he has to tell us of current events is that 'the triumphant Cardinal now thought only of enjoying himself with his chosen friends, including the most honest men in France, at whose head was the Maréchal de Gramont . . . never was Court more joyful, the Courtiers with pockets full of gold, extreme magnificence in dress, and good cheer everywhere . . . made our Court the first in the universe'.

The dewy morning, in fact, of 'the beautiful years' in which Louis, backed by expert ministers, and his swaggering, reckless nobility, was to become the pest of Europe; with the whole rout happily ignorant of the lowering afternoon and dark sunset which was to usher in the night.

Antoine's daughter Charlotte, now firmly established at Court, was still apparently Lauzun's mistress; she had tried to quarrel with him, found that he had become a habit, and their liaison had acquired the status of honorary marriage, when a thunderbolt struck the lovers. The Maréchal announced that he had found Charlotte a husband. In vain Charlotte stormed, entreated, burst into tears, her father was inflexible; for Mademoiselle de Gramont all that remained was to ask sulkily who was to be her bridegroom. When she was told that it was Louis de Grimaldi, Duc de Valentinois, heir to the principality of Monaco, she despaired; to be married at all was bad; to become the wife of a greedy, vainglorious Italian, 'round as a cask, who could not see the end of his belly', was worse; but infinitely the worst aspect of the business was that she was to be married out of France. However, there was no help for it, and on 30 March she was wedded to her unprepossessing groom, who by the way was three years her junior.[1]

[1] Montpensier, *Mémoires.*

But once married, her sky cleared unexpectedly. The Prince de Monaco had been married under duress also, and immediately after the wedding he dumped his wife at the French Court and set out alone for Monaco; leaving Charlotte 'with the privileges of a Princess and the liberties of a married woman'. Though it is difficult to see what liberties she had denied herself in the unmarried state; liberties which had apparently even included loving the future 'Madame' 'with a too tender affection'.[1]

The great Court event of 1660 was the return of Louis XIV with the new Queen, who made her ceremonial entry on 25 August; more reminiscent of the circus than of royal dignity, with the little Queen enthroned on a chariot decorated with allegorical figures. Through the heat, noise, stench and magnificence we here and there catch sight of a familiar figure – 'The Comte de Guiche marched alone, very much got up with embroidery and precious stones which sparkled delightfully in the sun; he was surrounded with a handsome turn-out of men in livery, and followed by some officers of his Guard...' Further down the line was Philibert, 'covered in flame colour, and very magnificent'.

According to reporters the new Queen was of course the quintessence of all bodily and mental perfection, but she made a poor impression on the inner ring. That she was pretty we must believe, seeing that the fact was granted by the Court ladies, but their further verdict, that she was utterly lacking in charm, seems also to have been true. And she was stupid, which at the Court of Louis was a sin, not a misfortune; especially when as in this case it was combined with immense pride. The unceremonious life of the Louvre shocked Marie Thérèse, and when she learnt that she must humiliate herself by offering her cheek to Duchesses and Maréchales, she burst into tears. Nor did she increase her popularity among these great ladies by protesting to Louis that sufficient honour would be done them if they knelt and kissed the hem of her skirt.

But in time the women's hostility towards her changed into a cynical appreciation of her naïveté; there was a fearful joy for these blasé worldlings in a woman who could produce as

[1] Palatine, *Lettres*.

evidence of her confessor's stupidity, his question whether before marriage she had ever loved any man. 'And how did you answer, Madame?' 'I said, how could that be? At the Court of Spain there was no other King than the King, my father.'

The spring of 1661 found Mazarin suffering from gout; or so at least it was announced. But it was clear to all except the sick man himself that his life was drawing to a close. Ghastly under the paint with which he was thickly daubed, Mazarin still tried desperately to persuade himself that he was the victim of a passing indisposition. 'That gentleman', said the Spanish Ambassador brutally as the Cardinal tottered past, 'bears a remarkable resemblance to the late Cardinal Mazarin.'

No one can have watched the situation with more anxiety than did Gramont, who throughout the spring was constantly in attendance on the Cardinal at Vincennes, where he had been conveyed for purer air. Antoine had done well out of Mazarin, and after his death, to whom was he to attach himself? It was the problem which had confronted him nearly twenty years earlier at the death of Richelieu, but with the important difference that this time the dying man would leave no obvious successor. Antoine was perplexed, and it is to his credit in the circumstances that he attended Mazarin faithfully until the end; 'he spent all his day', says Choisy, 'seated at the Cardinal's bedside'. And his conduct seems to have been dictated by one of the few genuine affections of his life; years afterwards, when his old patron was entirely forgotten, he wrote: 'The Maréchal de Gramont assisted the Cardinal until his last breath, and in him lost a protector and a friend such as he would never find again; and he never forgot the obligations which he owed him'.

Mazarin died as he had lived, 'more philosophically than Christianly', on 9 March, and everyone knows how dramatically the problem of his succession was solved by the young King; who himself took over the reins and continued both to rule and to govern France for the next fifty-three years. Gramont was one of the first to grasp the full significance of Louis' enfranchisement. He saw at once that here was a new France, one in which an ambitious man must depend absolutely on the King's will and pleasure. But how to adapt himself to a youthful régime was the problem, for Antoine was fifty-seven and the King twenty-three; he must have considered his approach to Louis with the same concentration which he had displayed in his dealings with Richelieu and Mazarin. At least he started with the advantage of never having neglected the King, and it was significant that it was to him Louis had turned at the moment of Mazarin's death, saying, 'Alas, Monsieur le Maréchal, you and I have both lost a good friend'. Gramont knew from the outset what course to avoid; he appreciated the mercilessness with which a young Court ridiculed the elderly seigneur such as St Aignan[1] who dressed youthfully and talked of his conquests. Ultimately the much cleverer Gramont hit upon the pose of the bluff, plain-spoken old soldier, the man whose blunt reproofs to his King were in themselves the subtlest form of flattery; in short, he determined to play tough old Joey Bagstock to Louis' Dombey.

The King at twenty-three was a handsome, grave young man, whose rare smile was charming; with a majestic air, polished manners, and the knack of saying the right thing to all and sundry; an incomparable actor of royalty, with a remarkable talent for keeping his own counsel. The secretiveness, the callousness, and the selfishness which underlay his genuine charm were already there, but were never to smother his more amiable characteristics. For the man was fundamentally amiable; and even his bitterest enemies admit that he was by nature both kind and just. His good qualities were innate, whilst his bad were acquired as a shield against the humiliations of his childhood and the frustrations of his adolescence. The only father he had ever known was Mazarin, who had treated him rather as an unwanted stepson than as his King, and though his mother loved him, she would hear no criticism of the Cardinal. The proud, shabbily dressed youth with the empty pockets had had to learn early to swallow his anger at the spectacle of the crowded brilliance of Mazarin's court, of his huge wealth, and his scant courtesy to Louis by the Grace of God, King of

[1] St Aignan, François Honorat de Beauvilliers, 1st Duc de, 1610–1687 'the perfect courtier'. Duke and Peer, 1661, elected to French Academy 1663. Chiefly known for his skill in arranging fêtes, ballets, etc.

France. Then with manhood had come the one great passion of his life. He had implored Mazarin, perhaps even knelt to him, in the urgency of his entreaties that he might make Marie Mancini his Queen; but Mazarin had been inexorable, and Louis had been forced into a State marriage with his dull Spanish cousin. Much had happened to the King in his twenty-three years, and intelligent Courtiers, meditating on that pale and unreadable face with the watchful eyes, speculated on what lay behind the façade. Nothing at all, said some, and lived to regret their mistake; for in fact Louis was no *roi fainéant*, but a man of remarkable though untrained ability, who was to come near to greatness, and whose place in history has not yet been fully evaluated. The man who succeeded in stamping his name on a century was no King Log whose name is remembered only because he was fortunate in his choice of lieutenants.

But to Gramont and his contemporaries in 1661, the King was primarily the leader of the smart set at Court, irresistible to women, envied by men, the ideal of a young seigneur bearing a great name. Embarrassingly acute though, and seeing much deeper into men's minds than one would suppose, as Gramont was to discover on the occasions when he was rash enough to abandon the Bagstock role for ordinary flattery. The writing of verses to one's mistress was in the 'sixties a social obligation from which even Louis himself was not exempt; and one day whilst he was conning a madrigal of his own composition, Gramont walked in:

LOUIS (*handing him the verses*): Here is a miserable performance.

GRAMONT: Ah, Sire, in the smallest as in the greatest of things, Your Majesty judges divinely; here we have the stupidest, the most insipid...

LOUIS (*laughing*): I wrote it.

GRAMONT (*horrified*): Sire, Sire, what treason! I read hastily; if Your Majesty would permit me to read it again...

LOUIS (*still laughing*): No, no, Maréchal, first thoughts are always best.

Madame de Sévigné, who tells the story, closes with a surprisingly modern comment which few of her contemporaries would have understood – 'I think it was a cruel trick to play on an old courtier'.

But if Gramont could descend to the odious flattery which was already poisoning the air of the Court, he could also speak to the King with a frankness which was rare in that atmosphere; here is an illuminating conversation which took place early in the personal reign, not from Gramont's own memoirs:[1]

LOUIS: I have just been reading a book with which I am delighted.

GRAMONT: What is that, Sire?

LOUIS: *Calcandille*. It pleases me to find in it arbitrary power in the hands of one man, everything being done by him or by his orders, he rendering an account of his acts to no man, and obeyed blindly by all his subjects without exception. Such boundless power is the closest approach to that of God. What do you think, Gramont?

GRAMONT: I am pleased that Your Majesty has taken to reading, but I would ask if he has read the whole of *Calcandille*?

LOUIS: No, only the preface.

GRAMONT: Well then, let Your Majesty read the book through, and when he has finished it, see how many Turkish Emperors died in their beds and how many came to a violent end. In *Calcandille* one finds ample proof that a Prince who can do whatever he pleases, should never be such a fool as to do so.

La Fare is no doubt right in saying that Gramont's influence waned after the death of Mazarin – as did that of every other noble in France. But that 'he began to live in that half-retreat necessary to a man much given to debauch' is an assertion disproved by most of the available evidence; on the contrary, no man is more prominent at Court than Antoine in these years, and the King's liking for him is clearly shown by his admitting him in 1661 to the Order of the St Esprit. In fact we can for once accept Gramont's account of his own standing without any reservations:

Although the Maréchal was much older than the King . . .

[1] Challes, *Mémoires*.

> he was young in spirit and pleased His Majesty . . . being so assiduous and agreeable that the King could not do without him, and insisted on the Maréchal being of all his pleasure parties.

Nor was he only of the pleasure parties; it is evident that he was also one of Louis' domestic circle, and amongst his most constant companions in those hours which were not set aside for business. For from matters of state everyone except the Ministers was rigorously excluded from the first day of the personal reign; even Anne of Austria, who seems to have cherished hopes of retaining some influence, and took her exclusion badly; 'I perceive', said she, 'that my son is about to give us a display of his qualities as a ruler'. Louis the man of fashion she knew, but not Louis the worker, and she no more believed in the second Louis than did the rest of France; it was only by degrees that the fact dawned upon the Court that Louis the ruler had come to stay. Philibert de Gramont's account of the startling change which came over the King in 1661 reflects the general feeling very accurately:

> Pleasure promised herself an absolute empire over a Prince who had been kept in ignorance of the necessary rules of government . . . when men were surprised to see the King on a sudden display such brilliant abilities . . . an application inimical to the pleasures which generally attract at that age, and which unlimited power very seldom refuses, attached him to the career of government; all admired the wonderful change, but all did not find their account in it; the great lost their consequence before an absolute master.

And when we remember that Louis the man of business continued to be also the man of pleasure, who hunted, bathed, climbed about the roof of his palace by night, and made love until three in the morning, we get some idea of his superabundant energy and vitality in these early years.

On 1 April 1661 was celebrated a marriage which in brilliance came second only to that of the King himself in the previous year. The bride was Henrietta of England, sixteen-year-old daughter of the murdered Charles I, the groom Philippe de France, Duc d'Orléans, 'Monsieur' to the Court. Louis had accepted the match without enthusiasm; like most Frenchmen, he disliked the English, and all he knew of Henrietta was a thin-faced, owl-eyed little girl, unlikely to cut any figure at Court. He was utterly unprepared for the transformation of the tiresome poor relation into the radiant Princess who now offered him her cheek as his sister-in-law. Louis was all his life susceptible, and as he gazed into those eyes whose appeal no man could ever refuse, and caught the fragrance of the young girl's charm, two thoughts chased each other through his mind; that not so many months ago he could himself have had Henrietta for the asking, and that she was unworthily sacrificed to his degenerate brother. Not of course, as he assured himself, that he was in love with her; it was merely that what he had looked forward to as a duty had unexpectedly turned out to be a pleasure. Instead of the King of France doing the formal honours of his palace to the second lady in the land, it had become a case of Louis exerting himself to make cousin Minette at home in her new surroundings; and as she happened to be a charming girl, elementary good-breeding demanded that Louis should let her see that he was fully conscious of the fact. Henrietta was perfectly ready for a flirtation with cousin Louis, and the more risky it became the more she would enjoy it; up to a point, or perhaps we should say, up to the point. Life had been cruel to her, and she felt that it owed her much. No child could have been expected to endure patiently a life of perpetual mourning for a father whom she had never seen, and who had been murdered when she was only five years old; a life of wretched poverty, in which to visit a convent was a diversion, and a rare trip to a dull spa an excitement. Kindly Anne of Austria indeed did what she could for her desolate niece, but that was little enough; for her invitations to her sister-in-law to bring the child to Court were generally refused on the ground that those who sorrowed should do so in solitude. Small wonder that Minette saw in marriage, even marriage with 'Monsieur', the opening of a gateway into an enchanted world.

And now the miserable years of shabby dresses, scanty food,

cold rooms, and grudging charity were over, and she opened her arms joyously to embrace her fill of pleasure and excitement. And what could be more exciting than the conquest of the greatest King in Christendom? She was confident of her ability to make that conquest, for in her sixteenth year she was a very lovely person. From some bygone Stuart she had inherited a beauty which to this day is typically Scots; blue eyes, chestnut hair, a perfect complexion, red lips, and an excellent set of teeth. And she knew how to make full use of every asset she possessed, for already she was a finished coquette, far too worldly-wise not to know that she had something which would rouse to madness a man whom mere beauty would leave cold. Says Guiche, and he certainly ought to know, 'She had a way of speaking to anyone which seemed to ask for their love, however trivial were the words'.

CHAPTER IX

★

THE spring of 1661 ripened into a beautiful summer, and the Court moved to Fontainebleau. There Louis and Henrietta, always together, spent enchanted days and nights in a constant round of picnics, suppers, ballets, wandering with beating hearts through woods odorous in the summer night, and returning together in an unlit coach at three in the morning. How far did they go, these two? We shall never know, for there is a secret which – unless one of the parties to it is a fool – remains a secret for ever. All we know is that discreet Madame de La Fayette says, 'They lived in a manner which left no doubt that there was something more than a deep friendship between them'.

But like all good things, it had to come to an end; for there was heavy metal against the pair. The Queen-Mother and 'Madame' were on anything but amicable terms; 'Madame' had not escaped from the governessing of a tyrannical mother to put herself under the tutelage of a mother-in-law, and told Anne so in terms which were as pungent as they were imprudent. 'Monsieur', who was just enough of a husband to show jealousy, was tearful in his complaints to Anne, and indeed to anyone who would listen, about the King's behaviour. And the neglected little Queen, who at the best of times bored Anne exceedingly, now took up such of her time as 'Monsieur' did not monopolize, with a catalogue of her own grievances against Louis. Anne, exasperated, read Louis a severe lecture on his wickedness and on the bad example he was setting his Court, and stirred up the Queen of England to give her daughter a sharp rap over the knuckles. The result was a conference between Louis and Henrietta at which, after condoling with each other over their respective mothers' stupidity, they agreed that something must be done to shut their mouths.

Everybody knows the sequel; how it was arranged that Louis

should gain access to 'Madame's' apartments by pretending to make love to La Vallière; and how La Vallière stole the fickle King from 'Madame' and became his first acknowledged mistress. It was a denouement received by the Queen-Mother with tempered satisfaction, by 'Monsieur' with spiteful joy, and by Guiche with considerable annoyance; for he was then engaged in a languid endeavour to seduce La Vallière himself. It is remarkable as showing how little the rank and file of the Courtiers understood Louis even now, that when the King began to pay his attentions to La Vallière, they predicted his speedy repulse; for, said they, M. le Comte de Guiche is not the man to tolerate a rival. But Armand was under no illusions; he was not sufficiently in love to risk a collision with the King, and he retired from the contest, though with a very ill grace. And on the surface, all was peace again.[1]

But there was a good deal of explosive material lying about. 'Madame', in a fury of hurt pride, was very anxious to give Louis public proof that he was not the only or even the most attractive pebble on the beach. And Guiche had had his vanity severely wounded.

So here were two young people, a beautiful Princess and the second most admired man at Court, both seeking an opportunity to annoy the King, and both thinking, correctly, that few things would irritate him more than a well-advertised affair between them. 'Madame' liked a spice of danger, Guiche enjoyed notoriety; both were expert players of the game of love, neither intended to take the matter too seriously. But both forgot that this is a game in which you cannot throw in your hand when the stakes become too high.

They drifted into a love affair which by July was everywhere recognized as serious. The Court was still at Fontainebleau, rehearsing a ballet in which Guiche played opposite to 'Madame'; and rehearsals gave him an excellent opportunity to push his fortunes. Guiche was a quick worker and wasted no time in attacking; before rehearsals were over he had asked 'Madame' if nothing was capable of touching her heart; a question to which she replied 'with so much kindness and charm' that

[1] Lair, *Louise de la Vallière.*

Armand ran away, crying out that he was in deadly peril. This sort of thing of course did not take long to reach the ears of 'Monsieur', who was sulking in the château and taking no part in the ballet; but all the spiteful women with whom he felt so cosily at home, came running breathlessly to open his eyes to 'Madame's' disgraceful conduct. 'Monsieur' exploded, and worse still, opened his heart to the whole Court; for he was an hysterical little man, lacking in the most elemetary self-control. And when he had a battle royal with Guiche, 'who broke with him as if he had been his equal', Gramont intervened with an order to his son to return to Paris and not reappear at Fontainebleau.[1]

Guiche had hoped to leave a strong ally behind him in his sister Charlotte, who was now not only 'Madame's' most intimate woman friend, but for whom 'Monsieur' 'felt as strong an affection as he was capable of feeling for any woman'. Guiche had asked Charlotte to plead for him with 'Madame', and according to the ideas of the time, it was her duty to do so; but in fact she took exactly the opposite line, assuring Henrietta that her brother had never had the audacity to think of raising his eyes to such an exalted personage. Nothing could have been more damaging to her brother's ambitions; for 'Madame', who up to this had been pleased to hear that Guiche was posing at Paris as her cavalier, was now so irritated at the suspicion that his love was mere vanity, that she got the King to forbid him to accompany the Court to Nantes in September. Nor was Charlotte successful in her one effort to serve her brother, namely in persuading 'Monsieur' that there was nothing whatsoever between 'Madame' and Guiche. Charlotte was no diplomatist, and when 'Monsieur' declined to believe her, she first quarrelled with him, and then proceeded to worry the King; until she had exasperated him into advising her to rejoin her husband in Monaco. It was a stunning blow for Charlotte, but there was nothing to be done about it; one did not neglect 'advice' from the King of France, and Charlotte had to leave for her husband's Court in September. But not unaccompanied; for careerist though he was, Lauzun risked Louis' displeasure

[1] Lafayette, *Mémoires*.

by absenting himself from Court to enjoy his mistress until the last possible moment. Not however as the Comte de Lauzun; sometimes he was one of her postilions, at others a pedlar offering his wares at the carriage window; or a wandering friar to whom she gave a lift, and whose ungodly ministrations alleviated the tedium of many hours of travel. But in whatever guise he appeared, they always spent the night at the same halting place.

Guiche was now banished to Paris, 'Madame' was about to leave for Nantes, and the intrigue was at a standstill, when new life was infused into it by one Mademoiselle de Montalais, a Maid-of-Honour to Henrietta. The whole of the young Court lived in an atmosphere of intrigue, billets-doux, assignations, and to Montalais intrigue was the breath of her nostrils. Though self-installed as the confidante of La Vallière, she soon found that the post offered an insufficient outlet for her restless busyness, and was now rapidly insinuating herself into the confidence of 'Madame'. She had watched the commencement of the affair between her mistress and Guiche with approval; it appeared to her that Henrietta was not unfavourable to the Comte's prayers; and she determined to tackle him on the subject:

> She questioned him at length, turned him inside-out, and extorted from him an admission that he was in love with 'Madame'. She promised her help, and kept her promise only too well.

Guiche himself gives a somewhat different account of the interview:

> I entered into conversation with Montalais ... I explained the most secret feelings of my heart to her; but all that I could get from her was that she wished to help me, but that I was to beware of asking anything from her which was contrary to the interests of her mistress, and that she was sorry to see me bent on such a dangerous undertaking.

But Montalais spoke merely to exaggerate the value of her services, and to do her justice, these proved to be both energetic and ingenious:

> Montalais fell on her knees before 'Madame' and spoke to her of Guiche's passion; talk which is not ordinarily displeasing to a young woman, and rarely earns a rebuke... On the following day she brought 'Madame' a letter from the Comte de Guiche which 'Madame' refused to open; Montalais opened it and read it to her... Some days later, as 'Madame' was entering her litter, Montalais threw in after her a packet of letters from Guiche... In short, the charm of the Comte de Guiche, but even more the persuasions of Montalais, drew the Princess into a gallantry from which she reaped nothing but annoyance.[1]

If Guiche was rash, 'Madame' was criminally careless; Armand was now writing to her four times a day, and instead of destroying his letters, Henrietta gave them to Montalais for safe custody, who in turn handed them on to her lover, Malicorne. No doubt Henrietta did not realize that this highly incriminating correspondence was now beyond recall, and potential material for a blackmailer.

But meanwhile all continued as Montalais had planned; Guiche was egged on by her to plead for a secret meeting at which to say farewell to 'Madame' before she left for Nantes, and Madame was coaxed into granting the first of what inevitably became a series of interviews:

> She did not realize the consequences, but found in these meetings a pleasant spice of romance. Montalais found them expedients which no one else would have thought of. Guiche, who was young and reckless, found that the risk increased the pleasure... 'Madame' allowed Guiche to visit her in full daylight, disguised as a woman who told fortunes, and in this guise he even had the audacity to tell the fortunes of 'Madame's' ladies, none of whom recognized him... On other occasions the Comte saw 'Madame' in other disguises, but always at great risk to both of them.[1]

But another storm was brewing. 'Madame' was ill in the

[1] Lafayette, *Mémoires*.
[2] *Ibid.*

autumn, and expecting her first child; Guiche and Vardes one day found themselves in a salon where someone remarked that the doctors dreaded 'Madame's' death in childbirth; and the words so affected Guiche that Vardes had to help him from the room. Vardes, who up to this point does not seem to have known of the relations between Henrietta and Guiche, was both curious and suspicious; and the half-fainting Armand, under his friend's skilful cross-examination, blurted out the whole story.

'Madame' was furious, and with good reason. For not only was Vardes a friend of 'Monsieur's' but he was an extremely dangerous man, notorious for slander and treachery. On a larger stage he might have risen to the dignity of a villain, but in the hot-house milieu of the Palais-Royal he never rose beyond being a cad.

1662 was a chequered year for the Gramonts, with the exception of the Maréchal, to whom it brought fresh distinction. For Louis abolished the Colonel-Generalcy of Infantry and conferred the honours of the extinguished appointment on the Colonel of the Guards, Gramont; and further decreed that in due course Guiche should inherit the Guards from his father.

In February Armand's intrigue with 'Madame' entered upon a new and startling phase:

> Montalais, who wished to turn this gallantry into an important affair, and who thought that by letting a number of people into the secret she could form a cabal to govern the State, told the whole story to La Vallière... exacting a promise from her that she would not pass on the information to the King.

Montalais' conduct was, for a not unintelligent woman, a masterpiece of stupidity. La Vallière, timid and utterly out of the stream of Court intrigue, was so oppressed with the dangerous secret that Louis easily guessed that she was keeping something from him. La Vallière gallantly admitted that she knew something which she must not disclose, and Louis, having pressed her in vain, flung out of the room in a passion. Very early on the following morning La Vallière fled to a convent, where later in the day she was discovered and retrieved by Louis; there were tears, there were fresh vows, and the whole story came out.

'Madame', who ought to have borne the brunt of Louis' indignation, was saved by a lucky accident; certainly, she was forced to admit that La Vallière's revelations were true, and was compelled to promise that she would have nothing more to do with Guiche. But Louis was more anxious that his sister-in-law should take back the fugitive La Vallière than to scold her for her naughtiness; was in fact in no position to scold, for 'Madame', seeing her advantage, took a high moral tone:

> The King had a great deal of trouble in getting what he wanted from 'Madame', but he begged her so hard, with tears in his eyes, that at last he got his way and La Vallière returned to her old quarters.[1]

To Anne, Gramont, and the older section of the Court generally, it looked as if the storm were over, but their hopes were doomed to disappointment when in March came the notorious business of *The Spanish Letter*. This was primarily a plot to dethrone La Vallière, and its chief engineer was the Comtesse de Soissons, known at Court as 'Madame La Comtesse'; assisted by Guiche, who was jealous of the King, and was still stupid enough to think of himself as leader of the smart set and of Louis as a man who was trying to oust him from that position.

Olympe Mancini, Comtesse de Soissons, was a thorough bad lot; in the late 'fifties Louis had fallen under her spell, and though she had never been his mistress, she had until recently maintained a considerable influence over him; and she now saw its diminution with a good deal of chagrin. She had tried unsuccessfully to make a tool of La Vallière, whom she had hoped to make the nominal head of a cabal which should 'govern' the King; or in plain English, La Vallière was to be the conduit through which the revenues of France were to flow into the pockets of Olympe and her lieutenants. A stupid plan, which ignored two facts; firstly that La Vallière was genuinely in love with Louis the man, and regarded Louis the King as the

[1] *Ibid.*

enemy of her happiness; and secondly that, even if she had been inclined to collaborate, she was utterly lacking in the talent for intrigue. Vardes joined the conspiracy apparently for no better reasons than a love of mischief, and vague hopes of unspecified benefits to be obtained by blackmailing Olympe if the plot failed; whilst Guiche, in addition to his desire to put the King in his place, wanted his revenge on La Vallière for her temerity in repulsing his advances. And perhaps too, he had hopes of replacing her by his sister Charlotte, who had recently escaped from Monaco and come to Paris.

The plan was that the Queen should be informed that La Vallière was her husband's mistress; that the resulting fracas should be so publicised that Louis, to kill the scandal, would be forced to exile La Vallière; and that 'Madame La Comtesse' should catch him on the rebound with a mistress selected by herself. Her cabal, 'indispensable to the King's pleasures', would cautiously extend its operations from the bedroom to the cabinet, undermining the existing Ministers and replacing them by its own 'creatures'.

How was the ball to be set rolling? It was apparently 'Madame La Comtesse' who hit upon the idea of writing a letter to the Queen purporting to come from the King of Spain, and calling the Queen's attention to the indignity which Louis was inflicting upon her. A genuine cover of an old letter of Philip IV's was stolen, a draft prepared, translated into Spanish by Guiche, and delivered at the Louvre by a Spaniard who was leaving France that day and did not intend to return. The famous document read as follows:

> The King is throwing himself into a debauchery of which no one but Your Majesty is ignorant. Mademoiselle de La Vallière is the object of his love. It is for you to consider whether you can tolerate the thought of the King in the arms of another, or if you will put an end to a situation so humiliating to your dignity.[1]

The plot miscarried from the outset. The servant who received the letter handed it on to Molina, Marie Thérèse's Spanish

[1] Motteville, *Mémoires.*

chamberwoman, who, brought up in the semi-Oriental atmosphere of the Court of Madrid, regarded all letters to wives as suspicious, if not actually contraband; and this letter in particular, which was oddly folded, and had been delivered on a day when no courier had arrived from Spain. Without more ado Molina opened the document and read it. Now unfortunately Guiche was not the Spanish scholar he thought himself to be, and he had made several howlers in his composition; and the conspirators had overlooked the fact that their text must necessarily be in a quite different hand from that of Philip IV's domestic secretary. One glance satisfied Molina, who showed the document to the Queen-Mother; and Anne, having read it, told her to hand it at once to the King in person. Which Molina did, calling Louis' attention to what she described as 'the Divine inspiration' which had prompted her impudence in tampering with the Royal mail. 'Has the Queen seen it?' asked Louis several times; and reassured on this point, he stumped off in such a fury as can be imagined.

The three conspirators had of course bound themselves by solemn oath not to betray the secret to any one in any circumstances; with the result that Guiche, having done his part, went off and told the whole story to 'Madame'; and 'Madame', as soon as she had got rid of him, passed on the exciting news to Montalais. So Louis was soon the only person at Court who was not aware of facts known to everyone in his own inner circle. Indeed so at sea was he that he actually asked Vardes if he could ferret out the authors of this iniquity, and Vardes acted as such a man might be expected to act. He knew that Louis cherished an unmanly resentment against Madame de Navailles,[1] Governess of the Maids-of-Honour, for her successful attempts to preserve the virtue of her charges; and he asserted that she was the culprit; or if not she, the only other persons capable of such treachery would be 'Monsieur le Prince' or 'Mademoiselle'. When last we heard of 'Monsieur le Prince' he was commanding the Spanish Army of Flanders, but he had managed

[1] NAVAILLES, Suzanne de Baudéan, Duchesse de, 1626?–1700, a bluestocking,t he friend of Costar, Benserade, and other well-known men of letters.

to get himself amnestied in the general balancing of accounts which had accompanied the Peace of the Pyrenees, and was now back in France, pardoned but not forgiven, living in the shadows.

'Madame', we may remember, had recently promised the King that she would break with Guiche; but she entirely agreed with Montalais that the essential preliminary to the breach was a series of meetings to decide how they were to avoid awkward public encounters after the separation. And thanks to the ingenuity of Guiche, their public encounters became almost private interviews; he gave out that he was suffering from a throat disease which prevented him from raising his voice above a whisper; and thus established a right to murmur into 'Madame's' ear whenever he pleased.

So far so good, but there were fresh complications for the lovers; Vardes, that amiable man, took it into his head that it would be amusing to cut out Guiche with 'Madame', and set about the adventure in a characteristic way. He obtained an interview with Gramont, to whom he said that he was becoming increasingly anxious for the safety of his best friend, the Comte de Guiche; who, so far from keeping his promise to the King, was seeing more of 'Madame' every day; this could only end in disaster; the command of the Nancy garrison was vacant; he implored Monsieur le Maréchal to secure the post for his son, and thus remove him from the danger zone. Antoine, who was beginning to regard his elder son not only as a menace but as an intolerable nuisance, jumped at the suggestion, to which the King readily agreed. Guiche was of course not consulted, and Vardes, having made sure that the commission was signed, hurried off to 'Madame' to condole with her on Armand's desertion, which was, he said, common knowledge; what further proof did she need than the fact that he had begged the Nancy command from the King so as to provide himself with a decent excuse for breaking with her? 'Madame' fell into the trap, and Guiche learnt that he was now commander at Nancy from Montalais, who arrived at his lodgings weighted with a stream of furious reproaches from Henrietta. There were comings and goings by Montalais, further reproaches, counter-complaints, until at last the lovers, in calmer mood, came to the conclusion that there was nothing to be done but obey the King; Guiche must take up his new appointment. Quite so, but Guiche flatly refused to set out unless 'Madame' granted him a farewell audience, a thing not easy to arrange in the circumstances. But the resourceful Montalais triumphed over all difficulties; about midday Guiche was smuggled into 'Madame's' oratory by a secret staircase, and there waited until Henrietta had finished dinner and returned to her room, into which the lover was hustled by the soubrette. All was well until, to their horror, a breathless servant rushed in to say that 'Monsieur' was even then ascending the staircase. What on earth was to be done? For there was only one door to 'Madame's' room. It was Montalais' quick wit that saved the pair. In summer the vast fireplaces of seventeenth-century rooms were blocked up with a sort of wooden penthouse which was almost a small shed, and catching hold of Guiche, she pushed him into the chimney; just two seconds before 'Monsieur' entered the room to find his wife in placid conversation with her *suivante*. But even now there was a further bad moment, and once more it was Montalais to the rescue. 'Monsieur', who ate intermittently all day, and whose pockets were always stuffed with fruit, biscuits, and sweets, pulled out an orange, and having prepared it, advanced to the firescreen with the obvious intention of throwing the peel into the grate. 'Oh, Monsieur,' said Montalais, 'are you going to throw away that lovely peel when you know I am so fond of it; give it to me, do.' Which 'Monsieur' of course did, and Montalais, with commendable fortitude, ate every bit of it.[1]

All would now have been saved had it not been for the unlucky fact that the presence of Guiche in 'Madame's' room had been detected by a third party, Mademoiselle d'Artigny,[2] who hated Guiche and had been on the watch for a chance to ruin him for some time past. Artigny wasted no time. She rushed to the Queen-Mother's apartments, and in Anne found a ready

[1] Bussy-Rabutin, *Histoires Amoureuse des Gaules*.

[2] ROURE, Claude Marie de Bérenger du Gast, Comtesse du, 'beautiful as an angel', but 'low-minded', and of very poor reputation. The Comte du Roure was 'induced to marry her' by Louis XIV in 1666. She died in 1723.

listener, who at once passed on this interesting item of news to 'Monsieur'; 'Monsieur' rushed off to the Queen of England to give her a piece of his mind about the way in which she had brought up her daughter; and the Queen of England, having smoothed him down to the best of her ability, sent for 'Madame', to whom she spoke in a way which rather surprises us in one of her prudish character:

> She scolded her a little, and then told her everything that 'Monsieur' knew as a fact, in order that 'Madame' might admit so much, and nothing more.[1]

'Madame', thus forewarned, played the meek and penitent wife to perfection at the subsequent interview with 'Monsieur'; yes, she had seen Guiche, but Montalais had been present throughout the meeting, which was the first one she had ever had with him; and she had written him perhaps three or four letters on trifling matters. 'Monsieur', at once the most credulous and the most suspicious of men, delighted at having caught his wife out, forgave her without much trouble after she had made the routine promise to break with Armand. And oddly enough he showed very little anger against Guiche, for whom he appears to have retained much of his old affection.

The only real sufferer was Montalais, who was banished from Henrietta's entourage and 'advised' by the King to make a retreat in some convent. But 'Madame' had to see to it that her Maid-of-Honour was let down gently, for that enterprising young woman had left the palace with a large quantity of her mistress's correspondence which had not yet been handed over to Malicorne; and furthermore, she knew all the details of the Spanish Letter plot, disclosure of which would mean ruin for Guiche.

Guiche had in the meantime set out for Nancy in complete ignorance of the treachery of Vardes, who was hard at work to provoke an irreparable breach between Armand and Henrietta. He had persuaded Montalais and Malicorne to give him Guiche's letters to 'Madame', ostensibly for him to burn them in her presence; and he had written to Guiche pointing out that

[1] Lafayette, *Mémoires*.

as these documents had been destroyed, it was only fair that Armand should surrender the letters which 'Madame' had written to him. The unsuspecting Guiche agreed, and sent orders to his mother at Paris that the package should be handed over to Vardes for destruction. Vardes now felt that he had all the game in his hands, and promised himself great things from pressure judiciously applied to 'Madame' and the Gramonts whenever he needed their influence. But he had entirely underestimated Montalais and Malicorne; that simple pair had indeed handed him a mass of perfectly genuine letters from Guiche to Henrietta, but they had not felt it necessary to call his attention to the fact that they had removed all the most compromising ones before surrendering the packet; in the last resort therefore it was Malicorne and not Vardes who held the ace of trumps.

It had been a trying year for Antoine as head of this troublesome House of Gramont; certainly he himself had got the Colonel-General's honours, and on 1 June had appeared, 'plumed and clinking, with a beautiful train', as Marshal-General of the Lists at the most famous *carrousel* ever given by Louis XIV. But Guiche had been a constant anxiety, Madame de Monaco had sneaked back to Paris where she was certain to get into some scrape or other, and then in the winter brother Philibert must needs elect to get into trouble, and that out of sheer perversity:

> La Motte-Argencourt was one of the Maids-of-Honour to the Queen-Mother... It was sufficient in those days for the King to cast his eye upon a young lady of the Court to inspire her with hopes... and if he spoke to her more than once, the Courtiers who had either pretensions or love for her, respectfully withdrew... but the Chevalier de Gramont thought fit to act quite otherwise, perhaps to preserve the singularity of his character. He had never before thought of her; but as soon as he found that she was honoured with the King's attention, he was of opinion that she was likewise deserving of his... She was in hopes that the Chevalier would change his behaviour; but finding him rashly persisting in it, she complained of him; and then it was that he perceived that if love renders all conditions equal, it was not so between

rivals. He was banished the Court, and not finding any place in France which could console him . . . he at last formed the resolution of visiting England.[1]

Philibert de Gramont, now in his fortieth year, was in his disreputable way one of the best-known men in France when in 1662 he set out for England. At Louis' Court his position was established; no room was ever so crowded that on entering it your glance did not soon fall on the man with the dimpled chin and the laughing eyes, whose impudence, wit, and cynicism formed a circle round him, however exalted the company. He was to live to make a complete conquest of the King, and to say anything he pleased to him, even about his Ministers. 'He was a very clever man, but showed his cleverness only in sarcasm, hitting off people's foibles and absurdities in a few stinging words which it was not easy to forget. He was like a mad dog, biting everybody.'[2] To me he is a near relation of Barry Lyndon; I am sure that Philibert would have agreed with Barry that if you run a man through who has caught you cheating at cards, the act proves that you are a person of the most scrupulous honour. But Charles II liked a rogue, and if he was a witty one, he loved him; the Chevalier's reputation for 'address' at the gaming table was unlikely to prejudice him at the Restoration Court.

Philibert had visited Cromwell's England, but he was to find things very different in that of Charles II. Not only had the atmosphere throughout the country changed out of all recognition, but the Court of Whitehall proved markedly unlike the dowdy, rather ludicrous affair which the French imagined it to be:

Accustomed as he was to the grandeur of the Court of France, he was surprised at the politeness and splendour of the Court of England. The King was inferior to none either in shape or air; his wit was pleasant, his disposition easy and affable.[3]

[1] Hamilton, *Memoirs.*
[2] St Simon, *Mémoires.*
[3] Hamilton, *Memoirs.*

And Charles received Philibert with open arms, for the two men were not strangers to each other; they had heard the chimes together at midnight during the exile, and Charles was the last man in Europe to stand on his new dignity; the Chevalier, with his easy morality and his obvious desire to please, was at once welcomed into the King's raffish entourage of mistresses and roués:

> The reception which he met with in this Court made him forget the other ... The Chevalier de Gramont had long been known to the Royal family, and to most of the gentlemen of the Court, and now had only to get acquainted with the ladies; and for this he wanted no interpreter; they all spoke French enough to explain themselves, and they all understood it sufficiently to comprehend what he had to say to them.[1]

And he had arrived at a lucky moment, for earlier French visitors had reflected little credit on their country:

> The Chevalier de Gramont was soon liked by all parties; those who had not known him before, were surprised to see a Frenchman of his disposition ... The French were rather in disgrace; for instead of persons of any distinction having appeared among the first who came over, they had only seen some insignificant puppies, each striving to outdo the other in folly and extravagance, despising everyone who was not like themselves, and thinking they introduced *le bel air* by treating the English as strangers in their own country. The Chevalier de Gramont on the contrary was familiar with everybody; he gave in to their customs, ate of everything, and easily habituated himself to their manner of living, which he looked upon as neither vulgar nor barbarous ... and ... all the nation was charmed with a man who so agreeably indemnified them for what they had suffered from the folly of the former class.[2]

Presumably his actual conduct was less patronizing than his account of it, for after a month in England, 'he found so little

[1] Hamilton, *Memoirs*.
[2] *Ibid.*

difference in the manners and conversation of those with whom he chiefly associated, that he could scarcely believe that he was out of his own country. Everything which could agreeably engage a man of his disposition presented itself to his different humours as if the pleasures of the Court of France had quitted it to accompany him in his exile'.[1]

It is a revealing picture of an exotic Court, in which the sturdy English vices had been French-polished to a point at which they were indistinguishable from those of the Louvre; governed with consummate skill and cynicism by a cosmopolitan diplomat possessing one of the best brains in Europe, who has succeeded to this day in impressing on popular imagination the mask under which he hid his ability. It is only within comparatively modern times that the revolt against the old school of history has begun to show us the real Charles hidden underneath the traditional picture of lazy, good-natured old Rowley, the Merry Monarch.

Philibert was lucky in striking up a friendship with the only other distinguished Frenchman in England, St Evremond,[2] who had been exiled in 1660 for satirizing Mazarin, and being now well established at the English Court, was able to give Philibert some valuable advice; avoid love and stick to gambling was the gist of St Evremond's sermons; 'for', said he, 'if you attempt to seduce a lady or supplant a lover, your gains at play will by no means suffice for presents and bribes'. And he went on to explain to the incredulous Philibert that amorous intrigues were not quite so easily embarked upon in London as in Paris:

> However docile the English may be with respect to their wives, they can by no means bear inconstancy on the part of their mistresses, or patiently suffer the advantages of a rival.

[1] *Ibid.*

[2] St Evremond, Charles de Marguetel de St Denis, Chevalier de, 1613–1703, prolific writer, whose collected works were published in London in 1705. Though pardoned by Louis XIV he never returned to France, but spent most of his long life in England, without ever learning a word of the language. In 1670 he was pensioned by Charles II, and the pension was continued to him by James II and William III.

> . . . You will certainly meet with no success with such as are unmarried; honourable views and good landed property are required here; and you possess as little of one as of the other. . . . Here it is a miracle if a young lady yields to any proposal but that of matrimony.[1]

And Philibert, having heard his friend's lecture, reluctantly convinced himself of its truth by making simultaneous and unsuccessful attacks on Mrs Middleton[2] and a Miss Warmestre, one of the Queen's Maids-of-Honour. Both were obdurate, though every week the Chevalier had over from Paris 'perfumed gloves, pocket looking-glasses, elegant boxes, apricot paste, essences, and other small wares of love, with a new suit of clothes for himself'. Then he met Miss Hamilton, and in a trice Middleton and Warmestre were forgotten: 'No longer was he inconstant; no longer were his wishes fluctuating; this object fixed them all; and of all his former habits none remained except uneasiness and jealousy . . . He soon found that he had seen nothing of the Court before this instant.'[3]

Like so many Cavalier children, Miss Hamilton, a remarkably independent woman, who paid very little attention to other people's prejudices, had been educated in France. Philibert of course thought her the perfection of all beauty, but his raptures would have little evidential value were they not corroborated by other testimony, which gives her a high place even among the beauties of Versailles; where she was to hold her own triumphantly. For as St Simon remarks, 'she had a beak and claws'. Frenchwomen soon found that she was too dangerous to be attacked, for 'she had a wit of the disquieting Irish-English sort which Frenchwomen could hardly sneer at, and felt to be too potent for them'.

Of the strength of character of the woman who tamed Philibert de Gramont, frightened Madame de Maintenon, and

[1] Hamilton, *Memoirs*.

[2] MIDDLETON, Jane Needham, Mrs, 1645–1692. Had Charles II, James II, and Archbishop Sheldon among her lovers. 'Her literary attainments were more than respectable.'

[3] Hamilton, *Memoirs*.

'accustomed Louis XIV to her free manner', we can have no two opinions. 'She was always on good terms with the King, who enjoyed her wit and had a strong personal friendship for her'; and contrary to all expectations she made a brilliant success of her marriage with Philibert.

The only fly now in the ointment for the Chevalier was that he had dangerous rivals, including the Duke of York, who 'talked to Miss Hamilton as much as he could, and ogled her with great assiduity'. But as the Duke's idea of love-making was to tell her 'miracles of the cunning of foxes and the mettle of horses; giving her accounts of broken legs and arms, dislocated shoulders, and other curious and entertaining adventures', Philibert thought that he had little to fear from him. But there were more dangerous competitors.

Philibert worked hard and spared no expense to win his Elizabeth; on summer evenings when the heat and dust of the park were too much even for that tireless walker Charles II, there were boating parties on the Thames, with music, fireworks, and picnic suppers, in which the Chevalier rarely failed to display 'some unexpected stroke of magnificence and gallantry':

> Sometimes he had complete concerts of vocal and instrumental music which he privately brought from Paris . . . sometimes he gave banquets which likewise came from France and which, even in the midst of London, surpassed the King's collations.

In this year Charles II offered Philibert what he described as a trifle, namely a pension of £1,500 a year until such time as he was restored to Louis XIV's favour; which Philibert refused, taking good care that 'Monsieur de Comminges[1] did not fail to represent properly the merit of such a refusal to the French Court'. And to let Charles see how little his affairs were deranged – though he was in fact existing on his card winnings – he im-

[1] COMMINGES, Gaston Jean Baptiste, Comte de, 1613–1670, Lieutenant of the Guard to Anne of Austria, 1644, Ambassador to Lisbon, 1657–9, and to London, 1662–5. Disliked by Charles, who describes him as 'good for nothing but to give malicious and wrong intelligence'.

ported from France as a present for the King of England 'the most elegant and magnificent calash that had ever been seen'. A present which caused its recipient a good deal of trouble, for there was keen competition amongst the women to be the first to ride in it through the Park; Barbara Castlemaine threatening to miscarry if she was not the favoured one, and Frances Stuart promising that the King had nothing to hope from her if Castlemaine was awarded the prize. Charles finally decided in favour of Miss Stuart, 'and', says the Chevalier, 'it is believed that this triumph cost Lady Castlemaine's rival some of her innocence'.

Suddenly Philibert's sky clouded. Richard Talbot,[1] 'in possession of about £40,000 a year in land', appeared as a suitor for Elizabeth; and even Philibert's optimism could not persuade him that any careful guardian would reject such an offer in order to bestow a penniless ward on a French younger son who lived by his wits. But it was some slight consolation to the Chevalier that he fleeced Talbot of four hundred guineas, thus laying him under contribution to his rival's war-chest. Talbot, 'who played deep, and was tolerably forgetful', somehow overlooked this trifle. But the Gascon proved a match for the Irishman; waylaying Talbot some time later as he was about to leave town, Philibert, by way of farewell, said, 'Adieu, be sure not to fall sick on the road; but if you do, remember me in your will'. The Chevalier got his money. 'He had', says Anthony Hamilton, 'a thousand genteel ways of refreshing the memories of those persons who are apt to be forgetful in their payments.'

Later in the year Philibert heard from his sister, Madame de St Chaumont, now Governess to 'Monsieur's' children, that Louis XIV had given him leave to return to Paris; and he was most reluctant to do so. Was in fact only persuaded to visit Louis by the positive command of Miss Hamilton, and 'the nearer he approached the Court of France, the more he regretted his absence from that of England'. That he should have been

[1] TYRCONNEL, Richard Talbot, Earl of, 1630–1691. 'Lying Dick Talbot', made an Earl, 1688, and fought against William of Orange in Ireland, 1690–1. 'A man of very good sense, obliging, but immoderately vain, and full of cunning.'

recalled from exile by a message transmitted in a private letter from his sister does not seem to have struck him as at all odd, and he duly arrived in Paris, blithely ignorant of the reception which awaited him; namely a visit from his brother the Maréchal, with orders for him to return to England at once. Philibert expostulated, producing Mme de St Chaumont's letter. 'And since when', said Antoine, 'has our sister been either Secretary of State or a Minister?' And he went on to give his light-hearted brother a full account of the situation:

> Some time ago the King told 'Madame' how you had refused the pension the King of England offered you. He appeared pleased with the manner in which Comminges had related the circumstances, and said he was pleased. 'Madame' interpreted this as an order for your recall; and Madame de St Chaumont, being very far from possessing that wonderful discretion she imagines herself to be mistress of, hastened to despatch you this consequential order in her own hand. To conclude: 'Madame' said yesterday when the King was at dinner, that you would very soon be here; and the King, as soon as dinner was over, commanded me to send you back as soon as you arrived. So set off at once.

But the Chevalier, having secured a few days grace to collect some debts, sneaked off to Vaugirard where he amused himself by impersonating a Huguenot pastor, 'administering the Sacrament in so solemn a manner that, as there did not remain a sufficient number of Swiss at Versailles to guard the Chapel, Vardes was obliged to acquaint the King that they were all gone to the Chevalier de Gramont, who was administering the Sacrament at Vaugirard'. After which Philibert set out for London 'on the wings of love'; and perhaps of fear, for though Louis would be mightily indifferent to the profanation of a Huguenot Sacrament, he would have wanted to know why the Chevalier was playing the buffoon at Vaugirard when he ought to have been on the road to Calais.

Once back in London, Philibert turned with renewed ardour to his interrupted courtship, and, it being still 'the fair and dry part of the season', he found to his surprise that the fashionable world was resorting to 'charming, delicious walks called bowling-greens, which are little square grass plots where the turf is almost as smooth and level as the cloth on a billiard table. As soon as the heat of the day is over all the company assemble there; they play deep, and the spectators are at liberty to make what bets they please . . . Near all these places ofdiversion there is usually a sort of inn, in which are sold all kinds of English liquors such as cider, mead, bottled beer, and Spanish wines. Here the rooks meet every day to drink, smoke, and try their skill'.[1]

Before the end of the year Philibert was as triumphant in love as he had been in play. 'As the reward of a constancy he had never before known, he found Hymen and Love united in his favour, and he was at last blessed with the possession of Miss Hamilton.' An idyllic ending to an honest love story? Possibly, but Philibert's account of the event is not the only one in existence; and I fear the alternative version has about it a smack of the Chevalier which carries conviction:

> Gramont, having at last obtained his recall from Louis XIV, was on the point of returning to France without the lady (Miss Hamilton), and had actually got as far as Dover when he was overtaken by Anthony Hamilton and his elder brother George, who after assuring him of their respect, explained that they had made the journey to ask him if he had forgotten anything. 'Ah,' said the Chevalier, 'true; I have forgotten to marry your sister.' Back he accordingly went with them, was duly married, and in the following year became the father of a son as beautiful as the mother.

[1] Hamilton, *Memoirs*.

CHAPTER X

★

In 1663 Louis began his long series of aggressions with a smash and grab raid on the Duchy of Lorraine; which concerns us only because Guiche was summoned out of Nancy to act as Lieutenant-General of the invading force; and rather to the surprise of the Court, the King treated him with marked graciousness during the time he was in Lorraine.

'Madame' had regarded a meeting between the two with uneasiness; she knew that Louis was inquisitive, and she knew how winning he could be when he was in search of information. She wrote hurriedly to Guiche, telling him that if he babbled about their affairs, he need not present himself before her again. Henrietta's fears were realized. Guiche expanded under the sun of Royal favour and said many things that he ought to have left unsaid; and by the time 'Madame's' letter reached him, the harm was already done. Worse still from Armand's point of view, Vardes assured Henrietta that Guiche had received her letter before his little talk with Louis, but had ignored it, saying that the sacrifice of 'Madame's' countenance was a small price to pay for his restoration to the King's favour. It is hardly surprising in the circumstances that the Princess's next letter to her lover should have been 'full of bitterness', and should have concluded with a refusal to see Armand again. Guiche, finding his humblest protestations of sorrow unavailing, returned to Paris to sue in person for Henrietta's forgiveness. We can guess the sequel; 'Madame' inflexible in her just wrath, Guiche threatening to run himself through with his own sword, promises, pardon, kisses, and soon the old liaison in full swing once more. Until the inevitable day when 'Monsieur', 'all in tears', went to his brother to demand vengeance on this insolent Guiche. Armand's offence was not one to rouse any very deep anger in Louis; but he saw clearly that if he was to avoid having his leisure hours made intolerable by a lachrymose Philippe, something drastic must be done. And having considered the problem, he sent for Gramont:

> M. le Maréchal, your son is an extravagant sort of fellow into whom it is difficult to instil any common sense; if it were not for the esteem in which I hold you, I would abandon him to my brother's resentment, for he has certainly shown himself lacking in respect towards 'Monsieur'. Send him off to fight in Poland; and to cover up our reasons for doing so, let him ask my permission to serve abroad, and let him take Louvigny with him.[1]

Guiche, all unaware of what was brewing, spent a late and enjoyable night at the Hôtel de Soissons, and on the following morning was awakened in a singularly disagreeable manner; by the entry of an enraged father into his bedroom, armed with an obviously set speech:

> So, Monsieur le Comte, we are *homme à bonnes fortunes* it seems, successful too, and what I particularly admire is our discretion. You have paid your court admirably. I am commissioned by His Majesty to inform you that he recognizes your merit and wishes to bestow upon you a fitting reward; namely that you set off at once and see whether the King of Poland[2] is prepared to accept you as a volunteer in his army.

And the Maréchal added 'a hundred other displeasing remarks which the Comte did not feel strong enough to dispute, so stunned was he by the news'.

So far as the public was concerned, Guiche emerged from the business with credit. *La Muze Historique* for 8 September informed its readers that 'M. le Comte de Guiche, rich in Nature's gifts, having wit, heart, beauty, gentleness, and generosity, being covetous of honour, has by permission of His Majesty, gone with the Comte de Louvigny to the Polish wars'.

And Armand did not go unrecommended, for Condé came

[1] Bussy-Rabutin, *Histoire Amoureuse des Gaules*.

[2] POLAND, Jean Casimir V, King of, 1609–1672, entered the Jesuits, 1643, and was made a Cardinal, 1647. In 1649 he succeeded his brother, whose widow he married; she ruled Poland throughout his nominal reign. Abdicated 1668 and settled in France.

to the aid of his old protégé with a letter to the Queen of Poland – 'The Comte de Guiche has merit and an established reputation; he should be a useful man'. To which in due course the Queen replied that she looked forward with pleasure to receiving the Comte, for whom she was preparing a hearty welcome.[1]

Guiche did not enjoy his exile among the savages; even at the so-called Court, only the Queen was worthy of his attentions; and there was neither glory nor experience to be gained in a war conducted with an imbecile brutality and inefficiency which made him shrug his shoulders. He neither knew nor cared why Poland was at war with Russia, despised both nations equally, and regarded his own services merely as a compliment paid by a French noble to a Frenchwoman of his own caste, a fellow-exile amongst this disgusting tribe of barbarians. It is significant that the only news of him which reached Paris was that 'he had succeeded in pleasing Her Polish Majesty'.

Philibert, who returned from exile at the close of the year, was apparently given a hearty welcome by Louis XIV; 'I am very glad', writes Charles II to 'Madame' in January 1664, 'that the Comte de Gramont is so well receaved there, and I hope he will receave the effects of it'.[2] One is surprised that in the circumstances he should have risked Louis' displeasure by setting off again almost immediately for England; but that he did so is evident from a second letter of Charles's, dated 18 January, in which he says, 'I am very glad I receaved yours before that which the Comte de Gramont brought'.

The Comtesse de Guiche appears for a moment in 1664, showing more spirit than we should have expected of her:

> There is trouble between the Maréchal de Gramont and his daughter-in-law, and it is making some noise . . . The King intends to select certain ladies for the Queen . . . and thought of choosing the Comtesse de Guiche for one; she is dying to be picked, and the Chancellor[3] has done his best to get the

[1] *Lettres sur la cour de Louis XIV*, 1660–67, ed. E. Magné.

[2] Hartmann, *The King my Brother*.

[3] Seguier, Pierre, 1588–1672, Chancellor of France since 1635. He was the uncle of the Comtesse de Guiche.

King to choose her; but the Maréchal does not think she should hold a post which would oblige her to be at Court from morning to night in the absence of her husband, and has let the King understand that he begs him to appoint some other lady. Society agrees with M. le Maréchal, but Mme de Guiche is very angry with her father-in-law, and has gone so far as to tell him that she refuses to see him again.[1]

Poor Louise de Guiche; only twenty-one, pretty and attractive, longing to escape from the dull monotony of her grass-widowhood to the Court where she hoped to forget the cruel farce of her marriage. We can imagine her home life from a letter which her husband wrote to his father, apparently in answer to one from the Maréchal, expostulating with Armand on his indecent neglect of his wife:

> He [i.e. Guiche himself] has no pleasant ties, because the woman he has married on M. le Maréchal's orders is disagreeable to him; and he will always live on bad terms with her, as is his present habit; it is a feeble argument to say that she is beautiful when that beauty leaves the Comte de Guiche entirely cold.[2]

Gramont was now beginning to look his age, judging from the news in June that 'the Nestor of the Court' is ill. A more annoying label for a man who was trying to impress the King with his youth and vitality it would be difficult to imagine, and if Gramont could have laid hands on that reporter it would have gone hard with him. But by July he was his jaunty self again, and back at Court to welcome his sons on their return from Poland.

> The Comtes de Guiche and Louvigny have returned so full of the honours which Your Polish Majesty showed them that they are unable to talk about anything else . . . The Comte de Guiche is extremely satisfied with Poland; he found it the best country in the world for the performance of gallant actions.[3]

[1] *Lettres*, 1660–67.
[2] Bussy-Rabutin, *Histoire Amoureuse des Gaules*.
[3] *Lettres*, 1660–67.

The truth is that Guiche was talking about nothing except how 'Madame' had saved his life, and in a dozen salons he was reverently exhibiting her shattered portrait which had deflected the bullet intended for his heart. But Guiche was not his father's son for nothing; that the portrait was shattered is undeniable, but who fired the bullet that smashed it? I have a strong suspicion that it was Guiche himself.

This ostentatious parade of devotion had two unpleasant consequences which Guiche had not anticipated; first, 'Monsieur' insisted that Armand should exclude himself from all places where he might be brought into contact with 'Madame'; and secondly 'Madame', remembering Guiche's indiscreet confidences to Louis in the previous year, demanded the return of the letters she had written to him whilst he was serving in Lorraine, and Armand was forced to surrender them. It was in fact a year in which he made small headway with Henrietta. During his long absence from Court Vardes had managed to establish a kind of intimacy with her, which he had used to blacken Guiche in every possible way, and some of the mud had stuck. Armand for his part was not as suppliant as the case demanded; he could not forget the stream of witty, carefully casual letters from Vardes, in which the tale of 'Madame's' infidelities had been told him at great length; he did not at heart believe that she had thrown him over, but he was tormented with jealousy and suspicion.

Late in the summer both 'Madame' and Guiche, acting independently, obtained convincing proof of the repeated treacheries of Vardes. That Henrietta had her eyes opened to Vardes' baseness is clear from his own conduct: 'he threw himself upon his knees before her, burst into tears, and begged her pardon, offering, if she would be his ally, to conceal her dealings with Guiche'. This abject blend of servility and insolence 'Madame' had the pride and good sense to reject with scorn. As regards Guiche, it may be that he got wind of Vardes' latest piece of treachery towards him; Guiche had entrusted Vardes with a letter to be handed secretly to 'Madame'; and Vardes, having opened and read it, took it to the King as proof that Henrietta was breaking her promise to have no further communication with Guiche. Or possibly Armand traced back to Vardes the lie now circulating in Paris that he was still having secret interviews with 'Madame'. At any rate in August Guiche broke openly with his erstwhile friend:

> M. le Comte de Guiche has had a big row with M. de Vardes, asserting that while he was in Poland, Vardes did not treat him honestly, and that he told the Archbishop of Sens[1] recently that his affair with 'Madame' was still continuing; the Archbishop told 'Madame' and Guiche this, and they are loud in their complaints . . . The King has forbidden the two to fight, and ordered them to behave civilly to each other.[2]

In October Condé intervened unsuccessfully to reconcile the two, and throughout the month his son, 'Monsieur le Duc', was working for the same end. The details of the quarrel were now common property:

> M. le Comte de Guiche asserts that, having given his letters to the other for safe custody, he [Vardes] used them to force his suit on 'Madame'; that he betrayed to her all his secrets; and that he did his best, both with the King and with the Maréchal de Gramont, to persuade them that as he [Guiche] had not broken with 'Madame', it would be advisable to keep him in Muscovy indefinitely.[3]

The publicity given to the affair seems to have frightened both 'Madame' and Guiche; even 'Madame' felt that this was not the time for further indiscretions, whilst Guiche behaved with a circumspection which he rarely showed:

[1] SENS, Louis Henri Pardaillan de Gondrin, Archbishop of, 1620–1674, appointed to Sens, 1646. In politics a Frondeur, and in ecclesiastical matters he refused to admit the infallibility of the Pope. A worldly prelate, whose disorderly life created much scandal. His nephew, the Marquis de Montespan, was the husband of Louis XIV's most notorious mistress.

[2] *Lettres*, 1660–7.

[3] *Lettres*, 1660–7.

'Monsieur' is quite at his ease about M. de Guiche; and well he may be, for M. Le Comte's behaviour is irreproachable. I don't think he has once been in a place where he could even see 'Madame' since his return from Poland, and he always leaves a room long before there is any chance of her entering it.[1]

Guiche could not see 'Madame', she refused to write to Guiche, and the famous intrigue seemed to be dead at last, when at the turn of the year an accident fanned the embers into a blaze again. Madame de La Vieuville gave a masked ball on 7 January 1665, to which came 'Monsieur' with 'Madame'; and at the door they meet 'a troop of masks' whose manners pleased 'Monsieur'. He suggested that they should join parties for the evening; it was agreed; 'Monsieur' took the hand of a lady, and a gentleman took that of 'Madame':

Judge of her surprise when she found that it was the crippled hand of M. de Guiche, who at the same moment recognized 'Madame' by the perfume which she always used for her hair. So surprised were they that they were within an ace of crying out. So agitated that they mounted the great staircase without saying a word. Later on Guiche recognized 'Monsieur', fell on his knees to him, and not only succeeded in justifying himself, but also found time to learn from 'Madame' all that had happened since they had last met... Everything seemed to aid their reconciliation, and it was accomplished. 'Madame' began to receive his letters again, and one evening when 'Monsieur' was at a masquerade, the two met at the house of the Comtesse de Gramont.[2]

Things were coming 'Madame's' way. She had a long score to settle with Vardes, who had sneaked back from the country to Paris, and in February he was fool enough to give her a

[1] *Ibid.*
[2] Lafayette, *Mémoires.*

magnificent opening. The Chevalier de Lorraine[1] was at the time making love to one of 'Madame's' Maids-of-Honour, Mademoiselle de Fiennes; and the matter was being discussed in the Queen's apartments when Vardes, turning to Lorraine, said, 'Why bother about the maid when you can have the mistress?' A remark which Philibert passed on to 'Madame', who at once made a formal complaint to the King; and Louis sent the offender to the Bastille.

Vardes would probably have been free again in a week or so, had it not been for the stupidity of his friends, who broadcast it that the detention was proof of his influence over the King; for, said they, 'Madame' had tried to have him banished, and had failed. These well-meaning blunderers could have adopted no more disastrous line; there was nothing about which Louis was so sensitive as the insinuation that he was being 'governed', and when the story reached his ears he immediately took Vardes out of the Bastille and banished him to Aigues-Mortes; where in well-deserved exile he spent the next twenty years.

'Madame La Comtesse', who had been Vardes' mistress, was the only person who regretted his fall. She had always disliked 'Madame', liked her none the better for depriving her of Vardes, and after consideration she decided that the perfect revenge would be to ruin Guiche. As a first step towards this, she somehow persuaded Montalais to give her those compromising letters which were still in her keeping; and thus armed, she obtained an audience with the King:

> 'Mme La Comtesse' told the King that the Comte de Guiche had written letters to 'Madame' in which His Majesty was very disrespectfully handled; the King told 'Madame' of the charge, and 'Madame', seeing that the Comtesse had begun

[1] LORRAINE, Philippe, Chevalier de, 1643–1702, 'beautiful as an angel' and 'the most depraved man of his age', practised homosexuality not by inclination but as a matter of tactics; lifelong friend of 'Monsieur', with whom the nature of his relations was common knowledge. Showed great bravery whilst serving with the Dutch during his banishment. Accused of debauching Louis XIV's son, the Comte de Vermandois, 1682. 'A bad man, whose last words were infamies.'

to talk, and would undoubtedly go on to tell everything, decided to forestall her, and confessed everything.[1]

But at the same time she put Louis in possession of the facts of the Spanish Letter plot of 1662, thinking quite correctly that the information would act as a powerful counter-irritant. 'Madame' won.

> She asked the King to promise to pardon Guiche his share [in the 1662 plot] if she could prove that his fault was venial compared with that of Mme de Soissons, and of the Comte de Vardes; the King promised, and 'Madame' told him the whole story. They decided that 'Mme La Comtesse' should be banished and Vardes put in prison.[2]

But for 'Madame' it was a hollow triumph, spelling the end of her romance with Guiche; for Armand, though pardoned, was a man under a cloud, with whom it would in any case have been dangerous to associate, and she herself was now under such strict surveillance that any attempt to renew the liaison would be madness. Probably in any case she would not have reopened the affair, for 'she was no longer at that age when the most perilous adventures appear the most attractive'.

The scene which brought down the curtain on this romantic comedy was worthy of those which preceded it; 'Madame' had been wise enough to refuse Guiche a final interview, but Guiche was determined that there should be one; so disguising himself as a valet, he waylaid 'Madame' in her sedan chair on the road to the Louvre, said farewell, and fell fainting at her feet.

One by one the actors left the stage; Vardes to banishment, 'Madame La Comtesse' to exile in Champagne, and only Guiche remained precariously at Court.

But not for long. The Maréchal realized that his son was a ruined man; the King would never forget the insult which Armand had offered to the Royal dignity, and the sooner

[1] *Lettres*, 1660–7.

[2] Lafayette, *Mémoires*.

Guiche was out of France the better. His father ordered him to beg Louis' permission to pay a long visit to Holland, and Louis granted the request with unflattering readiness. While his hand was in, Antoine also got permission for Louvigny to accompany his elder brother; for Louvigny, though not such a nuisance as Guiche, had apparently not been behaving well this summer; he had got his name coupled with that of a Mademoiselle d'Ardennes, a Maid-of-Honour to the Queen, and the affair had ended in the girl having to enter a convent.

When anyone of importance was arrested in seventeenth-century France, it was routine police procedure to seize his private papers; and when their contents became public – as they invariably did – there was a good deal of unpleasantness and embarrassment all round. The Vardes case proved no exception to the rule. Amongst his correspondents had been Madame de Mecklembourg[1] who had given free rein to a caustic wit, of which 'Madame', Gramont and Madame de St Chaumont were the victims, 'and all were very angry'. Especially Madame de St Chaumont, accused of 'governing' 'Madame'; which was exactly what she was trying to do.

Scarcely had the noise died down when Madame de Monaco brought the family into a ludicrous publicity. She had never given up hope that she was destined for something better than to be the wife of a dull little Italian and the mistress of Lauzun. And now that glittering prize Louis XIV seemed to be within her grasp; she had been entrusted by the Prince de Monaco with some trifling business at the French Court, and had contrived to make the affair a pretext for a series of interviews with the King; her charm, 'the fascination of the Gramonts', made an impression, and at last came the day when she accepted Louis' invitation to pay him a visit in his private room. But unfortunately Lauzun had heard of the assignation from Charlotte's maid, and he determined to wreck it. The arrangement was that

[1] MECKLEMBOURG, Isabelle de Montmorency, Duchesse de, 1627–1695, younger sister of the future Maréchal de Luxembourg, known at Court as 'Bablon'. She married, firstly, the Duc de Châtillon in 1645, and then in 1664, Christian Louis, Duc de Mecklembourg.

Bontemps[1] should bring Charlotte up the private staircase to the secret door of the King's room, which should be locked with the key on the outer side. Lauzun took the immense risk of creeping up the forbidden stairs half an hour before the appointed time, satisfied himself that the door was locked, then removed the key and threw it into a privy opposite the door; and from that post of vantage he enjoyed the scene which followed. Charlotte arrived; there was a frantic search for the missing key on the dark stairs; Bontemps at last dared to scratch on the door; the King asked what was the matter; the valet explained; and the baffled lovers, so near and yet so far, were forced to part with their hunger unsatisfied. Lauzun's audacity did more for him than he had dared to hope; it was in no way Charlotte's fault that the meeting had not taken place, but she had, however innocently, been the means of making the King feel and look ridiculous, and that was something for which with Louis XIV there was no forgiveness. A passing affair she undoubtedly had with the King, but her misadventure lost her any hopes she ever had of becoming *Maîtresse en titre de France*.

Armand had an unexpectedly good send-off from Louis XIV. 'The Comte de Guiche', writes Condé on 10 April, 'left yesterday for Holland, and the King treated both him and his father with all the kindness in the world.' Early in May he and Louvigny arrived in the country of their exile.

The Holland of 1665 was a small country, very wealthy, enjoying a high standard of living; having large overseas interests; with a huge mercantile marine and a powerful navy; yet unwarlike, grudging every penny spent on the fighting services, and especially on its small and inefficient army. A state with an unimportant aristocracy, in which the wealthy merchant was the most respected figure; disliked by its neighbours for its arrogance and for its unconcealed contempt for all other nations.

[1] Bontemps, Alexandre, 1626–1701, began life as a Parisian blood-letter, and became First Valet de Chambre to Louis XIV, Governor of Marly, and Governor of Versailles. He managed all the King's confidential affairs, and was 'as silent as the tomb'. An excellent man, unspoilt by his position, and 'all his life a father to the poor'.

Though appearing strong, Holland, or more correctly the United Provinces, had all the inherent weaknesses of an autonomous federation, and in addition, one peculiar to itself; namely that the country was split into Orangists wanting the restoration of the Stadhoulderate, and Republicans who upheld the *coup d'état* of 1650 which had abolished it. The latter now held power, and to maintain it recruited the army on a purely political basis; which was disastrous to its efficiency, for any military talent which there was in the republic was to be found in the Orangist ranks. And lastly, this army, when it went on active service, found itself under the control of Field Deputies, civilian delegates of the provinces, armed with full powers to dictate to the Commander-in-Chief on all matters of strategy and even of tactics. Small wonder that the Dutch forces had, as Guiche remarks, 'nothing about them of an army but the name and the scarves'.[1]

When Armand reached Holland in May, the Republic had been at war with England since 4 March; officially that is, for in the colonies and at sea individuals of the two nations had been fighting each other for the best part of a year. Louis XIV, a very reluctant ally of the Dutch under a treaty which he had inherited, was using all his political dexterity to preserve the friendship of Charles without openly repudiating his treaty obligations. Within a few days of Guiche's arrival the Dutch fleet had lost the battle of Lowestoft; and the first we see of Armand in Holland is when he makes one of the crowd standing on the beach at Scheveling, listening to the booming of the guns out to sea, and contemplating the battered Dutch ships at anchor in the offing. What he saw and heard seems to have fired him with the ambition to try his luck in a new profession, for within a day or two he applied without success to Louis XIV for permission to serve with the Dutch fleet. Being thus reduced to the role of an idler, he went to the Hague where, to his great indignation, he found that public prayers were being offered 'that it may please God to deliver us from our two great enemies, the French and the English'. An illuminating sidelight on Dutch

[1] Guiche, *Mémoires*.

opinion, a shrewd appraisement of things to come. Shortly afterwards we find Guiche attached to the Dutch forces in the field as an observer.

The reader may well ask at this point how the Dutch army came to be on active service in a sea war. The explanation is that Charles II had stirred up the Bishop of Munster[1] to attack the inland provinces of the Republic. Munster had his own grievances against the Dutch, and thoroughly enjoyed a war. He is still remembered for two things; first, he was the only sovereign who ever succeeded in extracting a subsidy from Charles II, and second, that he invented the first poison-gas shell, whose efficacy he demonstrated against the population of his own cathedral city.

Guiche, as a freelance observer, elected to go to Zwol, which he thought offered promising opportunities for a fight. But 'there I found the situation entirely different to what they thought at the Hague. It will hardly be believed that the States, who wished to plan everything from their own homes, could never get two reports of the same situation which corroborated each other, and could not agree among themselves, even on geographical matters of fact'.[2] Thus early it must have dawned upon the Frenchman that the Dutch army was a very different one from those with which he had been accustomed to serve.

In the meantime Louis XIV had at last been goaded into taking the preliminary steps towards sending his contingent to the help of his allies, and Turenne was sent to reconnoitre a line of approach. On hearing which, Guiche 'to show my zeal, however useless, for the service of His Majesty', set out to bring Turenne up-to-date information. The two met in the Ardennes, where the Maréchal asked what was being said about his journey; Guiche replied that some thought he was on his way to take over command of the Dutch army, others that he would command the French contingent only; but that he, Guiche, thought that the King was seeking a pretext to quarrel with

[1] MUNSTER, Christoph Bernard von Galen, Bishop of, 1607?–1678, had been made Bishop in 1650.

[2] Guiche, *Mémoires*.

Castel-Rodrigo,[1] the Governor of the Spanish Netherlands, and wished to have Turenne on the spot to exploit the breach. Turenne admitted that Guiche was not far out, but said that the King was not yet quite ready to swallow the Low Countries; though he would do so if Castel-Rodrigo refused leave for the French contingent to march through his territories.

When at last the French troops arrived they proved to be an exasperation rather than a help to the worried Dutch authorities. But the faults were about equal on both sides. On the march across Dutch territory to the front, there had been what Guiche airily describes as 'some little disorder', caused as he says, and no doubt truly, by the fact that the Dutch commissaries had failed to arrange either rations or billets for their visitors – 'and when one does not give a soldier anything for his subsistence, it is only fair that he should forage for himself without any punishment'. Which I take to mean that the French lived as if they were in a conquered country. Pradel,[2] the French commander, took as instant a dislike to the Dutch as they took to him, he being a stiff-necked professional soldier, with all a ranker's contempt for foreigners and military slovens, and with no hesitation in showing it. Even the French Ambassador was unable to get Pradel to adopt a less difficult attitude towards his allies; Pradel knew nothing about the Dutch, and did not want to know anything about them; he knew his duty to His Majesty. 'He never even approached the haziest notion of the structure of the Republic', says Guiche, who was now an unofficial member of his staff.

The first result of the French commander's intransigeance was that the Dutch commissaries paid less attention than ever to his requisitions, and the hungry French soldiers took matters into their own hands; seizing a bread convoy and caning the

[1] Castel-Rodrigo, Don Francesco de Moura Cortréal, Marquis de, Grandee of Spain, Councillor of State, 1641; Governor of the Spanish Netherlands, 1664. Died 1675.

[2] Pradel, François, Sieur de, 'a soldier of fortune', entered the French service in 1638, and became a Lieutenant-General, 1657. Lieutenant-Colonel of the French Guards, 1667. Died, 1690.

waggoners – 'a most respectable body of men', says Guiche – and the whole matter was reported to the Hague. Furthermore, 'the soldiers' quarters were near towns, in which they got drunk and created disorders', and fresh complaints went to the Hague until Pradel ended the scandal by hanging three or four men.

It was a futile campaign, enlivened only by the grotesque cowardice of the Field Deputies, and by a trifling siege, that of Lochem, where we notice Louvigny in command of a Dutch regiment. The Dutch army made an even worse showing than Guiche could have believed possible; on one occasion the Deputies sent four hundred horse 'to recapture the country house of one of their number'; and all went well until the attackers were fired upon from its windows, when the four hundred wheeled as one man and galloped home again. On another occasion Guiche was sent out with the Household Cavalry to support a French detachment which was in contact with the enemy, and called at a Dutch post where there were eighty men, to ask for a guide. The Dutch officer in charge unwillingly permitted him to call for a volunteer, 'but I could not find one man who thought that he had any business in a district where the enemy might be'. Food, ammunition, material, all were lacking, though Guiche admits that every now and then they received 'a strong reinforcement of Field Deputies'.

Meanwhile at home his sister Charlotte had been restored to 'Monsieur's' favour; so much so that the gossips of Paris were asserting that 'Monsieur' had at last fallen in love with a woman. For in June Madame de Monaco had been invited to St Cloud when Philippe was not entertaining, and no one but the Princess-Palatine had gone with her. The Palatine would certainly have been a broad-minded chaperone, but in fact her services were not required in that capacity.

Charlotte had had an uncomfortable year; there had been that bad business about the missing key, followed by an unpleasant quarrel with Lauzun in her own rooms, where the Comte, having abused her savagely for her conduct with the King, had underlined his indignation by reducing her dressing-mirror to smithereens; and had wound up by promising to ruin her by exposing some of her past tricks. Charlotte, who knew that Lauzun had letters of hers which would be highly damaging if they came to Louis' notice, determined to forestall him, and complained to the King about Lauzun's rudeness. Louis, who at the time was conducting an *amourette* with Charlotte, felt that for the moment he could get along very well without Lauzun's company, and ordered him off to Béarn on military inspection duty. Whereupon Lauzun, who knew perfectly well why he was being ordered south, lost his temper; he forced his way into the King's presence, refused point blank to obey, drew his sword, and, having broken it across his knee, dropped the pieces at Louis' feet. But if he had reckoned on provoking a quarrel, to be followed by a reconciliation, he had mistaken his man. No one ever succeeded in playing Louis off the stage, and all that Lauzun accomplished was to give him the opportunity for one of his finest impersonations of a great King. Strolling to the window, Louis dropped his cane out, remarking tranquilly that he would have been sorry if any provocation could have induced him to strike a man of quality. After which he sent Lauzun to the Bastille, and Madame de Monaco breathed more freely.[1]

Philibert was much in evidence about Paris this year, and his English connections had made him a prime favourite with 'Madame'. True to that 'singularity' upon which he always prided himself, he had chosen the moment when Louis XIV and Charles II were at war to become an ostentatious Anglophil; 'the Chevalier de Gramont', 'Madame' writes to Charles, 'is more English than any man in the world, and every day I wonder that he does not get into a thousand scrapes on account of it'. But in fact Philibert was taking small risk of incurring Louis' displeasure, for he had correctly estimated the lukewarmness of the King's attachment to the Dutch cause.

In August Madame de Monaco was once more the chief topic of conversation in society, to 'the great mortification' of her father; though for once Charlotte seems to have behaved

[1] St Simon, *Mémoires.*

very properly. Young Villeroi[1] had taken it into his head that he was in love with her, and had behaved with that fatuity which was to distinguish him throughout his life:

> He has been ass enough to work up a passion for Madame de Monaco... and though she has several times told him to give up these ideas, he persisted... for having the highest possible esteem for his own merit, he cannot be persuaded that any woman finds it possible to resist him; he is persuaded therefore that the King is in love with her... so he and Mme de La Baume, having talked his difficulties over, determined to send an anonymous letter to Mlle de La Vallière telling her of the King's affection for Mme de Monaco[2]...

In fact a variation on the old Spanish Letter theme; and nothing shows more clearly the strength of Louis' affection for Villeroi than that when the truth came to light he forgave him unreservedly. As far as Charlotte was concerned the result seems to have been to strengthen her position with Louis; 'the King treats her with distinction, and she is of all his pleasures'. And in December she had the unusual honour of receiving him as a guest in her own house.

In the autumn her brother Armand had also been in the news, when an exciting rumour went round Paris that he had come home in disguise and was visiting 'Madame' secretly; 'the wickedest lie in the world', says Monsieur le Duc. And so it was, for Armand did not leave Holland until the winter, and when he did, it was to visit the Elector of Brandenburg at Clèves. Early in 1666 he went back to the Hague, where he was struck by the growing pressure on the government for the restoration of the House of Orange. 'My own impression', says Guiche, 'is that they will not be able to hold Prince William down for long.'

The Bishop of Munster, who had spent his subsidy and could

[1] VILLEROI, François de Neufville, 2nd Maréchal and 2nd Duc de, 1641–1730, had been educated with Louis XIV and was the King's lifelong friend. Succeeded his father, 1685, created Maréchal, 1693. Louis' most incompetent Commander-in-Chief.

[2] *Lettres*, 1660–7.

not get another, was glad to make peace in this year, leaving the United Provinces free to concentrate on the naval struggle. The collapse of military operations dismayed Guiche, who records the event in a sentence which perfectly reflects the attitude of his race and caste towards war:

> And so, after the delightful promise of a long and great war, all we got was a prompt peace, which was primarily the *fault* of Spain; for it was only in consequence of her actions that the whole party collapsed.

In disgust at the extinction of all his hopes, Guiche relapsed into his most fantastic mood; appearing on the fashionable promenade at the Hague in the most outrageous disguises:

> The fancy took ... the Comte de Guiche ... to draw the eyes of the spectators upon him; to put which noble design into execution, he resolved that his Dress should have all the magnificence which this part of the world was able to afford, and at the same time discover the nicety of his invention. The Comte distinguish'd himself by a thousand singularities; he had a tuft of feathers in his hat, which was buckled up with diamonds ... He wore about his neck some Point de Venise which was neither a Cravat nor a band; but a small ruff, which might gratify the secret inclination he had contracted for the Golilla when he lived at Madrid. After this you would expect to find him in a doublet after the Spanish manner ... but it was a Hungarian vest. Next, the ghost of Antiquity haunted his memory, so he covered his legs with Buskins, but infinitely sprucer and genteeler than those the antient Romans used to wear; and on which he had order'd his Mistress's name to be written in letters that were extreamly well design'd upon an embroidery of pearls.[1]

But Guiche soon realized that he must turn his attention to more serious matters. 'The peace', he says, 'having ruined all my plans, I was in great uncertainty how to act; I had the idea of going to sea.' And while he was reflecting gloomily on the boors with whom he would have to associate if he did so, there seemed

[1] St Evremond, *Letters*.

a chance of seeing further service in Poland. But his hopes were disappointed; 'the King did not judge it à propos that I should pay a second visit to that country'. And Louis went on to add that if Monsieur le Comte cared to take a turn with the Dutch fleet, his doing so would be very pleasing to His Majesty; which of course left Armand no option but to become a sailor. Taking with him his brother-in-law the Prince de Monaco, who had left the French Court for reasons which will presently appear, Armand reached the fleet late in May when it was preparing to go to sea. In this alien world he showed an unwonted modesty:

> We embarked with the resolve that should guide all foreigners and volunteers, to be humble and win our host's affection... and as magnificence is rare among the Dutch, who dislike spending money, it was easy to gain the friendship of the officers and soldiers.

Armand's wish to see a naval battle was speedily gratified. At six on the morning of 1 June the Dutch fleet, with de Ruyter[1] in command, arrived at the Downs, and about nine the English under Albemarle hove in sight. The famous Four Days Battle had begun. The sea was rough, or at any rate it appeared so to Guiche, and Terlon, his Captain, told him there was no prospect of executing his promise to transfer him to the flagship in such weather; which probably meant that he was not going to waste time putting the boat over the side at a moment when he had more important matters to think of. But if Guiche was wholly ignorant of sea warfare, he at least understood fighting:

> Seeing an English ship pretty near, I begged Terlon to go for it; which he did with much pleasure, getting close alongside it... so that we were able to fire point blank at him, and even use our pistols... we stood higher in the water than he did, and were able to fire our lower deck guns whilst his were out of action, and that saved us from being entirely

[1] RUYTER, Michel Adrien de, 1607–1676, was, in the opinion of the Duke of York, 'the best sea commander of his time. His good sense was only equalled by his courage'.

> smashed up. But all the same he killed the devil of a lot of our people, broke our masts, and set us on fire ... Some sailors, entering the cabin, found our baggage burning ... and coming out half burnt, told us to give up all hope ... Some people ran to the boat, but it had been broken with cannon balls, so I went into the eyes of the ship and hailed the neighbouring Captains to send their boats ... but though I was sufficiently well-dressed to cut a prominent figure ... they refused all help.

However, as the burning ship drifted off she came alongside another Dutchman and 'the skilful boarded her, whilst the clumsy and the unlucky were crushed between the two hulls'. Guiche managed to jump, and when next he could think connectedly, he found himself on the forecastle of the stranger with his left arm jammed under the anchor cable, 'expecting every moment to feel the arm break'. When at last he managed to get free, he found himself under the orders of a harassed ranker, little disposed to investigate the niceties of Armand's social status:

> To tell the truth I was shown less consideration than the meanest sailor, being refused permission to remain on the poop with the Captain, who sent me to the lower deck to serve a gun with some five or six of my people ... and in order to be taken to the flagship on the following day, I had to bribe the fellow with two hundred ducats.

This treatment so offended Guiche that when after dark they grappled with another enemy, he remained a spectator:

> I did not put myself to any trouble; for the treatment I had received did not dispose me to show any great zeal. Also I was weaponless, and wounded in several places ... Still, had there been a trifle more courtesy, I would have made an effort.

On the morning of the 2nd he and Monaco thankfully transferred themselves to the flagship, but not until their prudent Captain had extorted from them a draft on Amsterdam for two hundred ducats for the hire of the ship's boat. Ruyter received them 'with all the kindness imaginable', and Guiche constituted himself his aide-de-camp. 'I set about following Ruyter, carrying his orders, and seeking to earn his good opinion.' All this appears to have taken place before six in the morning, when the English fleet once more came down upon them, 'marching', says Guiche, 'in as careful formation as an army'. A calm had succeeded yesterday's breeze, and the morning passed languidly; 'we were often able to relax for an hour at a stretch'. Things flared up however in the afternoon, when Guiche notices how ragged is the Dutch line of battle compared with the English – There is nothing to equal the good order and discipline of the English navy', he says. Ruyter's own ship lost a mast towards the close of the engagement, and was otherwise so badly damaged that for a moment he considered transferring his flag. But the damage cannot have been as serious as Guiche thought, for dawn of the 3rd found Ruyter still on board, sailing through a sea 'sown with barrels, gear, and the debris of a burnt English ship'. It was a day of indecisive ship-to-ship engagements, culminating so far as Guiche was concerned in the surrender to Ruyter of one of the enemy Admirals whose ship was hard aground. Night falling soon after, and the last thing seen by the Dutch being the junction of Albemarle's and Prince Rupert's fleets, the Dutch drew off.

The cold morning of the 4th began a day of confused and savage fighting, indecisive as had been the previous three; and from Guiche, who was in the thick of it, we naturally get only glimpses of what happened. The English, he says, were uncommonly lucky in that the Dutch fireships were so badly handled; and he had time to notice the astonishing way in which the English squadrons rallied and returned to the attack 'with the same degree of order and discipline as if they had not fought at all'. And further, as the afternoon lengthened, he was vividly aware that the Dutch morale was weakening. Gradually the two fleets fell apart, and Ruyter, satisfied that the battle was over, went below to sweep out his cabin and feed his hens.

At dawn on the 5th the Dutch anchored in their home port, and Guiche, who had seen enough of the sea and sailors, went ashore at once:

> I admit that when I considered those for whom I had been risking my life so freely... my reflections gave me a lively wish to be quit of them. I took a boat and came ashore in Holland, stripped of all I possessed.

De Witt, the Dutch Dictator, was one of the first to visit the flagship, and on board it he wrote the exuberant despatch in which he claimed a great Dutch victory. Or as Guiche puts it, 'He killed six thousand English with his pen, and with his candle burnt twenty English ships which were lying at anchor in the Thames':

> And therefore I wrote to the Duc de Gramont that if it was to the King's interest to assume that the despatch was true, I would say nothing to the contrary; but that if the States tried to tempt him into some action based on their version of the damage done to England, he could assure His Majesty that in fact the damage was slight... The King said that they must accept the Comte de Guiche's version.

De Witt acted as Armand had foreseen; Louis politely declined to be drawn into any military gamble; and De Witt found himself reduced to 'taking London two or three times a day with the armies of His Majesty'.

Guiche himself was left with a very clear impression of the relative naval strengths of the two countries:

> For my part, that which I saw of the two nations persuaded me that, except where there was an entire inequality of forces, a Dutch fleet cannot save itself against an English one.

Louis XIV, under treaty to aid the Dutch at sea, could not postpone the sailing of his squadron indefinitely, and when the Dutch were beaten at Southwold Bay on 4 August, he decided that he must aid them; but even then he declined to order out his ships until he had emerged triumphant from an acrimonious dispute with De Witt on the subject of salutes.

Ultimately Beaufort was appointed to command the French

squadron, and Bellefonds,[1] who, by the way, had been a soldier all his life, was sent to the Hague to arrange details of the junction of the two fleets. The plan was such as one might have expected from the deliberations of a soldier and a civilian. In Guiche's words, 'it was decided that the two fleets, in order to unite, must sail in opposite directions on the same wind'. Not content with sending Bellefonds to see De Witt, Louis sent La Feuillade,[2] another landsman, to give Ruyter the benefit of his advice. Ruyter, a stolid, humourless professional sailor, was rendered speechless by the supple, voluble landsman, who answered his criticisms with the comforting assurance that 'the King's fleet would proceed against both tide and wind; M. de Beaufort had received His Majesty's orders to that effect'.

[1] Bellefonds, Bernardin Gigault, 1st Marquis and Maréchal de, 1630–1694, made his fortune by showing attention to Louis XIV when Mazarin was King; Louis never forgot it, and Bellefonds remained one of his favourites to the end of his life.

[2] Feuillade, Louis d'Aubusson, 4th Comte and 1st Duc de La, 1623–1691, head of a House which was noble before A.D. 887.

CHAPTER XI

★

GUICHE in the meantime remained unemployed, and it looked as if he was to continue at leisure indefinitely, for there was no sign of the King relenting. He had moved from Clèves to Aix, a spa of repute, whose waters had been recommended to him for his old wound in the hand, and there he was visited by gleams of hope; the Swedes were attacking Bremen, and surely, thought Guiche, he could make a place for himself with either the attacking or defending forces. But alas, in October Louis refused his consent; 'I had the routine answer that as the King wished to remain neutral, he could not permit me to take sides'. As nothing better offered, Guiche then asked permission to make a tour of the Low Countries (i.e. the Spanish Netherlands) to see its finest cities; which being granted, and Castel-Rodrigo having endorsed his passport, he arrived in due course at Brussels. There he was cheered up, not only by 'very good company in agreeable suroundings', but also by a letter from his father warning him that France would declare war on Spain in 1667, and that there were great hopes of his recall.

A stupider man than Guiche would not have found it difficult to foresee that the Netherlands could offer no serious resistance to Louis XIV; for the Spanish Empire was visibly dying, and everywhere Armand could see the unmistakable signs; unpaid garrisons, mouldering fortifications, empty magazines, and a bankrupt administration. Evils which had been aggravated by the conduct of Caracena,[1] the late Governor:

> He had always treated the Low Countries as if it was a house which he was leaving without any intention of ever reoccupying it; he had removed everything down to the padlock and key.

[1] CARACENA, Don Luis de Benavides Carillo y Toledo, Marquis de, Governor of Milan, 1648, and then of the Netherlands until 1664; defeated by the Portuguese at Villa-Viciosa, 1665, died 1668.

Castel-Rodrigo was a very different type; brave, proud, arrogant, and honest, sternly refusing bribes, determined to do his best in the position in which he found himself. But by the time he took over the government, the whole rotten fabric was on the point of collapse, and there was little he could do to prepare for the coming storm. Though to Armand he was civil, and even friendly, he disliked Frenchmen and did what he could to eliminate French influence throughout his government:

> He forbade the wearing of clothes and fashions in vogue at our Court, and wished Brussels to take Madrid as its model; but as these cities are not further apart in distance than their inhabitants are in their humours, he found it impossible to make an instant change in the Low Country way of life.

Towards the end of the year Guiche, who had used his eyes during his tour, reported to his father in Paris that 'without any doubt the Spaniards were on the point of losing the Netherlands, for Fortune had apparently blinded their Ministers to the signs of coming trouble which were sufficiently obvious to everyone'.

At Paris on the last day of April the Maréchal de Gramont had the honour of entertaining Louis XIV to dinner; and let us hope that he drew much comfort from this striking evidence of high favour. For he was to have little further cause for self-congratulation during the year. Not only were his two sons in exile, but in addition Madame de Monaco was in May the heroine of a much discussed affair, the portentous business of Monsieur de Lauzun's heel.

When last we heard of Lauzun he was on his way to the Bastille, and there he remained for three months, a prey to fury, despair, and hatred of Charlotte de Monaco. In December 1665 he had won his liberty by dint of abject flattery; and now to all appearances he was as firmly established in Louis' favour as ever. But his anger against Charlotte was still hot, and he was determined on revenge; which he took in a form so puerile and so caddish to modern eyes, that we are suddenly reminded of how distant from us and how alien is this world of three hundred years ago.

In mid-May there was gambling going on in the salon at Versailles, and for coolness' sake many of the ladies were sitting on a plank on the floor; and the best description of what then happened is that of Louis XIV himself, in a letter to his Ambassador at the Hague:

> I was standing watching the game... I went back two paces to see better, and those who were between me and the wall were obliged to move, among them Lauzun, who leaving his place hastily to give me room, unfortunately trod by mistake on Mme de Monaco's hand... which was covered by her skirt so that it was impossible to see it... The said Princess began to cry, threw down the book which she was reading, and ran out into the anteroom... where we could not calm her, nor make her believe that it had been an accident... Lauzun... did everything to show his despair at what had happened... Meanwhile the Maréchal de Gramont was informed... and became very angry, declaring that on certain occasions honour obliged a man to revenge himself at any cost. I spoke to them all... to try to make them hear reason... and it seemed to me that the Maréchal had become more tranquil... but I have just heard that contrary to my hopes, the Prince de Monaco has been advised... to go to the Hague to consult MM. de Guiche and de Louvigny... (so as) not to let the affront go unpunished... Never has advice been more foolish.[1]

And the letter concludes by charging the Ambassador to warn the two younger Gramonts and Monaco not to be drawn into any rash attempts to revenge an imaginary wrong.

'Monsieur le Duc's' version of the affair suggests that either he was misinformed or else that Louis had completely misunderstood the cause of the Maréchal's anger:

> M. le Maréchal de Gramont... went off to Paris in a fury against his daughter for having said that Lauzun had trodden deliberately on her hand, and is greatly embarrassed as to how he is to get out of the business; he has acted stupidly in making a thousand speeches against her, and in saying publicly that

[1] Louis XIV, *Oeuvres*.

> he will shut her up in a convent. And whilst in this temper he sent M. de Monaco off post haste to the Hague to see Guiche and Louvigny.[1]

Not as in the Louis XIV version that the family might debate jointly on a suitable form of revenge, but to reinforce the King's order that the exiles were not to move in the matter. But in such a trifling affair this discrepancy is itself a trifle, for we know the truth, which was not known to either Louis or to the Maréchal. Lauzun's act was, on his own boast, deliberate; and he was delighted with his 'revenge'.

The noise of this storm in a teacup died away slowly, but the incident conferred an unfortunate publicity upon Charlotte; so much so that when a friend of hers, Cavoye,[2] quarrelled with Lauzun in July, the comment is that 'the most annoying aspect of the affair is that it has restarted all kinds of scandal about Mme de Monaco, and it is a great misfortune for a woman of her quality to be mixed up so often in these sorts of businesses'.[3]

Louvigny, not banished but merely advised to pay a visit to Holland, obtained permission to return to Court early in 1667. And almost at once found himself involved in a disagreeable quarrel forced upon him by his sister Charlotte. At a masked ball in Paris in January, 'M. de Rohan[4] and M. de Louvigny had a quarrel, because the former had for a long time past been letting himself go with great freedom about Mme de Monaco, and Louvigny thought it his duty to resent Rohan's talk. M. de Rohan received him politely, and indeed promised not to speak

[1] *Lettres*, 1660–7.

[2] CAVOYE, Louis d'Oger, 1st Marquis de, 1640–1716, after a stormy youth, won Louis XIV's affection by his bravery at Tolhuis, 1672; Quarter-Master General of France, 1688. 'A man of great merit, with many friends, who was treated with consideration by everybody.'

[3] *Lettres*, 1660–7.

[4] ROHAN, Louis, Chevalier de, 1635-1674, son of the Duc de Montbazon. In 1669 he incurred suspicion by selling his office of Grand Huntsman and investing the proceeds of the sale in Holland. In 1673, in debt, discredited, and cast off by his family, he entered into a plot to admit the Dutch into Normandy. He was arrested in 1674, and beheaded on November 26 of the same year.

of Mme de Monaco in future; but so malicious is our world that someone must needs inform Louvigny that Rohan was broadcasting it in society that M. de Louvigny almost died of fright when Rohan spoke to him; Louvigny then wanted a second explanation . . . but Rohan, who was tired of the subject, merely replied that he would meet M. de Louvigny sword in hand on the following day; they agreed upon this, but as the quarrel had taken place in a gallery where numerous people were coming and going, it was seen that the matter was serious . . . and the rencontre was stopped. Poor Maréchal de Gramont, he is much to be pitied, for his children certainly give him plenty of trouble'.[1]

One hopes that it was Charlotte who bore the brunt of her father's anger; but if Louvigny came in for a share of it, he had the consolation of knowing that society approved of his behaviour; 'M. de Louvigny has conducted himself very well', writes Condé on 3 February.

One would have thought that Fate, having saddled the Maréchal with such children, might have rested content with her work. But there was also trouble brewing at the Palais-Royal, where the Maréchal's sister, Mme de St Chaumont, was Governess to 'Monsieur's' children; and she we may remember, rather fancied herself as a politician. Of all the disgusting crew that surrounded 'Monsieur' there was none viler than the Chevalier de Lorraine; his mere presence in her husband's house was an insult to Henrietta. And Lorraine, absolutely secure in his hold over 'Monsieur', treated 'Madame' with an open insolence which drove her to the point of frenzy. A wise confidante would have laboured to convince her mistress that what cannot be cured must be endured, but not so Madame de St Chaumont, who on the contrary was doing her best to goad Henrietta into violent action against Lorraine. Gramont, powerless to intervene, awaited the inevitable explosion with dread.

We can well understand that the Maréchal 'showed extreme joy' when at this very unsatisfactory juncture in Gramont history Louis made his steady brother Toulongeon King's Lieutenant of Béarn. The news must also have done something

[1] *Lettres*, 1660–7.

to offset his annoyance at Madame de Monaco's latest piece of ingenuity. Her husband had recently returned from Holland, and backed by the whole Gramont clan, had asserted his marital authority; Madame de Monaco was ordered to accompany her husband on a long visit to Monaco, and they were to set out at once. But Charlotte knew a trick worth two of that. Even the uninformed now realized that it would be only a matter of days before Louis XIV attacked the Netherlands; and Charlotte pointed out to her husband that she was prepared to forego her return to their beloved Principality in order that Monaco might win for himself on the plains of Flanders that military glory for which she was convinced he was destined; she for her part would await him at Court, under the care of 'Madame'. Her barrel of a husband swallowed the bait, and Charlotte laughed at her father's helpless indignation. And to add to Antoine's troubles, Louis was adamant about Guiche:

> The Maréchal de Gramont fell on his knees to the King and implored him to permit the return of the Comte de Guiche, who would cleanse himself of his offences by carrying a musket in the ranks. The King . . . charged Le Tellier to tell the Maréchal that it was useless for him to speak to him of his son, for as long as he was King of France, Guiche would not return.[1]

On 24 May Louis, at the head of a magnificent army, crossed the Spanish frontier into the Netherlands and the War of Devolution had begun. A war which was of course brilliantly successful, and lasted for a bare two months, but was on the long-term view disastrous to France; for there was just enough opposition to lend a spice of danger to what was really a military promenade, and Louis XIV emerged from a war which it would have been impossible for him to lose, with a conviction that he was not only a King but a General; a delusion which was to bring him within an ace of losing his Crown in years to come.

For Antoine Louis always had a soft spot in his heart; and if he was determined not to pardon Armand, he would at least let the old Maréchal see that his own standing was unaffected

[1] Gramont, *Mémoires*.

by the crimes of his son. So he took Gramont to the war with him. For this favour Antoine was proportionately grateful, and we can feel his exuberance when he records the operations at Douai; where, with his usual astuteness, he had elected to serve not as a Marshal but as Colonel of the French Guards:

> He could now offer the spectacle of a Marshal of France, in his eagerness for the good of his master's service, appearing as a simple Colonel, taking his orders from General Officers whom he had seen wearing bibs, and who had been his aides-de-camp when he was commanding armies with the great Condé.[1]

It was an admirable *tour de Gascon*, and the delicate flattery was fully appreciated by the King. Actually of course Antoine was only too pleased to have a good excuse for serving in the unexacting role of Colonel, where nothing was expected of him but a display of that physical courage in which he had never been lacking. It was nearly twenty years since he had carried his bâton at Lens, and those years had taken their toll of the man in whom there had always been a self-indulgent streak; wine, women, and good cheer had softened his moral fibre and induced a lethargy which unfitted him for high command; and he knew it.

But even the pleasure of taking the field under the King could not dispel Antoine's grief at the position of his House; he was getting old, and what was to become of the Gramonts if he died with his son unforgiven and in exile? He had seen that tragedy happen too often not to know that the whole family would be relegated to the twilight of semi-disgrace. No wonder he was down at heart; 'The Maréchal de Gramont', writes St Maurice, 'has withdrawn to his government in the sulks'. Perhaps the King missed him, perhaps he was genuinely distressed at his old friend's sorrow; at any rate he did him a favour which was not only striking in itself, but so far as I can remember, unique. He, who prided himself on the fact that his decisions once made were irrevocable, decided to recall Guiche; and a courier left for Holland with orders for Armand to pro-

[1] Gramont, *Mémoires*.

ceed to Bayonne and stay there during His Majesty's pleasure. And whilst Louis was about it, he decided to round off the transaction handsomely by appointing the Comtesse de Guiche a Lady of the Palace to the Queen. Guiche however cannot have regarded his position as greatly improved; what he wanted was an invitation to reassume his place at Court. And from this he was as far away as ever; indeed Bayonne was further from Paris than was the Hague, and Gascony was a backwater; whereas in Holland he had at least frequently met Courtiers fresh from Versailles and primed with the latest gossip.

Any chance that Armand might have had of returning to Court was extinguished when 'Monsieur' came home from the front to learn that whilst he had been wreathing himself with laurels in the Netherlands, that terrible Guiche had been visiting 'Madame' surreptitiously at St Cloud. This was of course untrue, but it served the purpose of detaining Armand at Bayonne, the prisoner of his own bygone audacities. The relations between father and son while they were together in the south cannot have been agreeable; for Guiche, in addition to his numerous faults, had committed the unpardonable crime of throwing away a valuable piece of family property. Louis, as the price of his recall, had exacted from him the surrender of his patent to inherit the French Guards; and the Maréchal would have been more than human if he had not recapitulated the tale of Armand's misdoings and pointed the moral, with irritating frequency. One wonders why Gramont did not try to get the inheritance transferred to the younger brother, and we can sympathize with Louvigny's annoyance. 'My brother', he says, 'would not agree to my having it, and so my father sold it.'

In February 1668 Louis XIV helped himself to another slice of the Spanish cake; in mid-winter he fell upon the almost defenceless territory of Franche-Comté, 'in pursuance of his just claims'. It was a trifling operation which Philibert de Gramont brought perilously near to the ridiculous by offering to take Dôle, the capital, single-handed; and by succeeding without drawing his sword. The town was held only by the city militia, who allowed Philibert to approach the gates unchallenged; and by the time instructions reached the guard to order him away, it was too late; Philibert was already on the best of terms with the citizen soldiers, laughing, joking, behaving as if there was not a war within a hundred miles. At the gate he remained for four hours until the magistrates decided that the only way to get rid of him was to have him into the Town Hall and hear his business. Once before the city fathers, Philibert adroitly seized the initiative; he had not of course seen one of them before in his life, but that did not hinder him from embracing each of them most affectionately. And before they had recovered from the warmth of his greeting, Philibert had begun his speech. He had come, he said, to offer his best services to extricate them from the embarrassing position in which they found themselves. Were they going to offend the kindest King in Christendom in order that the glories of Dôle should pass to her impudent rival, Besançon? He felt sure that their answer would be, no. And what of the impossibility of the officers restraining the soldiery in the first flush of victory? Would they be guilty of the crime of sentencing their wives and daughters to death by rape? Of course not. 'And yourselves?' concluded Philibert with tears in his eyes; 'Oh, gentlemen, gentlemen, what a disagreeable operation it is to be put to the sword!' An hour later the Comte de Gramont was back at French headquarters with Dôle's surrender in his pocket.[1]

Louvigny, who had about him a good deal of his uncle Philibert, married this year under circumstances which recalled the Chevalier's matrimonial adventure of 1663. For Louvigny, like Philibert, 'had carried gallantry a little too far', and he also encountered a brother who was not inclined to put up with any nonsense.[2] We cannot suppose that the marriage increased Gramont's satisfaction with his younger son, for Marie de Castelnau[3] was no great catch, even for a cadet of the Gramonts; nor was Antoine in the best of humours, for he had just been notified that the King 'hoped' he would sell him the Hôtel de Gramont for demolition, in order that the Louvre might be

[1] Hamilton, *Memoirs*.

[2] St Simon, *Mémoires*.

[3] Louvigny, Marie Charlotte de Castelnau, Comtesse de, *ob.* 1694, only daughter of the Maréchal de Castelnau; a celebrated beauty.

enlarged. However, Madame de Monaco was even now on her way south to rejoin her husband, which was something; but Antoine's relief at her departure was short-lived, for in 1669 she was back again in the capital, drawing attention to herself by the fervour of her welcome to the twenty-year-old Duke of Monmouth.

1669 saw an important change in the orientation of the Court. For some time past it had been obvious that Louis' passion for La Vallière was cooling, and the star of Madame de Montespan[1] was in the ascendant; and by the end of the year it was an open secret that she had become the royal mistress. When, too late, La Vallière realized her helplessness and isolation, she was naïve enough to unburden her heart to Gramont. But Antoine knew, if she did not, that a dead flame cannot be rekindled, and moreover he was the last man in France to support a falling cause. To her plaints he merely replied, 'Ah, Madame, while you had cause for laughter you should have made others laugh with you if, when the time came for tears, you wished others to weep for you'.[2]

This year saw the explosion in 'Monsieur's' household which destroyed Madame de St Chaumont. In exacerbating 'Madame's' resentment against the Chevalier de Lorraine she had a powerful ally in 'Monsieur's' ex-Almoner, the Bishop of Valence,[3] an ambitious Gascon who became 'Madame's' champion in her unending quarrels with her husband. And to Henrietta he had rendered important services, notably in buying up and destroying the whole edition of a Dutch libel, *Les Amours de Madame et du Comte de Guiche*. But services rendered to 'Madame' were not calculated to advance the Bishop with 'Monsieur', and their relations rapidly worsened until a day came when Monsieur de Valence told his master, with complete and morti-

[1] MONTESPAN, Françoise Athénais de Rochechouart-Mortemart, Marquise de, 1641–1707, Louis' mistress from 1670 to 1678; she bore him numerous children, of whom two boys and two girls survived childhood.

[2] Lair, *La Valliere.*

[3] AIX, Daniel de Cosnac, Archbishop of, 1630–1707, Bishop of Valence, 1655, Almoner to 'Monsieur', 1660. 'Madame's' confidential adviser, 1661–7. Archbishop of Aix, 1687. 'No man was ever so fitted for intrigue.'

fying frankness, what he thought of his useless and vicious existence. 'Monsieur' promptly dismissed him. Henrietta, horrified, urged the Bishop to remain in the hope that Philippe would calm down. 'Oh, come, Madame,' protested Valence, 'a Bishop should walk out by the door, not wait to be thrown out of the window'; and he left. But to 'Monsieur's' indignation he not only refused to quit Paris, but continued to appear in society just as if he had not been 'disgraced' by a Son of France. 'Monsieur' then sent a gentleman to him with orders to retire to his diocese; and the messenger brought back, all unsweetened, the Bishop's dry comment that he had not heard that the power of inflicting banishment had been delegated to 'Monsieur'. But Cosnac had gone too far; the King heard of this strange lack of respect to his brother and exiled the Bishop to Valence, from where he maintained a confidential correspondence with Henrietta. In 1669 Charles II was busily engaged in trying to sell his *Grand Design,* the restoration of Roman Catholicism in England, to Louis XIV, and 'Madame' was the intermediary through whose hands passed the dangerous correspondence between the two kings. And she had communicated a good deal, if not the whole, of the secret to Cosnac. Louis and Charles had already arranged that the finishing touches to their treaty should be supplied by 'Madame' in person during a visit to England in the near future; and 'Madame' who, unlike her brother, was sincere in her wish to see the religious articles of the treaty executed, thought that if she could take Cosnac to England with her, he would be just the man to act as her liaison officer with the English Catholics. She insisted to Cosnac that at all costs she must have a conversation with him on this vitally important matter, even if it meant disobeying the King. Cosnac, who saw his danger very clearly, protested, was overruled, and late in November arrived in Paris, disguised, and loaded with memoranda. He had, he hoped, made himself tolerably secure, for not only was he lodged at an out-of-the-way tavern, but before leaving Valence he had furnished himself with an alibi by getting the King's permission to go to Limousin on urgent private affairs – 'I cannot say what a distaste I had for the whole idea of this journey, nor how often I represented to 'Madame' and Madame de St Chaumont the risks I ran . . .' His forebodings were justified; someone betrayed him, and whilst he lay in bed on his first morning in Paris, a police officer entered, saying, 'Ah, rascally coiner, you will make no more false money; get up and follow me'. Cosnac protested that so far from being a coiner, he was a Bishop; but the policeman laughed at him. And Cosnac, racking his brains for some method of concealing at least the most damning of his papers, was saved by a miracle. In his consternation he had forgotten that on the previous night he had ordered an enema for the following morning, and here in the nick of time was the apothecary entering his bedroom. The policeman raised no objection to the man's ministrations; and in a few minutes, after some skilful sleight of hand on Cosnac's part, the most dangerous of the papers left the room in the Bishop's commode. After which Cosnac spent a very uncomfortable twenty-four hours in a dirty lock-up, and was then released with profound apologies for the 'mistake' of his arrest; and was ordered to return at once to Valence.[1]

But though the most damaging documents were out of the King's reach, enough remained to give him a pretty clear idea of what had been going on, and also of the part played by Madame de St Chaumont in the domestic politics of the Palais-Royal. Her banishment was decided upon, but Gramont got wind of what was coming, was perhaps given a strong hint by Louis XIV himself. At any rate Antoine was in time to order his sister to hand in her resignation, which she did, much to the annoyance of 'Monsieur', who had looked forward with spiteful glee to the pleasure of dismissing his wife's favourite companion. 'But you have forestalled me', he cried with naïf anger when Madame de St Chaumont requested permission to retire. But though the governess had saved herself from dismissal, she was in deep disgrace, and Louis curtly refused her permission to reside in a Paris convent. There was a strong suspicion that Guiche had had a finger in the pie, and though that suspicion was unfounded, it was regrettable, for it directed Louis' attention to Armand and his extravagances at a time when Antoine had hoped that his son's shortcomings were being forgotten. It

[1] Choisy, *Mémoires*.

was sorry news for the exile, yawning his head off down in Gascony.

During the summer Philibert and his wife paid one of their frequent visits to England, where they were as popular as ever; 'The Comtesse de Gramont', writes Charles to Minette, 'is as good a creature as ever lived'. A view not fully endorsed by French society when Elizabeth was in one of her more arrogant moods:

> The Comtesse de Gramont is an Englishwoman who carries her head high because she claims to be related to the King of England; but this is laughed at here; it causes her to do many things with an ill grace; the other day the Queen was going out in her carriage, when this lady got in too; the Queen told her to enter the second carriage; she replied boldly that she was not of such a condition as to travel in the second carriage, and the Queen had not a word to say.[1]

On 26 May 1670 Charles II took Henrietta into his arms on board the English Flagship in Dover harbour, which was for 'Madame' the prelude to the only three weeks of unalloyed happiness which she had ever known, a happiness now increased by the recollection of all the difficulties which had stood in the way of its attainment. For 'Monsieur' had done his utmost to prevent the visit from taking place. Philibert de Gramont may have travelled in her suite, for he is mentioned as being in England this June, charged with a semi-official mission to Charles on some details connected with the sale of Dunkirk. At the English Court he seems to have been an even more welcome visitor than usual, for Charles, 'out of the kindness and partiality' which he entertained for him, wished to present him with a jewel. This was of course very gratifying, but what Philibert wanted was not jewellery but cash; and to pawn the royal gift immediately after his return home would not create a very good impression when the news leaked out – as it certainly would. And furthermore, Charles had not hinted at the value of the jewel. With a dexterity which both men must have enjoyed, Philibert managed to insinuate that he was too humble a person

[1] Sévigné, *Lettres*.

to receive such an extravagant mark of the royal favour, and that in dealing with a person of Philibert's sort His Majesty would better maintain the distance between them if instead of the jewel he gave him the three hundred pounds or whatever it was, in the form of a draft on Paris. He got his money, for Charles, who loved the rogue, was in high good humour and could afford to be generous; for the money was Louis XIV's, not Charles's. On 12 June 'Madame' returned from England, gay, triumphant, 'lovely as an angel', and much in favour with the King. She had another eighteen days to live.[1]

At half-past five on Sunday afternoon, 29 June, she took a glass of chicory water, and immediately after swallowing it, cried out with pain, turned white, and almost fainted. Her terrified women sent for the doctor, who laughed at their fears, saying that it was only a touch of colic; while Henrietta, writhing in agony, made the historic remark about poisoning which created a sensation that has lasted down to our own times. So let us be clear as to what she did actually say. As generally quoted, she said to Gramont when near her end, 'I think I have been poisoned', whereas what she really said was, 'I think I have been poisoned *accidentally*'. Which is not at all the same thing. And the whole sensational story of her having been murdered by 'Monsieur's' horrible favourites is probably without foundation; the modern diagnosis is that she died of acute peritonitis. She died at half-past two on the morning of Monday, 30 June, nine hours after she had been taken ill, aged twenty-six.

Sorrow was a short-lived emotion at the Court of France; Louis' was sincere, but within twenty-four hours he was saying to 'Mademoiselle', 'My cousin, here is a place vacant at my Court; would you care to fill it?' 'Monsieur' had certainly shed tears, but when his wife was obviously dying and had asked for a confessor, he had replied, 'We must think of someone whose name will look well in the *Gazette*'. To Charles II, however, her death was a lasting sorrow, and there was real grief amongst the ladies of the dead Princess's household; Madame de St Chaumont for instance 'never recovered from her pain at

[1] Lafayette, *Mémoires*.

parting with her beloved mistress and her children, and after "Madame's" death she took the veil and became a Carmelite nun'.[1]

And Armand de Guiche, still mouldering in Gascony, what were his feelings when the news filtered down into the provinces? He does not tell us.

With fear, gloom, and hatred the states bordering on France watched that country's feverish military activity in 1671. Louvois[2] was now at full stretch, working day and night to perfect the great war machine which he had built, ruthlessly sweeping aside the last of its anachronisms and abuses. Amongst others the *roulement*, the absurd system whereby when two or more Marshals found themselves serving in the same army, they exercised the supreme command in turn, each taking a day. Louvois' much discussed order that the senior Marshal should be permanently in command, seems to us the merest common-sense, but to Louis' generals it appeared nothing less than a revolution, and it provoked a mutiny. Several Marshals refused point blank to obey the new regulation, and had to be retired before the remainder could be induced to give their written assurance of obedience. We need hardly say which side Gramont took in the fracas; he was among the first to offer Louis an unconditional acceptance of the new rule, which gratified the King at no expense to Antoine. For he knew quite well that there was no possibility of his ever again being called upon to serve as a Marshal of France.

In May Philibert was entrusted with some trivial mission of compliment to Charles II, and that he once again had a distinguished reception is evident from the fact that on the 25th Charles sent him back to France in the royal yacht. At Versailles Philibert, by his wit and his calculated insolence, managed this year as always to keep himself prominently before the eyes of his circle; though probably his latest exploit amused the King

[1] St Simon, *Mémoires.*

[2] LOUVOIS, Francois Michel Le Tellier, Marquis de, 1641–1691, son of the War Minister, Michel Le Tellier; encouraged Louis in his policy of calculated aggression, and was responsible for some of the worst crimes of the reign.

less than it did the Courtiers. There was in these days at Versailles a certain Langlée, of obscure birth and mysterious wealth, a specimen of a type which became increasingly common at Court towards the close of the reign; a great gambler, often admitted to the King's own card table, for Louis was not particular in his choice of gambling companions. One evening this worthy had the impudence to clap Philibert on the back as he was playing, a feat which earned him – and the King – a stinging rebuke: 'Langlée, be so good as to reserve that sort of familiarity for when you play with His Majesty'.

The Maréchal de Gramont, sick and worried, is little in evidence this year; cheered no doubt in his illness by the signal honour of a visit from the King, but harassed by the troublesome business of the inheritance of the Guards, about which Louvigny was still very bitter. And in November he was angered when the downfall of Lauzun focused public attention on Madame de Monaco's levity and indiscretion.

De l'audace et encore de l'audace was Lauzun's chosen motto, and it had served him well; up to a point. But his head had been turned by the King's favour, and he had thought that nothing would be forbidden him. When he should have been silent he had boasted, and he had sulked when he should have been complaisant. Also he had two very powerful enemies, Louvois and Madame de Montespan, who, working hand in hand, brought about his ruin, carefully reporting to the King all of Lauzun's frequent and tactless criticisms of Louis himself. The King became convinced that his erstwhile favourite was ungrateful, disobedient, and a menace not only to his domestic peace, but in matters of high policy; for was there not a suspicion strong enough to amount to certainty that he had recently married 'Mademoiselle' secretly, in defiance of the King's express prohibition? On 25 November he was arrested, taken to to the Bastille, and two days later was transferred to the fortress of Pignerol, where he was to spend the next ten years in strict confinement.[1]

His arrest was followed by the usual seizure of all the prisoner's effects and papers; which were found to include

[1] Montpensier, *Mémoires*.

many of Madame de Monaco's letters, and, even more piquant discovery, several portraits of her, all with the eyes gouged out. By somebody's indiscretion these facts soon became public property; possibly by a calculated indiscretion of the King's, for Louis was naturally horrified at the discovery that the woman to whom he had deigned to throw the Royal handkerchief was the mistress of one of his own Courtiers. Charlotte was news again, and the family did not thank her for it.

CHAPTER XII

★

EXCEPT for anxiety about his family, Gramont's position in 1672 was an enviable one. Not too old to enjoy his favour with the King, yet old enough to win indulgence on the score of his age, he was one to whom all liberties were permitted. Even his breaches of decorum drew smiles from Louis instead of the frowns which would have been bestowed upon lesser mortals:

> Maréchal de Gramont was so carried away the other day by Bourdaloue's sermon that he shouted at the top of his voice, 'Sdeath he's right!' 'Madame'[1] exploded with laughter, and the sermon was so interrupted that no one quite knew what was going to happen.[2]

An amusing illustration of the eternal boy in Antoine? Or the veteran character actor adroitly forcing an easy round of applause? The older Gramont became, the more Gascon he grew. He had never wavered in his conviction that to be a Gascon of the Gascons was the role which he could play most effectively, and he was now saving money by trading on that reputation for thrift which made his countrymen a standing joke. About this time Louis honoured him by sending his band to play outside the Maréchal's lodgings in the early morning. An expensive compliment for most people, but not for Antoine. Thrusting his head out of the window he asked what the strength of the band was; 'Monseigneur, we are twenty-four', replied the leader hopefully. 'Well, gentlemen,' said Gramont, 'divide a thousand thanks between you'; and then shut his window with a bang.[3]

Charlotte had apparently reached the conclusion that it was

[1] ORLEANS, Elizabeth Charlotte of Bavaria, Duchesse d', 1652–1722, daughter of the Elector-Palatine, married 'Monsieur', 1671.

[2] Sévigné, *Lettres*.

[3] Tallemant des Reaux, *Historiettes*.

wise to disappear until the Lauzun scandal died down; and was now living in Monaco and disliking it intensely. But her trial was to be a brief one, for in July she wormed her way back to Paris.

On 6 April France declared war on the United Provinces, and on the 23rd Louis left for the front.

It was, for a variety of reasons, his most popular war, and he had the whole country behind him. King, Church, *noblesse*, diplomacy, and big business were enthusiastically committed to the destruction of Holland; and as the state of the Dutch army was well known to the French War Office, all were confident that one summer's work would reduce these impudent cheesemongers to their proper place in the new Europe, namely that of unimportant satellites of France.

To Antoine the great fact was that Guiche was to be allowed to serve; he was to have the one chance of rehabilitation open to a French gentleman. The Maréchal, and for that matter Armand, would not have cared if the war had been against all Europe and had meant the ruin of France.

Dutch strategy and tactics proved even worse than the invaders had anticipated, for the Field Deputies, leaving the Rhine short of men and munitions, and the strong places in disrepair, had crammed most of their available strength into Maastricht. The first task which fell to Guiche was to support Condé in the capture of Wesel, a farcical operation in which the attackers lost one man, though the French had 'neither powder, lead, or artillery'; but then the key position of the defence 'had on it nothing but some handsome trees, and a few seats on which to smoke a pipe'. This happened on 1 June, but there was more serious business ahead; on the 10th the army was in sight of the Rhine; and the problem was how to force a passage. At the outset Louis tended to make heavy weather of the task, whilst Condé thought the operation a simple one. But as the situation clarified it was the King who urged a dashing manœuvre and Condé who preached caution.

Operations began on the 12th with an attempt by Condé to throw his right flank cavalry across the river, but this failed somewhat ignominiously, and 'Monsieur Le Prince' informed the King that the ford was impracticable. 'Well,' said Louis, 'but I am assured that there is a ford on the left flank, opposite the Toll-house.' This was all very well for Louis, who did not propose to cross with the first wave of the attack, but Condé was less enthusiastic:

> 'M. Le Prince' replied that he had heard of this ford, but that on the far bank it emerged at the foot of a strong tower, and that it was not a crossing which he himself would choose. It struck me [Guiche] that he was tired of having to counter impracticable proposals made to the King, and thought that, having no materials with which to build a bridge, an engagement at the Toll-house would merely advertise to the enemy the French intention to cross the river.[1]

At this point Guiche, who had all to gain and nothing to lose but his life, intervened in the discussion:

> I now offered to reconnoitre the ford of which they were speaking. I was given a faint-hearted guide whom it was necessary to refresh with brandy at frequent intervals. When I got to the place I rode into the water with some of my people, noting carefully where we had to ride in, and where come out on the other bank. The entry was capable of taking eight to ten men abreast, and the other side was flat, offering sufficient ground to form up a squadron . . . Going back to hunt for 'M. Le Prince', I found the King himself, and I promised him that we would most certainly either cross or perish in the attempt. The King . . . seemed very pleased at my offer . . . and the Courtiers smiled and whispered in each other's ears.[2]

But Condé merely grunted, 'Well, let us go and look at this ford of yours'. And after seeing it he liked the idea less than ever; 'This is a job for Polish or Tartar cavalry,' he said, 'and while you and a few of your officers may do all right, your men will either be drowned or else cut in pieces as soon as they land'. But Guiche refused to be discouraged, and ultimately

[1] Guiche, *Mémoires*.
[2] *Ibid.*

extorted from Condé a half-hearted blessing on the enterprise; and the famous crossing began, Guiche being the first into the water. The next half-hour gave him all the excitement which even he required:

> The enemy right flank did its duty well, and even came out as far as where I was still swimming; with the result that Pilois' horse, startled by the firing, stumbled against mine, and I was within an ace of being drowned . . . But my horse, which was a good one, jumped on the crupper of that of Pilois and got me out of my difficulties.[1]

What happened to Pilois he does not say; perhaps he did not notice his friend's fate in his anxiety to hold the bridgehead which he had now established; and having secured enough of the enemy bank to give him elbow room, Armand galloped back to the ford to hasten his reinforcements:

> There I was confronted with one of the most pitiful sights in the world, more than thirty officers drowned or drowning, with Revel[2] at their head; the Rhine was full of men, horses, standards, hats and suchlike; for the fire of the enemy's right had been hot enough to frighten the horses, which swerved into a current from which no one escaped alive . . . I saw Brassalay, Cornet of Cuirassiers . . . swimming with one hand and holding the regimental standard with the other.[3]

But though there were still some critical moments, the issue was in no real doubt after Guiche had made good his footing on the Dutch bank; reinforcements were pouring in as fast as they could get across, Louvigny and his musketeers among them, and by seven in the evening the French engineers had completed a bridge; and Louis, having crossed the river, sent for Guiche. It was Armand's hour.

The King embraced him in public and said that he would

[1] *Ibid.*

[2] Revel, Charles Amedée de Broglie, Comte de, served in this and the next two major wars, receiving the St Esprit for his conduct at Cremona, 1703. Died, a Lieutenant-General, 1707.

[3] Guiche, *Mémoires.*

forget all his past conduct, and that he would give him his friendship once more; that he was sorry M. le Maréchal had sold the Guards, in spite of his advice and warning; but that in the future there would be no other charge in the King's gift to which Guiche might not aspire. These charming words were accompanied by all those things which the King knew so well how to say when he wished to enchant . . . and M. de Guiche returned to Court overwhelmed with honours.[1]

And late though it was Louis, who never did things by halves, sat down to make the father a happy man:

I assure you that amongst the things which have moved me most today, none has touched me more than the distinction which the Comte de Guiche has earned. No one could have shown more valour or more good conduct. I share this with you so that, whilst all seems to smile in this part of the world, you will for more than one reason be able to enjoy the success of my enterprises.[2]

The Rhine was the only defensive line in the country, and to save Amsterdam the Dutch were compelled to play their trump card three days later; the sluices were opened and the Low Country inundated. A fortnight afterwards Louis, who was suffering from a bad attack of swollen head, refused the abject terms offered by Holland, and on 1 August he returned to France. Guiche seems to have had a mixed reception on his arrival at Court; the King's feelings towards him were no longer in any doubt, but others found him presumptuous and supercilious. However, adverse opinions troubled Armand very little so long as he could count on Louis' support; and that he could do so was evident in 1673, when he reaped the harvest of his showy gallantry of the previous year. The area of conflict had now spread, another front had opened, and Turenne was given command of the Army of Germany, with Guiche as his Lieutenant-General. Probably not at all to Turenne's satisfaction, for Guiche was more intent on advertising himself than

[1] *Ibid.*

[2] Louis XIV, *Oeuvres.*

on conforming to the tactical plans of his superiors; and on the Tauber this year he nearly involved the army in a pitched battle under very disadvantageous circumstances.

In Holland Maastricht was taken by Louis and Vauban[1] on 29 June; and there we find Philibert, who though he was no great soldier, had rather a taste for swaggering his way through a royal campaign. If he had no military triumphs to show for his pains, he at least made social history by publicly rebuking the King for his sarcastic references to courtiers on active service; and being Philibert, emerged scatheless from that enterprise.

Meanwhile Charlotte the irrepressible was not only back at Court and on the best of terms with 'Monsieur', but she had managed to become Lady-of-Honour to the new 'Madame'; whom she sought to captivate by that old display of charm which had served her so well with Henrietta:

> Mme de Monaco no longer uses rouge; she came to see me [Mme de Sévigné] the other day, very white; she is all taken up with the new 'Madame', just as she was with the other... one is a little disgusted to see her playing off the same little mannerisms and affectations which she showed to the other 'Madame'.

What time Charlotte could spare from the conquest of 'Madame' she appears to have devoted to getting into trouble with brother Louvigny, now serving with Guiche in Germany; society could not ferret out the details, but the burden of Louvigny's complaint was that Charlotte had 'been putting ideas into Mme de Louvigny's head'.

Early in December the utterly unexpected news reached Paris that Armand, Comte de Guiche, had died in his brother's arms at Kreutzenach on 29 November; 'of grief at the loss of a convoy which had been entrusted to his charge', said some; 'of ill-health and debility' according to another and more likely account.

To the father it was a stunning blow. Armand had caused

[1] VAUBAN, Sebastien Le Prestre, 1633–1717, the foremost military engineer of his day.

him much sorrow, had provoked great anger; but in his heart of hearts the Maréchal had been proud of his son, proud even of his languorous insolence, his foppery, and his audacious love affair; and it had all ended in a peasant's death in an obscure German village at the age of thirty-seven:

> The Maréchal cleared everyone out of the room; when he was alone [with Bourdaloue] he threw himself on his neck and said he knew only too well what he had come to tell him; that it was a death-blow to him, and that he had lost the only object of his tenderness... he threw himself on his bed, but did not weep.[1]

After which Bourdaloue took the stricken man to the neighbouring church of the Capuchins, which Antoine entered, 'stumbling, trembling, dragged rather than walking on his feet'.

> Mme de Monaco is inconsolable; Mme de Louvigny is not afflicted. What a bit of luck for her! Here she is, all in a moment the future Duchesse de Gramont.[2]

Guiche, says Madame de Sévigné, left behind him 'a rich and happy widow'; but for once she shows less than her usual charity. The poor, neglected woman, on hearing of her husband's death, said with tears, 'I would have loved him passionately if only he had loved me a little. I always hoped the day would come when he would change towards me'. It is pleasant at this stage to remind ourselves that the widow was to marry again,[3] and in true story-book fashion live happily ever afterwards.

The contemporaries of Guiche saw chiefly his follies, affectations, and audacities; but there was more in him than the romantic lover and the man of fashion. His political abilities were by no means contemptible, he had a background of culture rare in his generation, and he was decidedly something of an author. Personally I rate his memoirs high amongst those of

[1] Gramont, *Mémoires*.

[2] Sévigné, *Lettres*.

[3] On 6 February, 1681 she married Henri de Daillon, Duc du Lude, the marriage being 'one of affection on both sides'.

the century; higher certainly than the better-known Gramont memoirs which the Maréchal dictated to Louvigny.

Armand's body was brought home from Germany by his brother, and was buried in the chapel of St Antoine of Padua at the Capuchin monastery in Paris. By the turn of the year he had been forgotten by everyone except his mother, and his uncle Toulongeon who succeeded him as King's Lieutenant for Navarre.

In 1674 Louis had little except the reoccupation of Franche-Comté upon which to congratulate himself. The hereditary Stadhoulderate had been revived in favour of William of Orange, and the effect on Dutch morale had been astonishing. The Dutch navy looked like gaining command of the sea, which made Louis nervous about his Achilles heel, the coastal territory in the far south-west. Turbulent, indisciplined, full of Huguenots, within easy reach of friendly Spanish sea bases, it was the ideal place for the enemy to attempt a large-scale diversionary landing with the support of French traitors and malcontents. Gramont, within whose jurisdiction most of the danger points lay, was the obvious person to go south to take the necessary precautionary measures, but he was laid up with gout at Paris; so the King replaced him by Louvigny, who was sent with instructions to throw himself into Bayonne, where a combined Dutch and Spanish attack was expected hourly. Six days later he entered the city and immediately set to work to repair the dilapidated fortifications. If his own account is to be trusted, Louvigny certainly showed great energy and resourcefulness; seven hundred gentlemen were enlisted, five thousand peasants collected and armed; and of the latter we note that twelve hundred 'I brought from my own estates'. Which gives us some idea of the wealth of the House of Gramont.

In due course the Dutch fleet appeared, but not that of Spain; and the Dutch, seeing that there was now no hope of taking Bayonne by surprise, returned to the Channel.

Louvigny's had been a creditable piece of work, competently performed, and we can sympathize with his feelings when his gouty old father lumbered into Bayonne just in time to usurp the credit of having frightened off the Dutch. However,

Louvigny had at least the satisfaction of carrying the news to Louis, and doubtless he showed no bashfulness in appropriating the credit which he felt to be his due. As for the Maréchal, 'he returned to Court, for he could not accommodate himself to the life of the provinces, which was so little suited to a man of his condition.[1]

Louvigny appears to have spent this winter in the siege of Madame de Bouillon;[2] who, we may imagine, proved no very difficult conquest. For her way of life was so notorious that no woman with any shred of reputation would even call at the Hôtel de Bouillon. But she was on the whole the best of the Mancini girls, though that to be sure is not saying much.

When not in pursuit of Madame de Bouillon, Louvigny spent a good deal of the year in quarrels with his wife; for in spite of his passion for the Duchess, he remained the Comtesse de Louvigny's lover until her death. In July they were in a quarrelsome phase of their domesticity:

> They say that Louvigny has caught his wife writing a letter which did not at all please him; it has created no end of a stir.[3]

Curiously enough, whilst Louvigny was paying his court to the Duchesse de Bouillon in Paris, his uncle Philibert was conducting an *amourette* with her even more notorious sister the Duchesse de Mazarin[4] in London. 'He was enraptured of her.' Hortense had been married in 1661 to La Meilleraye, to whom Mazarin left the bulk of his wealth on condition that the groom adopted the name and arms of Mazarin. The marriage turned out a fiasco from the outset, but Hortense cannot be much blamed for its failure, seeing that the Duke was what polite society described as an 'original', and what we should call

[1] Gramont, *Mémoires*.

[2] BOUILLON, Marie Anne Mancini, Duchesse de, 1646–1714, a very wealthy heiress, married 1662 'the most eligible parti in France', Maurice Godefroy de La Tour d'Auvergne, Duc de Bouillon.

[3] Sévigné, *Lettres*.

[4] MAZARIN, Hortense Mancini, Duchesse de, 1644?–1699, seventh child and fourth daughter of Michel Mancini. She died in England, poor and forgotten, 2 July, 1699.

slightly insane. His mental instability showed itself in what was a very unusual form for a noble of his day, that of a prudery which bordered on madness; he it was who had clothes made for the late Cardinal's huge collection of classical statues, and forbade the dairymaids on his estates to milk the cows lest it should put improper thoughts into their heads. Hortense, whose head contained few thoughts which were not improper, deserted him early in her married life, shouting through her friends' salons the war cry of the Fronde, *Point de Mazarin! Point de Mazarin!* And since those days she had been leading a sort of Becky Sharp existence in most of the capitals of Europe. She was now a very beautiful woman, not yet thirty, and according to Philibert, much improved since he had last seen her as a bride – 'all the mistresses of Charles II were eclipsed by her'. And some of them realized it; notably the Duchess of Cleveland,[1] who in March was preparing to go on a sulking expedition to France, with her temper warmed up to an impressive pitch by the refusal of the French authorities to allow her to bring over what she pleased, duty-free. Charles, anxious to get rid of her, begged Philibert to squire her across the Channel, and he agreed to do so; which showed considerable good nature on his part, for Barbara in a rage must have been anything but an agreeable travelling companion. And not only did Philibert escort her through to Paris, but 'he took care to warn the customs officers to ask no money and overwhelm her with civilities, for such was the King's good pleasure'.

At the Palais-Royal Charlotte no longer enjoyed the favour which had been hers a few years earlier; for 'Madame' had begun to see the real woman hidden under Madame de Monaco's pretty little ways. And the blunt, frigid German girl was disgusted at what she saw:

> They say that Mme de Monaco is not on such good terms as she used to be with 'Madame'. You know 'Madame's' views on gallantry; and she has imagined – *what* an injustice! – that

[1] CLEVELAND, Barbara Villiers, Duchess of, 1641?–1709, 'enormously vicious, ravenous, foolish, and imperious', married Roger Palmer, Earl of Castlemaine, 1659, and became the mistress of Charles II in the same year.

Mme de Monaco has not the same aversion to kindness of heart as she has.[1]

In 1677 Louvigny earned further notoriety in one of those rather sordid quarrels which seem to have occupied so much of his time:

> D'Effiat[2] went to the Bastille yesterday for having raised his cane at Mme de Soissons' against Louvigny; the Comte de Gramont [Philibert] got between them; and the threats were lively. Louvigny said that d'Effiat was a coward, and that in any other place he would not have raised such a quarrel . . . it began about a sum of sixty pounds.[3]

In this summer Antoine left Court for good and settled on his estates. Up to the moment of his departure he continued to be 'received marvellously well' by the King; but he could no longer keep old age at bay, nor blind himself to the fact that his day was over; and the bitterness of the realization is apparent even in his own unemotional prose, which gives a strong impression that Louis, in spite of his show of tenderness, was beginning to find the old Maréchal a bore:

> Gramont began to feel both his age, and the difference between this Court and the one he used to know; the Comte de Guiche was dead, and neither he nor the Comte de Louvigny held a charge at Court. He could no longer ignore the fact that old men, subject to incommodities, fatigue the young in spite of all their wit, and that the young avoid them when they can. He saw that of the crowds who used to throng his house, only a few now called, some out of good manners, some because their parents had ordered them to do so. Sometimes he was all alone and reduced to his own thoughts. . . . So, like a sensible man, he resolved to quit the Court and put an

[1] Sévigné, *Lettres*.

[2] EFFIAT, Antoine Coiffier de Ruzé, 3rd Marquis d', 1638–1719, 'a clever, intriguing, unprincipled man, living in open contempt of morality and religion'. Certainly a pervert, possibly a poisoner, he was First Equerry to 'Monsieur'.

[3] Sévigné, *Lettres*.

> interval between his life and his death; though he was not scrupulously devout.[1]

But even now the poor old out-of-date Courtier could not nerve himself to make a clean break with the past; and with all his former ingenuity he left himself a loophole for return in case he found the provinces unendurable:

> The Maréchal de Gramont, on the pretext that Bayonne might run the same risk this year as last . . . petitioned the King that whilst I [Louvigny] was serving in Flanders, he might be allowed to return to Bayonne to guard the place against any hostile demonstrations . . . This was the reason which he advanced, and it had a plausible air, but it merely cloaked a retreat which had already been determined upon. All the same, his departure was a grief to the King, who did all that was humanly possible to dissuade him.[2]

Almost a year later Antoine paid his last visit to Court, where Charlotte de Monaco lay dying; she had turned out to be one of the Gramont bad bargains, but after all she was his daughter, and decorum insisted on his presence at her horrible deathbed:

> Mme de Monaco has departed this life [4 June] showing a dubious contrition confused with the pain of a cruel illness. She became much disfigured before death . . . so dried up as to outrage nature by the ravages inflicted on her face . . . the disease of which she died forced penitence upon her . . . she will be one of those labourers of the parable who were paid for the last hour as if they had been hired in the morning.[3]

She received a characteristic viaticum from her father:

> I have just heard of the death of Mme de Monaco, and that the Maréchal de Gramont, taking leave of her, said that it was time to pack the baggage; that Guiche had gone on ahead to mark the billets, and that he would follow them shortly.[4]

[1] Gramont, *Mémoires*.

[2] Gramont, *Mémoires*.

[3] Scudéry, *Lettres*.

[4] Sévigné, *Lettres*.

By the ideas of the time this was an admirable farewell, and society applauded.

This is our last sight of Antoine as well as of Charlotte. Immediately after the funeral he returned to Bidache, where he died on 12 July, aged seventy-four. Louvigny succeeded him as second Duc de Gramont, and only in the ducal branch was the family name continued. Toulongeon survived Antoine by thirteen months only, dying unmarried on 1 September 1679, and his brother Philibert, who lived until 1707, left no son; of Philibert's two daughters the elder, Claude Charlotte, married Henry Howard, Earl of Stafford, in 1694, whilst the other, Marie Elizabeth, who died in 1706, was Abbess of St Marine de Poussay.

Louvigny was to consolidate the family position which his father had won. He became Viceroy of Béarn and Navarre, Knight of the St Esprit, Knight of the Golden Fleece, and in 1704 revisited Madrid after an absence of forty-five years; this time as French Ambassador. His son, the third duke, another Antoine, was to become a Maréchal, to marry a daughter of the Duc de Noailles, and better still, to bring back into the family that much regretted piece of property the Colonelcy of the French Guards; whilst the third duke's sister, who had the doubtful privilege of being christened Cathérine Charlotte in memory of her notorious aunt Madame de Monaco, became Duchesse de Boufflers and a Lady-of-Honour to Louis XV's Queen.

★ ★ ★

Sixty years had passed since Antoine III, the little cadet from Gascony, had run about Paris in search of a crust to stay his hunger, and in the long struggle towards the sunlight he had been fortunate beyond his own dreams. Duke of France, Peer of France, Marshal of France, Knight of the St Esprit, Colonel of the French Guards, *Porte-Oriflamme* of France, Sovereign of Bidache, Minister of State, Governor of Béarn and Navarre, Governor and Mayor of Bayonne. Such were the prizes snatched in a long and toilsome journey. Did he ever ask himself if it had all been worth while? His mind was ambitious, complacent, trained for acute observation in a small field, and quite lacking in power of introspection; but perhaps some uneasy suspicion may have occurred to him during his last days that he had grasped the shadow for the substance. For the struggle had demanded every ounce of drive and concentration of which he was master, and during the climb all the comfortable baggage of life had perforce been cast away. Notably friendship, for this is a luxury with which the climber dare not burden himself; unless we call that friendship which is in reality nothing more than a contract of mutual aid, to be executed only so long as both parties to it keep level in their ascent. And who had been Gramont's friends? Condé perhaps, and for a few years only; and even there, the friendship did not go much deeper than a sharing of the pains and pleasures of army service. To the envious and the superficial he had been the King's friend, but for Louis on his pinnacle friendship was as impossible as it was for the climbing Gramont, and no one understood that fact better than Antoine himself. And love he never seems to have encountered, but only its pitiable substitute, lust; for his marriage had been merely a foothold in the assault on Olympus.

It is a success story if ever there was one. And yet that passage in which he speaks of his own retirement breathes sadness and disillusionment. Like all men of his stamp, Gramont obviously failed to escape the nemesis of the unloved and friendless; and as the last darkness closed in upon him he may have seen as by a lightning flash, the emptiness of that 'magnificence' which he had always worshipped.

But perhaps this is to attribute modern pessimism to a man of three hundred years ago, who saw life very differently. His was a small-minded day of intense concentrated strife for prizes which strike us as tawdry and childish. But though King-worship may be in itself a poor religion, where it is practised with the devotion shown by Gramont and his contemporaries, it has perhaps the compensation of leaving no time for regret over the sacrifices which it entails. And for all we know, Antoine's last thought may have been that he was the good and faithful servant who had done well with his talents; for had he not found the Gramonts country gentlemen and left them one of the great Houses of France?

BIBLIOGRAPHY

★

ANDILLY, *Mémoires de Robert Arnauld d'*, Petitot, Paris, 1824.

ANON, Travels as Ambassador Extraordinary to the Emperor Ferdinando II in 1636, 1 vol., London, 1637.

ANON, Marshal Turenne, 1 vol., London, 1907.

ANSÈLME, de Ste Marie (P. de Guibours), *Histoire Genéalogique et Chronologique de la maison royale de France, des pairs, des grands officiers, etc.*, 11 vols., Paris, 1712.

ARNAULD, *Mémoires de l'Abbé . . . depuis 1634 jusqu'a 1675*, Vol. XXXIV, Collection Petitot, Paris, 1824.

AULNOY, Baronne d', Memoirs of the present state of the Court and Council of Spain, 1 vol., London, 1701.

AVENEL, G., *Richelieu et la monarchie absolue*, 2 vols., Paris, 1883.

BAFFITOL, L., *Au temps de Louis XIII*, 1 vol., Paris, 1904.

BARINE, A., *La jeunesse de la Grande Mademoiselle*, 1 vol., Paris, 1909.

BASSOMPIERRE, *Mémoires du Mareschal de*, 2 vols., Amsterdam, 1692.

BEAUVAU, Marquis de, *Mémoires . . . Histoire de Charles IV, Duc de Lorraine*, 1 vol., Cologne, 1688.

BERTHOD, *Père, Mémoires du*, 1 vol., Paris, 1825.

BONNEAU-AVENANT, Comte de, *La Duchesse d'Aiguillon*, 1 vol., Paris, 1882.

BOULENGER, J., The Seventeenth Century, London, 1920.

BRIENNE, *Mémoires du Comte de, Ministre, etc.*, 3 vols., Paris, 1699.

BUSSY, *Les Mémoires de Messire Roger de Rabutin, Comte de*, 2 vols., Paris, 1696.

BUSSY-RABUTIN, Le Comte de, *Histoire Amoureuse des Gaules, et La France Galante*, 2 vols., Paris, 1857.

CALLOT or CALOT, J., *Fructus Belli*; les misères et les malheurs de la guerre, 1 vol., Paris, 1633.

CAMBRIDGE MODERN HISTORY, The, Vol. IV, *The Thirty Years War*; Vol. V, *The Age of Louis XIV*.

CAMPION, H. de, *Mémoires*, edit. Moreau, 1 vol., Paris, 1857.

CARLYLE, T., *History of Frederick the Great*, 8 vols., London, 1897.

CHALLES, *Mémoires de Robert*, ed. A. A. Thierry, Paris, 1931.
CHOISY, *Mémoires de l'Abbé de, pour servir à l'histoire de Louis XIV*, ed. Lescure, 2 vols., Paris, 1888.
CHOUPPES, *Mémoires du Marquis de*, 1 vol., Paris, 1861.
CONDÉ, *The Life of Lewis of Bourbon*, late Prince of, digested into annals, etc., 1 vol., London, 1693.
COULANGES, *Mémoires de M. l'Abbé de*, 1 vol., Paris, 1820.
DELAVAUD, L., *Le Marquis de Pomponne*, 1 vol., Paris, 1911.
ERLANGER, P., *Monsieur, frère de Louis XIV*, Paris, 1953.
ESTRADES, *Letters and Negociations of the Count d', etc.*, 3 vols., London, 1711.
FARET, N., *L'Honneste homme, ou l'art de plaire à la cour*, 1 vol., Paris, 1632. (English translation, Birmingham, 1754.)
FÉDERN, C., *Mazarin, 1602–1661*, 1 vol., Paris, 1934.
FEILING, K., *British Foreign Policy, 1660–1672*, London, 1930.
FEILLET, A., *La misère au temps de la Fronde*, Paris, 1886.
FONTENAY-MAREUIL, *Mémoires de Messire du Val, Marquis de*, 2 vols., Petitot, Paris, 1826.
FROMAGEAU, P., *Isabelle de Montmorency*, 1 vol., Paris, 1913.
GODLEY, E., *The Great Condé*, 1 vol., London, 1915.
GOURVILLE, *Mémoires de*, edit. Lecastre, 2 vols., Paris, 1894.
GRAMONT, *Mémoires du Maréchal de*, 2 vols., Petitot, Paris, 1826–7.
GRANT, J., *Memoirs and Adventures of Sir John Hepburn*, commander of the Scots Brigade under Gustavus Adolphus, 1 vol., Edinburgh and London, 1851.
GREEN, J. H., *Callot, Jacques*, A catalogue and description of his works, etc., 1 vol., London, 1804.
GRIMMELSHAUSEN, H. von., *The Adventures of Simplicissimus*, 1 vol., London, 1912.
GUICHE, *Mémoires du Comte de*, 1 vol., London, 1744.
GUISE, *Les Mémoires du feu Duc de*, 1 vol., Paris, 1763.
HAMILTON, Count Anthony, *Memoirs of Count Gramont*, edit. Goodwin, 2 vols., London, 1903.
HANOTAUX, G., *Histoire du Cardinal de Richelieu*, 2 vols., Paris, 1893.
HARTMANN, C. H., *The King my Brother*, London, 1954.
HASSALL, A., *European History chronologically arranged, etc.*, 1 vol., London, 1920.
HUME, M., *The Court of Philip IV*, 1 vol., London, N.D.
JOLI, Guy, *Mémoires de, etc.*, 2 vols., Paris, 1677.

LA FAYETTE, *Mémoires de Madame de*, 1 vol., Paris, N.D.
LAIR, J., *Louise de La Vallière*, 1 vol., Paris, N.D.
LAVEDAN, *Monsieur Vincent*, 1 vol., Paris, 1928.
LENET, *Mémoires de Mr, etc.*, 2 vols., Paris, 1729.
LODGE, R., *Richelieu*, 1 vol., London, 1896.
LORET, J., *La Muze Historique*, 4 vols., Paris, 1857.
LORRAINE, *Histoire de l'Emprisonment de Charles IV, Duc de, etc.*, 1 vol., Cologne, 1688.
LOWNDES, M. E., *The Nuns of Port-Royal*, London, 1909.
LOUIS XIV, *Oeuvres de*, 6 vols., Paris, 1806.
MAGNÉ, E., *Le Grand Condé. . . .* Lettres inédites sur la cour de Louis XIV, 1660–67, 1 vol., Paris, 1920.
MAGNÉ, E., *Ninon de Lenclos*, trans. Stevenson, London, 1926.
MAINTENON, *Correspondence générale de Madame de, Lavallée*, 4 vols., Paris, 1865.
MAYNARD, T., *Apostle of Charity*, 1 vol., London, 1940.
MONTGLAT, *Mémoires de François de P. de Clermont, Marquis de, etc.*, 3 vols., Petitot, Paris, 1825-6.
MONTPENSIER, *Mémoires de Mademoiselle de*, edit. Chéruel, 4 vols., Paris, N.D.
MONTRÉSOR, *Mémoires du Comte de*, 1 vol., Petitot, Paris, N.D.
MOTTEVILLE, *Mémoires de Madame de*, edit. Riaux, 4 vols., Paris, 1869.
MUNRO, Robert, *His expedition with the worthy Scots regiment called Mackay's, etc.*, 1 vol., London, 1637.
NEMOURS, *Mémoires de Madame la Duchesse de*, Paris, 1677.
NOAILLES, Vicomte de, *Episodes de la Guerre de Trente Ans*, 1 vol., Paris, 1906–8.
OGG, D., *Europe in the Seventeenth Century*, London, 1931.
ORLÉANS, *Mémoires de Gaston, Duc d'*, Petitot, Paris, 1824.
PALATINE, La Princesse, *Lettres inédites de la*, 1 vol., Paris, N.D.
PATIN, Gui, *Correspondence de*, 1 vol., Paris, 1901.
PEREY, Lucien, *Le Roman du Grand Roi*, 1 vol., Paris, 1894.
POINTIS, *Mémoires du Sieur de*, 2 vols., Petitot, Paris, 1824.
PORT-ROYAL, *Mémoires pour servir à l'Histoire de, et de la Revde. Mère Angèlique . . . Arnauld*, etc., 3 vols., Utrecht, 1742.
RETZ, *Mémoires du Cardinal de*, 4 vols., Paris, 1912.
RICHELIEU, *Mémoires du Cardinal de*, 10 vols., Petitot, Paris, 1823.
ROCHEFOUCAULD, *Mémoires du Duc de La*, Petitot, Paris, N.D.

ROHAN, *Mémoires du Duc de, etc.*, 1 vol., Petitot, Paris, 1822.
ROSTAND, E., *Cyrano de Bergerac*, 1 vol., London, 1914.
ROUSSET, C., *Histoire de Louvois*, 4 vols., Paris, 1864.
STE BEUVE, *Causeries du Lundi*; *Bussy-Rabutin*, 10th February, 1851: *Count Hamilton*, 12th November, 1849: *Cardinal de Retz*, 20th October, 1851.
ST EVREMOND, *The Letters of*, 1 vol., London, 1930.
ST MAURICE, Marquis de, *Lettres sur la cour de Louis XIV, 1667–1670*, 1 vol., Paris, 1910.
ST SIMON, *Mémoires du Duc de*, various editions.
SANDARS, Mary F., *Lauzun: Courtier and Adventurer*, 2 vols., London, 1908.
SCUDÉRY, *Lettres de Mesdames de, de Salvan, de Saliez, et de Mademoiselle Descartes*, 1 vol., Paris, 1806.
SÉVIGNÉ, *Lettres de Madame de*, edit. Aimé-Martin, 6 vols., Paris, 1876.
TALLEMANT DES RÉAUX, *Les Historiettes de*, Monmerqué, 6 vols., Paris, 1862.
TALON, Omer, *Mémoires de*, 1 vol., Paris, 1839.
TAVANNES, *Mémoires du Comte de, 1649–53*, 1 vol., Paris, 1691.
TOPIN, M., *Louis XIII et Richelieu*, 1 vol., Paris, 1876.
TRENCH, Archbishop, *Gustavus Adolphus*, some social aspects of the Thirty Years War, 1 vol., London and Cambridge, 1865.
VILLARS, Madame de, *Lettres*, 1 vol., Amsterdam, 1760.
VILLERMONT, Comte A. C. de, *Tilly, ou la guerre de Trente Ans*, 1 vol., Paris and Tournai, 1860.
VINCENT, P., *The Lamentation of Germany*, London, 1638.
VISCONTI, P., *Mémoires sur la cour de Louis XIV*, edit. Lemoine, 1 vol., Paris, 1908.
VOITURE, *Lettres et autres oeuvres de Monsieur de*, 2 vols., Amsterdam, 1709.
WALISZEWSKI, K., *Marysienka . . . Queen of Poland*, 1 vol., London, 1898.

INDEX